OFFERING CHRIST

OFFERING CHRIST

JOHN WESLEY'S EVANGELISTIC VISION

JACK JACKSON

KB™
KINGSWOOD BOOKS
An Imprint of Abingdon Press
Nashville, Tennessee

OFFERING CHRIST:
JOHN WESLEY'S EVANGELISTIC VISION

Library of Congress Cataloging-in-Publication Data has been requested.

ISBN 978-1-5018-1422-8

17 18 19 20 21 22 23 24 25 26—10 9 8 7 6 5 4 3 2 1
MANUFACTURED IN THE UNITED STATES OF AMERICA

To Anna and Mom

In Memoriam

Glenn Jackson

Contents

Acknowledgments

I would like to express sincere thanks to a number of people who helped this work come to fruition. First and foremost I give thanks to my family—Anna, Sophie, and Toby—for all their support and encouragement as I wrote this book. Thank you, Toby, for your almost daily texts of encouragement! This book originated as part of a doctoral dissertation at the University of Manchester, U.K., and Cliff College under the direction of Dr. Phil Meadows whose guidance and friendship I continue to cherish. My PhD studies were encouraged and supported in part by the Foundation for Evangelism, and I continue to appreciate our partnership through the Foundation's support of the E. Stanley Jones Professors of Evangelism at a number of United Methodist Schools, including at Claremont School of Theology. Thanks to Jane Boatwright Wood, Dr. Stephen Gunter, and all my colleagues in the ESJ chairs for your support. I'm grateful for the encouragement I've received from Claremont School of Theology, especially Dr. Jeffrey Kuan, Dr. Sheryl Kujawa-Holbrook, Dr. Karen Dalton, and the Board of Trustees for my research sabbatical. Thanks to Matthew Hambrick and Jacob Martin who helped me in the preparation of this manuscript. I also appreciate Rev. Dr. Ken Carter, resident bishop of the Florida Conference of the United Methodist Church, for allowing me the privilege of teaching some of the church's next generation of clergy leaders. I am also indebted to Dr. Rex Matthews and David Teel for their guidance and encouragement during this project.

My wife, Anna, and I are deeply grateful to a number of friends who supported our lives and ministry through the years: Ginger Jackson, Billie Strickland, Jim and Martha Harnish, Gordon and Meade Owens, Amy Wasserbauer, Karen Thomas, Scott Smith, Lyndol Lloyd, Tim and Cindy Carson, Pat Boren, Brian Yeich, David and Sally Johnston, Elaine Heath, Kirsten Oh, Scott Russell, Grace Kao, Nathaniel Walker, and Steve Moore. I am especially thankful to Paul Cantor for his friendship through the years and guidance on this manuscript.

INTRODUCTION

For a man whose ministry is as synonymous with evangelism as John Wesley's (1703–1791), it often comes as a surprise to both his contemporary devotees and detractors that he never actually used the word. He and his brother Charles Wesley (1707–1788), who together helped found the Methodist movement in Great Britain in the eighteenth century, used the term *evangelists* only when they referred to the movement's preachers, and never any other forms of the word. For all practical purposes, the founders of one of Christianity's great evangelistic movements never used the terminology of evangelism, which many contemporary Christians understand as essential to the nature of the church!

There is actually nothing unusual about the fact that eighteenth-century Methodists did not use the term, even if their activities were "evangelistic" in the contemporary sense of the word. The term *evangelism,* as well as its various Greek derivatives, fell out of use in Christian communities around the end of the fifth century CE and did not become common again until the nineteenth century. For centuries, the terminology simply was not used to describe any aspect of the church's ministry, even in ministries that are today considered evangelistic in nature. The current terminology did, however, gain traction in both Great Britain and the United States in the nineteenth century, when the practice of evangelism became associated with two particular Christian practices: public preaching and calling persons to an immediate conversion to Christ through faith and repentance.

These two practices, and their corresponding importance to the contemporary concept of evangelism, are perhaps best exemplified in the lives and ministries of Dwight Moody (1837–1899), Charles Spurgeon (1834–1892), and Billy Sunday (1865–1932). These nineteenth- and early twentieth-century evangelists drew enormous crowds, and over the course of their lifetimes hundreds of thousands, if not millions, of people responded to their message. They understood evangelism as a practice that consists almost solely of preaching, with the only desired result being personal conversion through repentance of sin and a confession of faith in Jesus Christ. These twin characteristics became the hallmarks of what is now typically considered evangelistic ministry, both in Western churches and the rapidly growing Christian communities in the global south. Not surprisingly, Methodists of many denominations began to interpret Wesley's evangelistic methods in light of preaching and conversion.[1] The result is that by the last half of the twentieth century, evangelism in many Wesleyan traditions was almost completely divorced from personal holiness and communal efforts for social reform in the name of Christ.[2]

By the 1980s many Methodists became concerned that preaching and conversion alone do not adequately capture Wesley's vision of evangelism. Evangelism was thus reconstructed along two fronts. The first reconstruction is best illustrated in the work of William Abraham. He argued that evangelists in the New Testament did more than just preach; they also taught, healed, and started faith communities, along with being apologists for the Christian faith.[3] Evangelism, he concluded, must include initiation and is best understood as "a polymorphous ministry aimed at initiating people into the kingdom of God."[4] The primary act of evangelism, he proposed, is not proclamation but any activity that helps initiate people into the Christian faith. The primary response is, correspondingly, not only conversion, but also beginning a process of Christian initiation. Fellow United Methodist Scott Jones, like most other Wesleyan theologians since Abraham, has since centered evangelism on initiation. Jones himself argues that the end of evangelism is initiation into discipleship or the church, while others argue the end is initiation into the reign of God.[5] This understanding of evangelism as a set of activities that initiates people into the reign of God and the church became for all practical purposes the theological vision of evangelism in much of the Wesleyan academic world.

The second reconstruction of evangelism insists that an evangelist's ethical life is integral to the practice of evangelism. This critique is perhaps best exemplified in the work of Laceye Warner. In her insightful book *Saving Women* Warner argues that the inclusion of a virtuous social ethic

[1]See Richard Green, *John Wesley: Evangelist* (London: Religious Tract Society, 1905); William L. Doughty, *John Wesley, Preacher* (London: Epworth, 1955); and A. Skevington Wood, *The Burning Heart: John Wesley, Evangelist* (Exeter: Paternoster, 1967). Each of these three highlights the importance of holiness in Wesley's theology and practice, but they do not link holiness with evangelism.

[2]William W. Dean, "Disciplined Fellowship: The Rise and Decline of Cell Groups in British Methodism" (PhD diss., University of Iowa, 1985), 301. Dean demonstrates that nineteenth-century link between preaching in public spaces outside churches and conversion distorted Wesley's focus on awakening.

[3]William J. Abraham, *The Logic of Evangelism* (Grand Rapids: Eerdmans, 1989), 40–69, 92–116.

[4]Ibid., 95.

[5]Scott J. Jones, *The Evangelistic Love of God and Neighbor: A Theology of Witness and Discipleship* (Nashville: Abingdon, 2003), 21–43. See also Phillip Meadows, "The Journey of Evangelism," in *Oxford Handbook of Methodist Studies*, ed. William J. Abraham and James E. Kirby (Oxford: Oxford University, 2009), 414.

that embodies the gospel is constitutive of evangelism.[6] Warner describes the problems that arise when people proclaim the story of God in Christ but fail to demonstrate Christ's ethical commands in their own lives. If an evangelist's ethical life does not approximate the ethical calls of the gospel, then any evangelism associated with the evangelist is flawed. She concludes that any conception of evangelism must move "beyond verbal proclamation" as the defining element of evangelism.[7] She makes this clear in an article coauthored with Stephen Chapman, where they argue that evangelism is more than just proclamation or initiation and includes virtually all of Christian mission: "The concept of evangelism should . . . be expanded to include the entire *missio Dei* of global reconciliation, particularly through the *imitatio Dei* of God's people in their care for creation and all its creatures. Social justice, peace, and ecological concern are not beyond the scope of evangelism."[8] Evangelism, they conclude, necessitates "a more complex theological future" than proclamation or initiation alone. Instead, it must embrace almost the entirety of the church's overall mission.[9]

And yet, despite the tendency to move away from proclamation as the central characteristic of evangelism, a number of Wesleyan scholars keep proclamation at the center. John Kurewa, while acknowledging various conceptions of evangelism, understands its primary task is to interpret "the work of God in Christ so that people understand God's love for the world."[10] John Hong argues that Wesley's method of evangelism centered on preaching, something he believes contemporary Methodists

[6]Laceye C. Warner, *Saving Women: Retrieving Evangelistic Theology and Practice* (Waco: Baylor University Press, 2007), 10.

[7]Ibid., 8–9, 280.

[8]Stephen B. Chapman and Laceye C. Warner, "Jonah and the Imitation of God: Rethinking Evangelism and the Old Testament," *Journal of Theological Interpretation* 2, no. 1 (2008): 43.

[9]Warner, 10. Bryan Stone and Paul Chilcote have a different take on this reconstruction. Instead of evangelism being everything the church does, evangelism is a constitutive element of every Christian practice. Stone, for instance, argues that evangelism is "an intrinsic characteristic of every Christian practice and of the comprehensive praxis of Christian faith itself." Bryan Stone, *Evangelism after Christendom: The Theology and Practice of Christian Witness* (Grand Rapids: Brazos, 2007), 27. Chilcote offers an even more clearly distinct vision of evangelism: "Evangelism is the core of all ecclesial practices. If practices of worship, discipleship, or pastoral care are pursued without an evangelistic orientation—namely an intentional proclamation and embodiment of the gospel of Jesus Christ—then such practices not only lose their motivation and power, but arguably cease to function as Christian practices altogether." Paul W. Chilcote, "Evangelism in the Methodist Tradition," in *T & T Clark Companion to Methodism*, ed. Charles Yrigoyen (London: T & T Clark, 2010), 236. In other words, not all that the church does is itself evangelism, but evangelism is a characteristic of all faithful acts of the church.

[10]John Wesley Zwomunondiita Kurewa, *Drumbeats of Salvation in Africa: A Study of Biblical, Historical and Theological Foundations for the Ministry of Evangelism in Africa* (Mutare, Zimbabwe: Africa University, 2007), 9.

need to reclaim.[11] Perhaps the most notable contributions come from Mortimer Arias and Walter Klaiber. While acknowledging that evangelism includes social justice and compassion toward all people, Arias argues that the primary characteristic of evangelism is the announcement of the reign of God.[12] Klaiber shares Arias's commitment to a narrow definition of evangelism as proclamation, arguing that evangelism's central task is a particular witness to the church's kerygma through public preaching and private conversation.[13] In sum, even after more than four decades of conversation, we are left with an imprecise mosaic of understandings of evangelism that typically includes proclamation, initiation, and embodiment, but no central and guiding vision of evangelism within the global Methodist community.

These various understandings can be problematic. For example, the relationship between evangelism and a Christian's ethical life is unclear. How does a Christian's ethical life itself proclaim the gospel, and perhaps invite others to it, when people from other religious traditions (or no religious tradition whatsoever) exhibit the same high ethical standards? Furthermore, why is one's ethical life associated primarily, if not solely, with evangelism? Certainly Christians' ethical lives influence how others perceive the truth of their spoken words. But a Christian's ethics also sway how others perceive the genuineness of their worship, their work for equality, and their efforts for social justice. The degree to which a Christian's ethical life reflects that of Jesus either adds to or detracts from the credibility of the person's entire Christian life, not just her evangelistic witness. Evangelism cannot simply consist of a Christian's ethical life.

Similarly, concerns regarding evangelism's association with colonialism lead to a claim that any and all work of the church can be thought of as evangelism as long as it does *not* proclaim the gospel and does not call anyone to an initial repentance and faith that leads to conversion. This assertion seems to take to heart the words erroneously attributed to St. Francis of Assisi: "Wherever you go preach the gospel. If necessary use words." This phrase has become a virtual mantra of many Western denominations, including many in Methodist traditions. This is unfortunate since there is scant evidence St. Francis actually spoke these words. Furthermore, it minimizes verbal preaching, a practice Francis understood as was the heart of his movement.[14] But the phrase's appeal to the idea that

[11]John Sungschul Hong, *John Wesley the Evangelist* (Lexington: Emeth, 2006), 10.

[12]Mortimer Arias, *Announcing the Reign of God: Evangelization and the Subversive Memory of Jesus* (Philadelphia: Fortress, 1984), 117–19.

[13]Walter Klaiber, *Call and Response: Biblical Foundations of a Theology of Evangelism* (Nashville: Abingdon, 1997), 26.

[14]Jack (Thomas Glenn III) Jackson, "St. Francis: Patron Saint of Evangelism through Social Ministry?," *Witness* 23 (2007–2009), 22–33.

people can share their faith without using words continues to find resonance. It gives credence to the many congregations in various Wesleyan traditions that seem to question whether proclamation is integral to an understanding of evangelism.

Perhaps these different visions do not contradict each other, but are rather different expressions of the nature and constituent practices that define evangelism. Nevertheless, the result is that there is disagreement within and between Wesleyan communities regarding the nature and practice of evangelism today. Even after forty years of rightly intuiting that John Wesley's evangelistic vision necessitated more than the preaching and call to conversion advocated by many nineteenth-century evangelists, Methodists continue to ask deep questions regarding the nature of Methodist evangelism that are worth investigating. Was the idea of evangelism as it is understood today important to early Methodists? If so, then what practices did they incorporate that would now be considered evangelism? Did John Wesley believe that the story of God in Christ must be specifically articulated so that people could respond emotionally and intellectually? What did early Methodists hope would result from evangelistic practices? If evangelism has anything to do with announcing the particular story of God in Christ, then how does evangelism take place through one's ethical life alone? Formulating answers to such questions from Wesley's perspective is a daunting, yet important, task.

Nevertheless, some may question the need at this time for a book-length treatment of John Wesley's view of proclamation and its role in evangelism. After all, the Methodist movement's heritage, in both the United States and Great Britain, is generally understood as evangelical in nature, and certainly the important role of preaching is well documented. The handful of Oxford University students who started meeting in 1729 and were given the derogatory name "Methodists," grew to more than 80,000 adherents in Great Britain by the time of John Wesley's death in 1791. Since his death Wesleyan movements have spread to virtually every corner of the globe. Furthermore, Wesley himself is typically seen as an evangelist extraordinaire, having over the course of his lifetime preached some 40,000 sermons and traveled approximately 250,000 miles as he carried out his ministry. Methodism's evangelical foundations seem strong. And yet, for a number of reasons, Wesley's conception of proclamation and the responses he desired from it necessitates a further look in light of current thought on evangelism.

First, the fields of Wesley Studies and evangelism remain topics of interest globally for Methodist students in graduate theological education as well as clergy and laity reflecting on their tradition. Over the past fifty years, through the initial work of Frank Baker, Albert Outler, and many others, Wesley has been reclaimed as not only a practitioner but also a theologian in his own right. The "practical theology" he advocated is as relevant in Methodist communities around the world today as it was in his day in England. Similarly, conversations on the subject of evangelism remain vigorous in Methodist communities in the United States and Europe and around the world. Having served as a pastor in several United Methodist churches for fifteen years, I have observed firsthand that evangelism is a regular topic of conversation in local churches throughout the United States. Pastors and churches still search for a practice of evangelism that is true to the Christian tradition, in general, and Wesleyan ones, in particular. As I pursued my doctoral work in the United Kingdom and as I teach, lecture, and otherwise engage Methodists around the world, I now see that conversations about the nature of a Wesleyan evangelism are nearly universal. Some people may define evangelism differently, and they may have contrary critiques of it, but one thing is constant: the study of early Methodism and its relevance to contemporary theologies and practices of evangelism is as pertinent throughout the global Methodist community as ever. From the most progressive and plural churches to the most orthodox and traditional, the challenges, opportunities, and critiques of evangelism continue to generate discussion, if not debate. Even some of those who shy away from the terminology of evangelism because of its association with Western colonialism often still want to understand the current intersections between a Wesleyan vision of evangelism and contemporary ecclesial practices.

Second, Wesley's vision of proclamation, and any corresponding relationship to evangelism, is important today because of the increasing awareness of the depth of religious pluralism around the world. Christians are more and more aware of the mosaic that is the global religious community. In light of the religious extremism and violence in some religious communities around the globe, including some Christian fellowships, many Methodists wonder how, or even if, evangelism has any place in the modern world. Some propose that in light of continuing conflict within faith communities, as well as the historical examples of various faith traditions oppressing others, the world would be better off if religious communities kept to themselves. Core beliefs, practices, and visions for the human community and for the planet should rarely be shared, they argue, and certainly people from one religious community should never invite people from another community to join theirs.

And yet, as different religions and traditions continue to mingle with the "other," many naturally begin to share their hopes and dreams and the perceived benefits that their worldview, tradition, or religion offers to a fractured world. Many Methodists find that they want to share their understanding of God's good news in Jesus Christ as well. They believe that their story of God coming to the world in Jesus Christ is one that brings hope and thus deserves to be shared with the world. The question they seek to answer is this: How do Methodists share that good news in such a way that people receive it and respond to it? These two reasons—along with the range of sometimes contradictory interpretations of John Wesley's conception of evangelism, the practices he associated with it, and the ends he desired from it—make this an appropriate time to take a fresh look at Wesley's evangelistic vision.

Third, and perhaps most importantly, I believe we Methodists have missed two critical aspects of Wesley's evangelistic vision. Some of us, I believe correctly, sensed that Wesley's notion of evangelism involved more than verbal proclamation of the gospel and a corresponding call to conversion through repentance and faith. But often our remedy was to expand the act of evangelism to such a degree that proclamation became optional in the church's evangelistic task; it became one of a constellation of practices that might make up evangelism, and no longer integral to evangelism itself. Furthermore, this same remedy also led to a radical deemphasizing of conversion, to such a degree that conversion is seen as optional in some parts of the Wesleyan community. In this book I argue that Wesley would tell us our instincts are correct—evangelism is more than proclamation and conversion—but that our remedy is flawed.

Instead of expanding evangelism to include all aspects of the church's ministry, Wesley believed we should expand our understanding of how people respond to the story of God in Christ through the power of the Holy Spirit. I believe Wesley would say that we "truncate" evangelism when we make conversion the only proper response to proclamation—not when we see verbal proclamation as the essential practice of evangelism.[15] Wesley believed, I argue, that repentance and faith that leads to a conversion is a necessary response to an encounter with the story of God in Christ. But it is not the only response. Rather it is one of three primary responses along with awakening and further repentance and faith that leads to holiness and sanctification. Wesley was aware that each of these three responses is critical to Christian maturity, and he designed the Methodist structure of ministry with them in mind. Following Wesley's death, however, the importance of this threefold response was minimized, and in some cases abandoned, with the result that conversion became the defining response of evangelism. Paul Chilcote expresses this reality well, along with its rise in the nineteenth century: "The revivalist milieu of the American frontier led to a shift from holiness of heart and life as the goal of the Christian life for Methodists to the experience of conversion as the defining event of redemption."[16] Today, instead of holding awakening, conversion, and

[15]Warner, 3, 7–10, 83, 266, 268, 271, 273, 277. Throughout this important book Warner argues that evangelism is "truncated" when evangelism is limited to verbal alone.

[16]Chilcote, 230.

sanctification as coequal responses to the gospel, Methodists unwittingly marginalize each one in favor of expanding the practice of evangelism to include virtually the entirety of mission. The remedy is not to expand the practice of evangelism beyond proclamation but to understand the full spectrum of response that the Holy Spirit seeks as people engage the story of God in Christ. Wesley shows us the way.

I propose we read Wesley again on his own terms. He believed the practice of a person telling the gospel story to another person or group of people was integral the church's ministry. This personal proclamation was multifaceted and included preaching, teaching, and exhortation.[17] Wesley was convinced that as people encounter the story of God through these various practices, the Holy Spirit works to encourage maturity in discipleship, from what Wesley called the "natural" person, through awakening, conversion, and sanctification. The result was a multifaceted practice of proclamation that encouraged these three responses; thus any description of proclamation in Wesley's evangelistic vision is incomplete if the various practices and responses are ignored. Furthermore, as I read Wesley, I encountered an idea that I believe is a significant contribution of this book—namely that the early Methodist practice of visitation was a critical component of Wesley's evangelistic vision, a vision that contemporary Methodists should not overlook. Visitation provided the most intimate setting in which Methodist preachers and laity could share the gospel story, and then in partnership with the Spirit encourage people to embrace the Spirit's awakening, converting, and sanctifying power. The central thesis of this book is that any discussion of Wesley's vision of evangelism must center on the proclamation of the story of God in Christ. Evangelism may have been more than mere proclamation to Wesley, but it certainly did not omit proclamation. I believe Wesley's writing and the very structure of the early Methodist community demonstrate that the heart of his evangelistic vision is the proclamation of the story of God in Christ.

Let me stress that I do not seek to challenge the importance of

[17]Proclamation of the gospel in particular, and the Bible in general, certainly took place in other ways. A prime example was through the singing of early Methodist hymns, especially those of Charles Wesley. Methodist hymnals were even structured around the various responses to grace. Other examples of proclamation include reading the Bible itself (which inherently entails proclamation of the biblical story), and the miraculous work of the Spirit to proclaim the gospel directly to a person with no other interpreter. I do not explore these other types of proclamation in great depth because my focus here is to explore the interaction between two or more people that is entailed, though at a distance in field preaching and society meetings, but quite intimately in class meetings and visitation. In this book I explore the primary ways the early Methodist community thought the Spirit partners with the proclaimer to encourage the listener. Hymns, reading the Bible, and the miraculous work of the Spirit do not necessitate what Tom Albin refers to as the human "catalyst" that partners with the Spirit to encourage maturity as a follower of Christ. Thomas R. Albin, "An Empirical Study of Early Methodist Spirituality," in *Wesleyan Theology Today: A Bicentennial Theological Consultation*, ed. Theodore Runyon (Nashville: Kingswood, 1985), 277.

embodying a Christian social ethic for any person who seeks to be true to Wesleyan evangelism or to minimize the role of initiation in discipleship. Warner and others are certainly correct that embodying a Christian social ethic is critical to people's perception of the value of embracing the Christian faith. In this way a personal or corporate Christian social ethic intimately relates to evangelism in that it serves to authenticate one's Christian faith. Absent a Christian ethical life, the seriousness with which an evangelist takes the story of God comes into question. But ethics also relate to other aspects of Christian life, such as worship. For example, if one who purports to worship as a Christian does not demonstrate a comparable Christian ethic in other areas of her life, then her worship will be seen as inauthentic. All aspects of a Christian's life and ministry, in order to be seen as valid and authentic by those not claiming the Christian faith, must correspond with one who models a Christian social ethic, not just evangelism.

Furthermore, Christian practices of initiation are vital to discipleship. Announcing the story of God hopefully and prayerfully leads to initiation into the work of the church and the reign of God. But in Wesley's mind proclamation of the gospel does more than just initiate people into the faith. The same gospel, through the inner work of the Holy Spirit, also provides the initial spark that can motivate people to see that the story of Christ is something worth investigating. The Spirit then keeps working in people's lives through the repetitive announcement of the gospel long after awakening and conversion, calling disciples to continually be molded into the image of God, namely the process of sanctification. In other words, the same story that encourages conversion also facilitates awakening and sanctification, as the Spirit works to reveal the power and presence of God in people's lives.

This threefold understanding of the work of the Spirit through proclamation is evident in a January 28, 1788, letter from Hester Ann Rogers to Wesley regarding some remarkable events that occurred in her Methodist community the previous month. She writes that during the preaching service on Christmas morning, "God was truly present to bless; many were awakened, and some converted."[18] Furthermore, at the New Year's Eve Watch-Night service a few days later, "Many more were awakened, and four justified." During the subsequent love feast, "several also found pardon." The covenant renewal service a few days later, however, "exceeded all: fourteen souls were that day born of God; some at their classes, and the rest at that sweet, solemn season of covenant... several were perfected in love and several backsliders restored." Over the next month, she writes, between thirty and forty joined the Methodist society, "several of whom date their awakenings from the covenant night."

[18]Hester A. Rogers, *An Account of the Experience of Hester Ann Rogers: And Her Funeral Sermon* (New York: Carlton & Porter, 1857), 270–71.

Rogers's letter hints at Wesley's understanding of the dynamic relationship in the early Methodist community between human proclamation and the work of the Spirit to nurture people through the stages of discipleship. The human task is to proclaim the gospel story in a variety of ways and in a variety of settings. In turn then the Spirit works in conjunction with proclamation to help people become aware of God, become disciples, and then mature as disciples. The proclaimer becomes, as Tom Albin writes, the human "catalyst" that partners with the Spirit to encourage maturity as a follower of Christ.[19] This relationship is integral to John Wesley's overarching evangelistic vision, but it is for the most part overlooked in contemporary conversations on early Methodist evangelism. Rogers's narrative points to a troubling reality, namely, that contemporary Wesleyan conceptions of the role of proclamation in evangelism often prune Wesley's vision of the ways in which verbal proclamation occurs and the responses it encourages and facilitates.

I propose that Wesley's evangelistic vision is best understood as a continual offering of God's gracious love in Christ Jesus. Through that proclamation, which takes place over the course of a lifetime of discipleship, the Holy Spirit works to facilitate various responses of deeper maturity of faith. The early Methodist community was structured around the conviction that God offers the grace of Christ in every moment, and that responding to Christ is the proper human posture. For as the early Methodist Hannah Ball wrote: "There is no state of life, but needs much grace."[20]

This book offers at once a broader and narrower interpretation of proclamation in Wesley's evangelistic vision. Based on my engagement with Wesley's writings, as well as original archival research on other early Methodists conducted at the John Rylands Library in Manchester, England, I propose that the dominant nineteenth-century vision of evangelism, as well as contemporary efforts that rightly seek to correct its errors, both abridge Wesley's evangelistic vision. His vision is best understood as a matrix in which the story of God in Christ is particularly announced in a variety of ways and a number of forums, and through which the Spirit encourages different responses in people, depending on their maturity as disciples of Jesus Christ.

The first element of the matrix is the various types of verbal proclamation in early Methodism. Wesley and the early Methodists believed proclamation to be critical to the church's very foundation and insisted that the story of God in Christ must be articulated in a way that people can respond both intellectually and emotionally. The story of God in Christ,

[19]Albin, 277.

[20]Paul Wesley Chilcote, *Early Methodist Spirituality: Selected Women's Writings* (Nashville: Kingswood, 2007), 14.

Wesley believed, is rarely intuited; therefore it must be announced in most situations. God works miraculously at times to tell the story of grace, but the Spirit's normative work is in partnership with a human conduit who announces the story. The people of God are called to specifically narrate the story of God, a practice Wesley understood as a means of grace, so that people might engage and experience the power of the Spirit in their lives. The Methodist system was designed to encourage continual proclamation and encounters with the Spirit in order to inspire people to maturity as disciples. His understanding of evangelism, therefore, is best understood as a set of practices that includes proclamation as its central, defining, and only constitutive practice. This particular proclamation in early Methodism ultimately included a number of activities, most prominently preaching, teaching, and exhortation.

The second element of the matrix involves Wesley's understanding of how the Spirit inspires people to mature as Christian disciples. Wesley believed that all people begin their lives in the "natural state," in a state of sin, having perhaps awareness of God but not of the story of God in Christ. He believed that as people encounter grace in the Christian story, they progress through three distinct stages of discipleship, though not always smoothly, linearly, or at the same rate.[21] The first stage occurs when one begins to "awaken" to the gospel story and to investigate its verity and relevance for life. The second stage occurs when one believes in Christ and repents for the first time, a stage that results in conversion and justification. The final stage is a constant journey of holiness that Wesley (and many of his followers since) sees as the apex of Christian discipleship. Wesley believed conversion to be critical, but not as an end in itself. Rather, Wesley believed conversion is critical because only after an initial repentance and faith could one then experience the New Birth and begin the journey of sanctification. In this way, Wesley anticipated nineteenth-century evangelists who called people to repent and believe and thus be converted. But unlike many of those evangelists, Wesley then invited people to the second aspect of salvation, namely, holiness of heart and life. Salvation for Wesley included both justification and sanctification.[22] In this way, Wesley differed significantly from nineteenth-century evangelists who almost exclusively sought conversion and justification.

The third element of the matrix includes the primary forums in which this particular proclamation took place, namely, field preaching, society

[21]Albin refers to the "spiritual transitions" people make with awakening/conviction, the New Birth, and sanctification. Albin, 277.

[22]*Sermons II: 34-70,* v. 2 in *The Bicentennial Edition of the Works of John Wesley* (Nashville: Abingdon, 1985). Sermon 43, "The Scripture Way of Salvation," §3, 2:157. Cited hereafter as *Sermons II.*

meetings, and, most importantly, class meetings and visitation.[23] Public preaching in the fields and in the large gatherings of Methodist societies was integral to Wesley's vision and is frequently included in discussions of early Methodist evangelism. As I note in the book, even class meetings are understood as an important place in which proclamation occurred in early Methodism. But visitation, and the private instruction it allowed, was essential to Wesley's evangelistic vision. Visitation was the most personal forum and therefore in Wesley's mind provided the most opportune setting for deep conversation, gospel proclamation, and an invitation to conversion or sanctification. And yet visitation is consistently downplayed, or even overlooked entirely, in contemporary discussions. That Methodists today overlook visitation's vital role in the early days is not unexpected since even in his lifetime Wesley had to work to maintain its central place in the ministry. Since his death, visitation has been almost universally overlooked as critical to Wesley's method of discipleship and the role of evangelism in it. Yet I believe his evangelistic vision simply cannot be understood apart from visitation.[24]

Wesley, I argue, believed that maturity through three responses or stages—not just conversion—results from engaging the story of God in Christ through the power of the Spirit. Proclamation of the gospel helps nurture people through the stages of discipleship, each of which is rightly considered a response to the gospel story. Wesley's evangelism is then best understood as an ongoing act of telling the gospel story which encourages a variety of responses throughout one's journey of discipleship. Thus proclamation continually engages all persons, Christians and otherwise, with the story of God in Christ and includes a corresponding invitation to grow and deepen as his disciples.

The framework I propose here demonstrates that Wesley's nineteenth-century interpreters did indeed misconstrue Wesley's concept of evangelism, but not in the ways so many twentieth- and twenty-first-century commentators assert. The mistake nineteenth-century Methodists made was not their emphasis on proclamation, but their failure to emphasize awakening and holiness as legitimate responses to proclamation. Furthermore they, along with most Methodists since Wesley, overlooked the importance of personal visitation in evangelism, an omission Wesley would have found unimaginable. I believe a fresh look at Wesley's understanding

[23]Rogers describes a number of activities that often included preaching or another type of proclamation in addition to society and class meetings. Some of these include Watch Night, Covenant Renewal, and Love Feast gatherings. These three gatherings, as I discuss in the book, are various gatherings of society members, not distinct communities themselves.

[24]Wesley uses various phrases such as "private instruction," "visitation," "visiting from house to house" to describe the practice of visiting. Visitation typically involved a private meeting, usually in a home, that allowed for private instruction and catechesis.

of proclamation will help our efforts to solidify evangelism as the heart of mission and proclamation as the heart of evangelism.

To give an overview: the book is divided into seven chapters and a conclusion. The first three chapters discuss the foundations for proclamation itself in early Methodism. Chapter 1 surveys the primary themes and characteristics of early Methodist proclamation. The chapter also explores early Methodist understandings of the nature of the gospel itself as the subject of Methodist proclamation. I highlight Wesley's insistence on articulating the gospel so that people can encounter the Spirit and then either reject God's presence or move toward faith and discipleship. Next I describe various characteristics Wesley thought integral to the proclaimer and the proclaiming community, including an embodiment of the gospel in one's ethical life, the presence of a Christian community, and the partnership of the Holy Spirit.

Chapter 2 addresses the means or methods by which the gospel is particularly announced in early Methodism, including preaching, exhortation, and teaching. This chapter includes discussions of how the gospel is announced through each method and its role in Methodism. I also outline how some of these methods were commonplace in Wesley's day and how he looked back to earlier Christian traditions, building upon them and molding them to fit his own vision of proclamation and its role in discipleship formation. This chapter addresses the human task of evangelism, namely, to proclaim God's grace while acknowledging the integral work of the Holy Spirit. The Spirit is the primary evangelist who usually, but not always, works in conjunction with a human proclaimer.

In chapter 3 I discuss the Spirit's role in encouraging the three primary responses Methodists sought as people matured in discipleship: awakening, initial faith and repentance leading to justification, and ever deeper faith and repentance leading to sanctification. The Spirit is always at work in people's lives, and the Spirit is the primary actor in evangelism. But those who encounter the gospel have a responsibility, as Randy Maddox argues, to respond to the work of the Spirit. In this chapter I argue that an initial response of repentance and faith leading to justification, while critical to discipleship, was never understood by Wesley or by most early Methodists as the sole response to proclamation of the good news of God in Jesus Christ. Rather the initial response of awakening and subsequent responses of repentance and faith that lead to greater depths of sanctification are just as important. This threefold progression in early Methodism is well known. What is less well understood, and what I explore in this chapter, is Wesley's assertion that the story of God in Christ encourages maturity through each stage.

The four primary forums in which early Methodists proclaimed the gospel—preaching abroad or field preaching, society meetings, class meetings, and visitation—are the subjects of chapters 4 through 7. Methodism in Wesley's day was structured to provide ever more private spaces for proclamation of the story of God in Christ. I trace the early Methodist understanding of the role of gospel proclamation in the various forums and the methods of proclamation in each. Furthermore, I clarify how proclamation leads to a variety of responses in each forum. I argue that Wesley, far from assuming that people respond in only one way in each forum, believed that different people respond in different ways, based on their maturity as disciples. Again, I identify historical precedents for each forum, demonstrating that Wesley not only looked back in church history for practices but also adjusted them to fit the specific needs and realities of his day. This threefold matrix demonstrates that practices associated with evangelism in early Methodism were much more nuanced than mere preaching leading to conversion or embodiment of a Christian ethical life. In John Wesley's evangelistic vision, human proclamation, in partnership with the inner work of the Spirit, offered grace within an intricate web that functioned throughout early Methodism to help people grow as disciples of Jesus Christ into the image of God.

This first book-length discussion of proclamation in John Wesley's evangelistic vision illuminates the nature and practice of evangelism in one of the greatest evangelistic movements in Christian history. This book's most distinctive contribution to the field of Wesley studies and the theology and practice of evangelism is the way it documents the importance of visitation in Wesley's thought, especially its function in facilitating discipleship. This study also offers important contributions to current conversations on evangelism. I propose that Wesley's understanding that conversion is one of three crucial responses to the gospel story sheds significant light on some of the current controversy in evangelism. Furthermore, this books demonstrates that proclamation is the central and defining characteristic of evangelism without minimizing the importance of a Christian's ethical life. The book helps illumine an important movement in church history and offers hope for improving the effectiveness of Christian ministry today.

CHAPTER 1

THE MESSAGE PROCLAIMED

I have long desired that there might be an open, avowed union between all who preach those fundamental truths, Original Sin, and Justification by Faith, producing inward and outward holiness; but all my endeavours have been hitherto ineffectual. God's time is not fully come.[1]

Given that John Wesley preached about forty thousand sermons and traveled upward of 250,000 miles in order to reach all those preaching points, one could be forgiven for thinking that the topics of his sermons would be too numerous to count. While it is hard to imagine listening to all those sermons, much less preaching them, the reality is that the content of Wesley's proclamation, not just his preaching, is actually not as hard to determine as it may seem.

THE BIBLE: THE SOURCE OF CHRISTIAN PROCLAMATION

In a very generic way, the subject of Wesley's proclamation was quite simple. It was the Bible. Much has been made of Wesley's statement regarding his being a "man of one book": "I want to know one thing, the way to heaven—how to land safe on that happy shore. God himself has condescended to teach the way: for this very end he came from heaven. He hath written it down in a book. O give me that book! Give me the Book of God... Let me be *homo unius libri.*"[2]

In many ways, the Bible was the preeminent source of Wesley's proclamation and theology, as well as that of the Methodist community. He writes in his sermon "On God's Vineyard" that the other original

[1]*Journal and Diaries IV: 1755–65*, v. 21 in *The Bicentennial Edition of the Works of John Wesley* (Nashville: Abingdon, 1992), 12 March 1764, 21:444. Cited hereafter as *Journal and Diaries IV*.

[2]*Sermons I: 1–33*, v. 1 in *The Bicentennial Edition of the Works of John Wesley* (Nashville: Abingdon, 1984). *Preface*, 1:105. Cited hereafter as *Sermons I*.

members of the Holy Club in Oxford were also men "of one book."[3] He continues:

> God taught them all, to make his "word a lantern unto their feet, and a light in all their paths." They had one, and only one, rule of judgement with regard to all their tempers, words, and actions; namely, the oracles of God. They were one and all determined to be *Bible-Christians*. They were continually reproached for this very thing; some terming them, in derision, *Bible-bigots*; others, *Bible-moths*; feeding, they said, upon the Bible, as moths do upon cloth. And indeed, unto this day, it is their constant endeavour to think and speak as the oracles of God.[4]

Wesley viewed the Bible as the "whole and sole rule of Christian faith and practice."[5] The Bible is the normative guide for Christian belief and discipleship. As he describes in *A Plain Account of Christian Perfection*, the Bible is "the only standard of truth, and the only model of pure religion."[6] Perhaps an example even more indicative of his views is found in his *Notes on the New Testament*. Here he writes that the scripture of the "Old and New Testaments is a most solid and precious system of divine truth. Every part thereof is worthy of God; all together are one entire body, wherein is no defect, no excess."[7] He writes in his journal, "If there be any mistakes in the Bible, it did not come from the God of truth."[8] In a letter to William Warburton in response to Warburton's assertion that there is "no considerable error" in the Bible, Wesley asks, "Will not the allowing there is an error in Scripture shake the authority of the whole?"[9]

Statements and questions such as those lead some scholars to assert that Wesley, as well as other early Methodists, believed in the Bible's "infallibility" and "inerrancy" as they are understood today. [10] But Randy

[3]*Sermons III: 71–114*, v. 3 in *The Bicentennial Edition of the Works of John Wesley* (Nashville: Abingdon, 1986). Sermon 107, "On God's Vineyard," 3:504. Cited hereafter as *Sermons III*.

[4]Ibid., Sermon 107, "On God's Vineyard," 3:504. Italics in original.

[5]*The Methodist Societies: History, Nature, and Design*, v. 9 in *The Bicentennial Edition of the Works of John Wesley* (Nashville: Abingdon, 1989)."Thoughts Upon Methodism," §2, 9:527. Cited hereafter as *Societies*.

[6]*Doctrinal and Controversial Treatises II*, v. 13 in *The Bicentennial Edition of the Works of John Wesley* (Nashville: Abingdon, 2013), §5, 13:137. Cited hereafter as *Treatises II*.

[7]*The Works of John Wesley*, 3rd ed., 14 vols. (Grand Rapids: Baker, 1978). Preface, *Explanatory Notes upon the New Testament*, §10, 14:238. Cited hereafter as *Works* (Jackson).

[8]*Journal and Diaries VI: 1776–86*, v. 23 in *The Bicentennial Edition of the Works of John Wesley* (Nashville: Abingdon, 1995), 24 July 1776, 23:25. Cited hereafter as *Journal and Diaries VI*.

[9]*The Appeals to Men of Reason and Religion and Certain Related Open Letters*, v. 11 in *The Bicentennial Edition of the Works of John Wesley* (Oxford: Clarendon Press, 1975). Letter to Bishop of Gloucester (1763), §II.5, 11:504. Cited hereafter as *Appeals*.

[10]Daryl McCarthy, "Early Wesleyan Views of Scripture," *Wesleyan Theological Journal* 16, no. 2 (1981), 103.

Maddox has recently challenged this idea.[11] Maddox points out that Wesley never uses the words *inerrant* and *inerrancy* and was aware of the Bible's inconsistencies and minor contradictions, especially in some genealogies and New Testament references to Hebrew Bible passages. Nevertheless, Wesley did find the Bible "infallibly true" in its identification of core Christian beliefs and its narration of the way of holiness.[12] The Bible provides the foundation for Christian teachings and is to be taught in a way that does not mix its teachings with the "heresies of others or the fancies of [one's] own brain."[13] The Bible is for Wesley, as Maddox concludes, the "trustworthy book of God."[14]

The Bible was integral to his life from his earliest days. As early as 1728 Wesley writes that the Bible is the word of God and that it is the content of Christian preaching. Indeed, the Bible's importance to Wesley is hard to overstate. Of all Wesley's sermons, we have no record of him using anything other than the Bible as the primary text from which he preached.[15] His preachers seem to have followed a similar pattern in most cases.[16]

The Bible Wesley usually read, cited, and proclaimed was the King James Version (KJV).[17] The other version that he frequently cited, especially for the Psalms, was the Miles Coverdale version, which was the text for the Book of Common Prayer. While he preached from the KJV, Wesley clearly emphasized reading and studying from the Greek and Hebrew texts. He wrote his own *Notes* on the Greek and Hebrew Bibles and encouraged his preachers to use the original languages in their own study. Furthermore, he believed that the original texts were so important that he abridged Greek and Hebrew grammars for the students at the Kingswood School.[18]

---

[11]Randy L. Maddox, "The Rule of Christian Faith, Practice, and Hope: John Wesley on the Bible," *Methodist Review* 3 (2011): 9–13.

[12]See *Sermons I*, Sermon 16, "The Means of Grace," §III.8, 1:388. See also ibid., Sermon 12, "The Witness of our Own Spirit," §6, 1:302–303; and *Sermons II*, Sermon 36, "The Law Established by Faith, II," §I.5, 2:37.

[13]Maddox, 13.

[14]*Sermons IV: 115–51*, v. 4 in *The Bicentennial Edition of the Works of John Wesley* (Nashville: Abingdon, 1987). Sermon 137, "On Corrupting the Word of God," §I.1, 4:247. Cited hereafter as *Sermons IV*. In his November 1, 1739, journal entry, Wesley seems to embrace the contents of a letter he received from Rev. Josiah Tucker, and which Wesley records in his journal entry of the day: "In all your sermons, writings, and practice, nakedly to follow the naked Jesus: I mean, to preach the pure doctrine of the gospel without respect of persons or things. Many Preachers, many Reformers, many Missionaries, have fallen by not observing this." *Journal and Diaries II: 1738–43*, v. 19 in *The Bicentennial Edition of the Works of John Wesley* (Nashville: Abingdon, 1990), 19:114. Cited hereafter as *Journal and Diaries II*.

[15]David Hempton, *Methodism: Empire of the Spirit* (New Haven: Yale University Press, 2005), 74.

[16]Ibid.

[17]Maddox, 102.

[18]Wesley, *Works* (Jackson), "A Plain Account of Kingwood School," 13:295. For the grammars see 14:78–160.

For Wesley, the entirety of the Bible, both the Hebrew Bible and New Testaments, was pertinent to Christian discipleship. He read the entire Bible and encouraged Methodists to do likewise. He insisted that the Hebrew Bible was part of the Christian tradition and that it was critical to a Christian's life of discipleship.[19] The New Testament's authority as the *final standard* of Christian faith and practice did not undermine the Hebrew Bible's importance in his mind.[20] Together, both testaments are the "whole counsel of God."[21] Wesley believed that the Bible included all that was necessary for salvation.

In order to best discern the intent of the biblical text, Wesley therefore believed the Bible was best interpreted in conversation with a variety of other resources such as the church and the natural world, and even itself. These other resources, read in partnership and in light of the Bible, help inform a Christian's understanding of faith and discipleship. He never claims that the Bible is the only book for Christians to read and study. In fact, he declares the opposite, writing in the 1770 *Large Minutes* that using only the Bible to gain understanding into life and faith is "rank enthusiasm" and that even St. Paul requested some other books.[22] Methodists must read more than just the Bible alone: "Read the most useful books [in addition to the Bible], and that regularly and constantly . . . at least five hours in twenty-four."[23] When some Methodists said they didn't have books, Wesley offered them up to five pounds to purchase books. Others said they didn't enjoy reading other books, to which Wesley replied, "Contract a taste for it by use, or return to your trade."[24]

IN CONVERSATION WITH THE CHURCH[25]

Wesley thought Christians needed the church and its tradition in order to correctly interpret the Bible for a number of reasons. The first reason was that he sometimes found the scriptures unclear. Second, and as importantly, Wesley recognized that people were sometimes wrong in their

[19]Matthew R. Schlimm, "Defending the Old Testament's Worth: John Wesley's Reaction to the Rebirth of Marcionism," *Wesleyan Theological Journal* 42, no. 2 (2007): 38–40.

[20]Maddox, 17.

[21]*Sermons III*, 3:258.

[22]*The Methodist Societies: The Minutes of Conference, Large Minutes*, 1770–72, §34.1, 10:887. Cited hereafter as *Minutes of Conference*.

[23]Ibid.

[24]Ibid., 10:888.

[25]Maddox, 1–35. Maddox provides a helpful analysis of a number of issues touched on in this chapter, including Wesley's understanding of the Bible in "conversation" with the Book of Nature, Christian tradition, and the Bible itself.

judgments. Wesley describes this reality, and the need for a bit of humility, in his sermon "Catholic Spirit":

> Although every man necessarily believes that every particular opinion which he holds is true...yet can no man be assured that all his own opinions, taken together, are true. Nay, every thinking man is assured they are not seeing *humanum est errare et nescire*—to be ignorant of many things, and to mistake in some, is the necessary condition of humanity.[26]

When biblical texts differed, Wesley believed that the clearer texts should inform those that were less so. "If any doubt still remains," Wesley writes, "I consult those who are experienced in the things of God, and then the writings whereby, being dead, they yet speak."[27] In other words, Wesley believed that Christians should read the Bible in conference with Christians from earlier generations, even as they try to make sense of the Bible in their own time and place.[28] Wesley encouraged his preachers to read beyond the Bible, going so far as to create a "library" of resources and even publishing materials himself to make available both to Methodists and non-Methodists alike. Wesley was especially cognizant of the place of the early church (especially the first three centuries) in interpreting the Bible and in setting "intentional patterns for Methodist beliefs and practices."[29] In a letter to Conyers Middleton, Wesley explains that some early Christian writings helped Christians avoid errors in their interpretation of scripture and that ignorance of those writings led people to emphasize current issues over those of the biblical text.[30] In this way the church's tradition became a conversation partner with the Bible.

In Conversation with the Book of Nature

A second conversation partner for the Bible in Wesley's mind is the "book of nature." Nature is another "revelation" of God that helps inform scripture. As Wesley writes,

> The world around us is the mighty volume wherein God hath declared himself...the book of nature is written in a universal character, which everyone may read in his own language. It contains not words, but things which

[26]*Sermons II*, Sermon 39, "Catholic Spirit," §1.4, 2:84.

[27]*Sermons I*, Preface, §5, 1:106.

[28]Maddox, 18.

[29]Ted Campbell, *John Wesley and Christian Antiquity: Religious Vision and Cultural Change* (Nashville: Kingswood, 1991), 106.

[30]John Wesley, *The Letters of the Rev. John Wesley*, ed. John Telford, 8 vols. (London: Epworth, 1931). "A Letter to the Reverend Dr. Conyers Middleton," 4–24 January 1749, 2:325. Cited hereafter as *Letters* (Telford).

picture out the Divine perfection. The firmament everywhere expanded, with all its starry host, declares the immensity and magnificence, the power and wisdom of its Creator...thus it is, that every part of nature directs us to nature's God.[31]

Wesley de Souza proposes that Wesley's use of nature as a conversation partner is so great that it should join reason, tradition, and experience as key theological partners with scripture.[32] Wesley believed that in studying the natural world Christians develop a deeper undrestanding of scripture, grow in faith, and become more appreciative of "God's power, wisdom and goodness."[33]

THE BIBLE IN CONVERSATION WITH ITSELF

As important as the church and nature were in Wesley's mind, the Bible itself was a crucial conversation partner for biblical interpretation. While Wesley believed that the entirety of the Bible was worthy of proclamation, he recognized two qualifications. First, the Bible had to be interpreted in light of its context. Wesley thought it was critical to read a passage in light of its context, that is, in light of "what precedes and what follows the text," instead of picking isolated passages.[34] This helped preachers to preach the natural and "obvious" subject instead of mixing it in with their own interpretations.[35] Second, some passages and themes are more important than others. The reason seems to be that Wesley thought some passages expressed themes that are pertinent to every age (as opposed to being relevant only to a time in the Hebrew Bible or New Testaments) or that ran throughout both testaments. Three examples of the first case suffice:

> Every truth which is revealed in the oracles of God is undoubtedly of great importance. Yet it may be allowed that some of those which are revealed therein are of greater importance than others as being more immediately conducive to the grand end of all, the eternal salvation of [humanity]. And we may judge of their importance even from this circumstance, that they are

[31]*A Compendium of Natural Philosophy: Being a Survey of the Wisdom of God in the Creation*, 3 vols. (London: Thomas Tegg and Son, 1836), 2:370. See also Howard A. Snyder, *Yes in Christ: Wesleyan Reflections on Gospel, Mission, and Culture*, Tyndale Studies in Wesleyan History and Theology (Toronto: Clements Academic, 2010), 52.

[32]Luis Wesley de Souza, "The Wisdom of God in Creation: Mission and the Wesleyan Pentalateral," in *Global Good News: Mission in a New Context*, ed. Howard A. Snyder (Nashville: Abingdon, 2001), 150.

[33]Maddox, 24.

[34]*Sermons IV*, Sermon 137, "On Corrupting the Word of God," §2.2, 4:249.

[35]Ibid.

not mentioned only once in the sacred writings, but are repeated over and over.[36]

> We know, "All Scripture is given by inspiration of God," and is therefore true and right concerning all things. But we know likewise that there are some Scriptures which more immediately commend themselves to every [person's] conscience.[37]

> There is nothing superfluous in [the word of God], relating either to faith or practice; and therefore they [those who are sincere] preach all parts of it, though those more particularly which are more immediately wanted where they are.[38]

Among these most critical passages are the Sermon on the Mount in Matthew 5–7, 1 Corinthians 13, and 1 John; these are among the chapters of the Bible he cites most frequently. Wesley believed that 1 John, as a "compendium of all the Holy Scriptures" (since it was, he thought, the latest biblical text), was perhaps "the deepest part of Scripture."[39] First John 4:19, "We love because God first loved us," was in Wesley's mind, "the sum of the whole gospel."[40] For these reasons it is not surprising that Wesley seems to have used verses from 1 John as his sermon text more frequently than any other book of the Bible.[41] On the other hand there is no record of Wesley ever preaching from Esther, the Song of Songs, Obadiah, Nahum, Zephaniah, Philemon, and 3 John.[42]

Wesley's understanding of the "whole tenor" of scripture relates to his use of the term "the analogy of faith." Until the Reformation, Roman Catholics applied St. Augustine's "rule of faith" as a way to clarify ambiguous passages in the creation of doctrine. The "rule of faith" incorporated more of the church's tradition in interpreting these difficult passages than Protestants would be comfortable with after the Reformation. Therefore Protestants began using the "analogy of faith," which looked more to scripture's grand themes, especially for interpreting more difficult passages. But the pattern is true not just for difficult or ambiguous passages, or those that discuss unusual commands or visions of God; rather, the "analogy of faith" becomes a way to the "deep pattern in the message

---

[36]*Sermons III,* Sermon 73, "Of Hell," §1, 3:31.

[37]Ibid., Sermon 91, "On Charity," Preamble, 3:292.

[38]*Sermons IV,* Sermon 137, "On Corrupting the Word of God," §2.3, 4:249.

[39]Maddox, 115.

[40]*Sermons II,* Preface, §6, 2:357.

[41]Maddox, 27.

[42]Ibid., 16.

of Scripture that helps us interpret it. Individual passages of Scripture are read in relation to each other according to how they fit into this pattern. What guides our understanding is not any single statement but a sense of the whole shape of Christian faith."[43]

Wesley most clearly expresses this use of the overall tenor of the Bible to interpret the Bible itself through his ideas of "getting the sense of the whole" pattern of scripture, or getting the "whole tenor of Scripture," not just an individual passage. For Wesley, the Bible was the centerpiece of Christian proclamation. It and it alone formed the essential content of Wesley's preaching.

PRIMARY BIBLICAL THEMES FOR PROCLAMATION

God's Love

The love of God for humanity and creation, and in turn God's call for people to love God and others, is the overarching theme of Wesley's proclamation. Two examples are found when Wesley writes,

> In my general tenor of preaching, I teach nothing (as the substance of religion) more singular than the love of God and man.[44]

> What religion do I preach? The religion of love; the law of kindness brought to light by the gospel.[45]

Wesley believed that God's love is the lens through which all of scripture should be read. He saw this theme most clearly in 1 John where John describes God's nature as love. Wesley believed that the writer of 1 John and Revelation was the "last of the inspired writers."[46] Therefore the themes found in these two books should be given priority in theological deliberation, since they reflect the final perspective of the inspired biblical writers. Not surprisingly then, Wesley emphasizes God's love over God's sovereignty, since he believed that the author of 1 John read the entirety of the scriptural narrative as stressing love over sovereignty. He never denied the sovereignty identified, for example, in Paul's letter to the Romans, but he interpreted that sovereignty through the later biblical writer's view of God's love.

---

[43]Joel B. Green and William H. Willimon, *The Wesley Study Bible* (Nashville: Abingdon, 2009)."Analogy of Faith," 1464.

[44]*Letters II: 1740–55*, v. 26 in *The Bicentennial Edition of the Works of John Wesley* (Oxford: Clarendon Press, 1982). 28 September 1745 letter to "John Smith," §18, 26:160. Cited hereafter as *Letters II*.

[45]Wesley, *Appeals, An Earnest Appeal to Men of Reason and Religion*, §19, 11:51.

[46]*Sermons II*, Sermon 40, "Christian Perfection," §20, 2:116.

Repentance, Faith, and Holiness

Out of this love flows what Wesley referred to in 1746 as Methodism's "main doctrines," namely repentance, faith, and holiness.[47] Everything that Methodism emphasizes, Wesley writes, flows from those three: "The first of these we account, as it were, the porch of religion; the next, the door; the third is religion itself." Wesley refers to these "main doctrines" or "grand scriptural doctrines" in various ways throughout his life, though rarely in exactly the same way, but rather introducing nuances on each occasion. For instance he sometimes summarizes the "fundamental" doctrines as justification and the New Birth.[48] In other cases, he describes faith and salvation as including "the substance of all the Bible, the marrow, as it were, of the whole Scripture."[49] In a letter to "John Smith" he writes, "Salvation by faith was my only theme."[50] In *Thoughts Upon Methodism*, he asserts that the "essence" of Methodist teaching is "holiness of heart and life."[51] Wesley emphasizes many other themes, such as assurance, Christian perfection, and the witness of the Spirit, to mention but a few. But as Wesley writes, each of these topics, as well as many others, falls under one of the three "main doctrines" mentioned above.

Wesley understood repentance as an ongoing acceptance of reality. First, "previous to faith," repentance is a self-awareness of one's sin. It is the knowledge "of that corruption of thy inmost nature, whereby thou are very far gone from original righteousness."[52] But repentance does not end with the faith that leads to justification; it continues, leading to deeper sanctification. As Wesley writes in his 1765 sermon "The Scripture Way of Salvation,"

> Faith, in general, is defined by the Apostle, ἔλεγχος πραγμάτων οὐ βλεπομένων—"an evidence," a divine "evidence and conviction" (the word means both), "of things not seen"—not visible, not perceivable either by sight or by any other of the external senses. It implies both a supernatural *evidence* of God, and of the things of God, a kind of spiritual *light* exhibited to the soul, and a supernatural *sight* or perception thereof.
>
> Taking the word in a more particular sense, faith is a divine evidence and conviction, not only that "God was in Christ, reconciling the world unto himself," but also that Christ "loved *me*, and gave Himself for *me*."[53]

---

[47]*Societies*, "The Principles of a Methodist Farther Explained," §5, 9:227.

[48]*Sermons II*, Sermon 45, "The New Birth," §20, 2:187.

[49]Ibid., Sermon 43, "The Scripture Way of Salvation," §2, 2:156.

[50]*Letters II*, Letter to John Smith, 30 December 1745, 26:181–82.

[51]*Societies*, "Thoughts upon Methodism," 9:529.

[52]*Sermons I*, Sermon 7, "The Way to the Kingdom," §2.1, 1:225.

[53]*Sermons II*, Sermon 43, "The Scripture Way of Salvation," §II.1–2, 2:160–61.

Rex Matthews argues that Wesley demonstrated three conceptions of faith over the course of his life, mainly as an assent to truth claims, as trust in God's love, and as an actual spiritual experience of God's love.[54] Holiness, or a steady growth in love for God and humanity, and "full sanctification" or perfect love, was the "grand depositum which God has lodged with the people called Methodist."[55]

Law and Gospel

During the Methodist revival two types of preachers—namely, gospel preachers and legal preachers—became common targets for critics of the Methodist movement, in particular, and the revival, in general; both types seemed to annoy Wesley. They came to signify a great difficulty in preaching: adequately balancing the proclamation of the law and the gospel, a practice that Wesley thought many do poorly but that is essential in order for people to actually repent, come to faith, and then grow in holiness.

"Legal preachers," according to some, were overly focused on God's wrath and original sin. Wesley acknowledges other terms for these preachers in his 1751 "Letter on Preaching Christ," in which he mentions some of the derogatory names for them, including "legal wretches," "doctors," or "doctors of divinity."[56] In his sermon "Law Established through Faith, Discourse 1," Wesley reminds readers that some critics use the phrase "a Preacher of the law" in a derogatory way to describe those who preach the law, "as though it meant little less than 'an enemy to the gospel.'"[57] Wesley was not entirely critical of "legal preachers," since he believed the ethical commands of Christ have to be announced and in turn lived. Wesley understood the law as a "complete model of all truth, so far as intelligible to a finite being" that endows souls with "the power to choose good or evil."[58] For Wesley the law is not simply a summary of human sinfulness. Rather, it is the ethical vision of the kingdom of God, especially as expressed by Jesus in the Sermon on the Mount. Jesus's Sermon on the Mount is, in Wesley's mind, the summary of "legal preaching": "By 'preaching the law' I mean explaining and enforcing the commands

[54]Rex Matthews, "'With the Eyes of Faith': Spiritual Experience and the Knowledge of God in the Theology of John Wesley," in *Wesleyan Theology Today*, ed. Theodore Runyon (Nashville: Kingswood, 1985), 406.

[55]*Letters* (Telford), Letter to Robert Carr Brackenbury, 15 September 1790, 8:238.

[56]*Letters II*, Letter to an Evangelical Layman or *On Preaching Christ*, 20 December 1751, §25, 26:487. Cited hereafter as Letter to an Evangelical Layman.

[57]*Sermons II*, Sermon 35, "Law Established through Faith, Discourse 1," §I.1, 2:22.

[58]Ibid., Sermon 34, "The Original, Nature, Property, and Use of the Law," 2:7.

of Christ, briefly comprised in the Sermon on the Mount."[59] In fact, before someone can truly hear and respond to God's love, Wesley believed, they first have to encounter the law and the reality of the sin rooted deep in their lives.

Gospel preachers, on the other hand, preach "the love of God to sinners, preaching the life, death, resurrection, and intercession of Christ, with all the blessings which, in consequence thereof, are freely given to true believers."[60] They preach one part of the message that must be proclaimed, namely, the gospel.

Wesley describes the gospel in his sermon "The Way to the Kingdom." He writes,

> "The gospel" (that is, good tidings, good news for guilty, helpless sinners) in the largest sense of the word means the whole revelation made to men by Jesus Christ; and sometimes the whole account of what our Lord did and suffered while he tabernacled among men. The substance of all is, "Jesus Christ came into the world to save sinners;" or, "God so loved the world that he gave his only-begotten Son, to the end we might not perish, but have everlasting life;" or, "He was bruised for our transgressions, he was wounded for our iniquities; the chastisement of our peace was upon him; and with his stripes we are healed."

But gospel preachers err, writes Wesley, in preaching the blessings of the gospel alone, and not in conjunction with the law. They preach the gospel without the law, with the result being that hearers "no longer bear sound doctrine…no longer hear the plain old truth with profit or pleasure, nay, hardly with patience."[61] They emphasized Christ's sacrifice and the results of eternal life for those who believe, without first describing the reason why Christ had to suffer and die. Gospel preachers offer an "unconnected rhapsody of unmeaning words" that

> Corrupt their hearers; they vitiate their taste, so that they cannot relish sound doctrine; and spoil their appetite, so that they cannot turn it into nourishment; they, as it were, feed them with sweetmeats, till the genuine wine of the kingdom seems quite insipid to them. They give them cordial upon cordial, which make them all life and spirit for the present; but, meantime, their appetite is destroyed, so that they can neither retain nor digest the pure milk of the word.[62]

[59]*Letters II*, Letter to an Evangelical Layman, 20 December 1751, §3, 26:482.

[60]Ibid.

[61]Ibid., §26, 26:487.

[62]Ibid.

In a letter to Mary Bishop, Wesley writes that he wishes no Methodist would use the term "gospel preaching" or "gospel preacher": "The term... has no determinate meaning. Let but a pert, self-sufficient animal, that has neither sense nor grace, bawl out something about Christ and his Blood or justification by faith, and his hearers cry out, 'What a fine gospel sermon!'"[63] Of all the types of preaching, gospel preaching is "the most useless, if not the most mischievous; a dull, yea or lively, harangue on the sufferings of Christ or salvation by faith without strongly inculcating holiness."[64] In Wesley's mind both the law and the gospel are intimately related, not doctrinal opposites. Without the gospel, the weight of the law is overwhelming. Without the law the gospel makes little sense.

The essence of the gospel for Wesley is God's love, a love that is seen most clearly in the life, death, and resurrection of Christ. This is God's ultimate love. Christ's suffering, death, and resurrection are not a form of divine child abuse, but rather a form of mutual self-sacrifice, a personal offering, of God's very own nature on humanity's behalf—indeed, on behalf of all creation. As Albert Outler writes,

> The gospel, in Wesleyan terms, is a joyous word from God to men, through men, in the depths of their existence... The gospel is a word of man's reliance and hope in God, of God's imperative that men should love him without stint and their neighbors without self-interest. It is a call to repentance, conversion, and new life. The gospel is an invitation from the Holy Spirit to fellowship in God's beloved community, in which men are inwardly moved to outward acts of thanksgiving, worship, and service.[65]

But Wesley believes that people encounter God's grace most profoundly when they see it in light of the law. Human sin, which God did not will but which God allowed, is what God deals with ultimately and finally in the life, death, and resurrection of Jesus. Jesus is the ultimate expression of God's love precisely because Wesley takes the law seriously. In fact, Wesley believed that God made known the law after "the understanding" of people was darkened because of God's love.[66] The law is, therefore, a sign not of God's wrath but of God's love. Wesley proclaimed the law because Christ is truly good news, because the law matters, and because the law must be taken into account.

In order to comprehend the gift of God's grace, people have to hear the depth of their sin. The law and gospel have to be announced, or told;

[63] *Letters* (Telford), Letter to Mary Bishop, 18 October 1778, 6:326–27.

[64] Ibid., Letter to Charles Wesley, 4 November 1772, 5:345.

[65] Albert C. Outler, *Evangelism and Theology in the Wesleyan Spirit* (Nashville: Discipleship Resources, 1996), 34.

[66] *Sermons II*, Sermon 34, "The Original, Nature, Property, and Use of the Law," §III.10, 2:14.

otherwise they would not be known. Some preachers were hesitant to proclaim the law because of its starkness. But Wesley was clear: preachers "must publish, as proper occasions offer, all that is contained in the oracles of God; whether smooth or otherwise."[67] Wesley warns more generally that Christians should avoid "taking from" the scriptures those parts they deem unpleasant, writing that those who do "corrupt the word of God" by taking

> Either the spirit or substance of it away, while they study to prophesy only smooth things, and therefore palliate or colour what they preach, in order to reconcile it to the taste of the hearers... they quite wash their hands of those stubborn texts that will not bend to their purpose, or that too plainly touch upon the reigning vices of the place where they are.[68]

Christian preachers are to

> Speak with plainness and boldness, and are not concerned to palliate their doctrine, to reconcile it to the taste of men. They endeavour to set it always in the true light, whether it be the pleasing one or no. They will not, they dare not, soften a threatening, so as to prejudice its strength, neither represent sin in such mild colours as to impair its native blackness. Not that they do not choose mildness, where it is likely to be effectual; though they know the "terrors of the Lord, they desire rather to pursuade men."[69]

Even more importantly, describing the life to which Christ calls people to live, Wesley writes,

> All that is written in the book of God we are to declare, not as pleasing men, but the Lord. We are to declare, not only all the promises, but all the threatenings, too, which we find therein. At the same time that we proclaim all the blessings and privileges which God hath prepared for his children, we are likewise to "teach all the things whatsoever he hath commanded."[70]

The ethical commandments of God have to be proclaimed if people are to truly understand and appreciate the good news of the gospel. The best way to preach is not to ignore either the law or the gospel but to preach both: "The most effectual way of preaching Christ, is to preach him in all his offices, and to declare his law as well as his gospel, both to believers and unbelievers. Let us strongly and closely insist upon inward and outward holiness, in all its branches."[71]

[67] *Sermons IV*, Sermon 137, "On Corrupting the Word of God," §II.3, 4:249.

[68] Ibid., §I.3, 4:247–48.

[69] Ibid., §II.4, 4:249.

[70] *Sermons II*, Sermon 35, "Law Established through Faith, Discourse 2," §I.5, 2:36–37.

[71] *Minutes of Conference, Large Minutes*, 1753–63, Q. 47, 10:860.

Preaching the ethical commands of Christ is not the same as preaching "fire and brimstone" as people today may understand but which Wesley referred to as "the terrors of the Lord." According to Wesley the motivation for obeying the ethical commands is God's love.[72] Rather, the point of preaching the law is to preach the blessings that come from faith.[73] Only in light of the law can a person truly understand the fullness of God's grace.

Christ, therefore, must be proclaimed in all his offices, as Wesley insisted throughout his life. Proclamation cannot be limited to a choice of Christ as prophet, or as priest, or as king, but must include all three. As Richard Heitzenrater summarizes, "Original sin, holiness of heart and life, love of God and neighbor, justification, salvation by faith, assurance of faith, witness of the Spirit, Christ in all his offices (law and gospel)—all part and parcel of the central gospel proclamation."[74]

The topic of the law and the gospel will be addressed again later in this book, since Wesley's understanding of the need to proclaim both is critical to understanding the message proclaimed and how that message encourages people through discipleship. At this point Wesley's statement in "Letter on Preaching Christ" sums up his basic position. For him, "the right method of preaching" is not preaching either the law or the gospel, "but duly mixing both, in every place, if not in every sermon," depending on the situation.[75]

CHANGING EMPHASIS

While these central themes are evident in Wesley's preaching and writing throughout his life, he emphasized particular themes at different times. Wesley himself records the trajectory of the themes he emphasized:

> From the year 1725 to 1729 I preached much, but saw no fruit of my labor. Indeed it could not be that I should; for I neither laid the foundation of

[72]*Minutes of Conference*, 1 August 1745, Q. 18. Wesley asks, "Need we ever preach the terrors of the Lord to those who know they are accepted of him? A. No: It is folly so to do; for love is to them the strongest of all motives."

[73]Hempton, 75. Hempton writes of Methodist preaching in America: "Based upon a survey of several hundred such sermons, my preliminary conclusion is that the Methodist message, to quote George Eliot, focused more often on 'The blessings of faith than upon the accursedness of infidelity.' The preoccupation with hell-fire preaching and scare tactics, the interpretation conveyed by satirical prints and anti-Methodist literature, is not as common as one might suppose In fact, the predominant themes of most Methodist sermons are grace, godliness, repentance, temporal and eternal joy, perseverance, vigilance, and assurance."

[74]Richard P. Heitzenrater, "John Wesley's Principles and Practice of Preaching" (paper presented at the Center for Methodist Studies at Bridwell Library: Lectures on Several Occasions, Dallas, 1997, 1999), 42, note 62.

[75]*Letters II*, Letter to an Evangelical Layman, 20 December 1751, §7, 26:483.

repentance, nor of *believing the gospel*; taking it for granted, that all to whom I preached were *believers*, and that many of them *needed no repentance.* (2) From the year 1729 to 1734, laying a deeper foundation of repentance, I saw a little fruit. But it was only a little; and no wonder: For I did not preach faith in the blood of the covenant. (3) From 1734 to 1738, speaking more of faith in Christ, I saw more fruit of my preaching and visiting from house to house than ever I had done before. Though I know not if any of those who were outwardly reformed were inwardly and thoroughly converted to God. (4) From 1738 to this time [1746], speaking continually of Jesus Christ, laying him only for the foundation of the whole building, making him all in all, the first and the last; preaching only on this plan, "The kingdom of God is at hand; repent ye, and believe the gospel," the "Word of God ran" as fire among the stubble; it was "glorified" more and more; multitudes crying out, "What must we do to be saved?" And afterwards witnessing, "By grace we are saved through faith."[76]

Extensive scholarly work confirms Wesley's shifting emphasis. For instance before 1748 Wesley emphasized justification more than sanctification. This is clear from his 1746 volume of sermons, which he prepared during the height of field preaching when many of those who gathered to hear preaching had not made a commitment to Christ through the Methodist movement. But two years later when the next volume of sermons was released, Methodists were focused more and more on building Methodist societies where preaching on sanctification was much more common than in field preaching. Therefore it is not surprising that the lead sermon in that volume is "Christian Perfection," and most of the other sermons focus on discipleship in the Christian life after justification.[77]

Further evidence for his changing emphasis comes in his preference for different scripture passages throughout his life. For instance, one of Wesley's favorite passages on justification was Ephesians 2:8, "You are saved by God's grace because of your faith." From 1738 to 1742 he preached on this passage thirty-four times. From 1744 to 1748, he preached on it only eight times. But there are no records of him ever preaching on the passage from 1749 to 1754.[78] A corresponding shift is evident in some of his preaching on sanctification. Before 1749 there is no record Wesley ever preached on Hebrews 12:28, "Serve in a way that is pleasing to God with respect and awe." But between 1749 and 1754 he preached on the passage thirty-one times. Wesley's emphasis in preaching shifted as the revival matured, a phenomenon that is discussed in depth in chapter 3.

[76]*Societies*, "The Principles of a Methodist Farther Explained," §6.1, 9:222–23.

[77]Heitzenrater, 45.

[78]Ibid.

CONCLUSION

The Bible as a whole provides the narrative for Wesley's proclamation. Wesley believed that the "whole tenor" of the Bible points to God's love revealed in Christ and exemplified through his life, death, and resurrection. First, one had to recognize the depth of one's sin and, in turn, the depth of God's love in Christ. After coming to faith in Christ and living in the light of this gospel, those who truly came to faith would naturally want to live out the moral law by living in concert with the principles emphasized in the Sermon on the Mount. In this way holiness is the natural outflow, in Wesley's mind, of a person who acknowledges the law and then believes the gospel. Holiness is the goal of preaching the law and gospel. Encouraging people toward holiness entails, as Heitzenrater writes, "Preaching both the law and the gospel; in effect, preaching Christ in all his offices."[79] And yet Wesley believed preaching is not the only way the law and gospel are proclaimed. In fact, limiting proclamation to preaching alone overlooks critical aspects of the early Methodist movement. To preaching, as well as these other types of proclamation, our discussion now turns.

[79]Heitzenrater, 44.

CHAPTER 2

THE MEANS OF PROCLAMATION

Rising to sing my Saviour's praise,
Thee may I publish all day long:
And let thy precious word of grace
Flow from my heart, and fill my tongue;
Fill all my life with purest love,
And join me to thy church above![1]

Contemporary Christians rarely, if ever, use the word *publish* in relation to speaking of God. They often employ the terms *preaching* and *teaching*, but the idea of "publishing" news of God in Christ is simply not common. Perhaps the reason for this is that many Christians in Europe and the United States today still believe that most people already know the "fundamentals" of the Christian faith and that the story does not need to be communicated. Yet as secularism continues to spread in Western cultures there is a growing awareness among Christians that the story of God in Christ might actually need to be "published" to a population that otherwise does not and will not know it.

Wesley was quite comfortable with the idea that the story of God must be proclaimed or announced—and yes, even published. He uses the latter term in a number of places. In part three of his *Farther Appeal to Men of Reason and Religion*, Wesley argues that all Christians, both lay and clergy, must "publish the Word of God," an act he "essentially equates" with preaching.[2] Wesley also invites Robert Brackenbury to preach at Methodist preaching houses; in a letter to Brackenbury, Wesley writes, "It is exceedingly clear to me, first, that a dispensation of the gospel is

[1]John Wesley, *A Collection of Hymns for the Use of the People Called Methodists*, v. 7 in *The Bicentennial Edition of the Works of John Wesley* (Oxford: Oxford University Press, 1983), Hymn #319, vs. 4, 475. Cited hereafter as *A Collection of Hymns*.

[2]Wesley, *Appeals, A Farther Appeal to Men of Reason and Religion*, Part 3, §13, 11:298.

committed to you; and, secondly, that you are peculiarly called to publish it in connexion with us [Methodists]."[3] "Publishing" this message was central to Wesley; in his "Preface to the Last London Edition" of the *Works*, Thomas Jackson (1783–1873) writes that Wesley felt that he "had a message from God to all men. The love of Christ constrained him to publish that message in all parts of the land, regardless of toil, contempt, and danger."[4] In Wesley's mind, while people might have the law "inscribed" on their hearts, Methodists are called to specifically announce the particular truths of the Christian tradition so that people can respond to them personally.

Wesley uses a wealth of terms to refer to the task of publishing the gospel. Skevington Wood points out that Wesley employs all of the following words and phrases to communicate the necessity of this announcement:

"I offered the grace of God"

"I offered the redemption that is in Christ Jesus"

"I proclaimed the grace of our Lord Jesus Christ"

"I proclaimed the name of the Lord"

"I proclaimed Christ crucified"

"I proclaimed free salvation"

"I declared to them all the grace of our Lord Jesus Christ"

"I declared the free grace of God"

"I exhorted the wicked to forsake his way"

"I began to call sinners to repentance"

"I invited all guilty, helpless sinners."[5]

For Wesley, each of these terms (and others like them) describes the various ways in which the good news of Christ was specifically articulated to the world. Early Methodists believed that there are certainly other ways in which the story of God can be verbally announced, such as hymns, witness, and testimony, as mentioned in the introduction. They also believed that the story was told through written mediums such as the Bible, letters, and journals. Furthermore the Spirit can mysteriously communicate the essence of the gospel directly to a person's spirit without an external mediator, such as a person or the Bible telling the story.

[3]*Letters* (Telford), Letter to Robert Carr Brackenbury, 9 March 1782, 7:113.

[4]Wesley, *Works* (Jackson), Preface to the Third Edition, 1:i.

[5]A. Skevington Wood, *The Burning Heart: John Wesley, Evangelist* (Minneapolis: Bethany House, 1978), 159.

The focus of this chapter, however, and the book as a whole, is on the particular practices of verbal proclamation Wesley encouraged that not only announce the story of God but also intend to encourage a response. The three primary practices evident in Wesley's corpus are preaching, teaching, and exhortation.

The Necessity of Proclamation

As noted in the previous chapter, Wesley believed that the fundamentals of the story of God as revealed in the Hebrew Bible and the New Testament, especially the law and its fulfillment in the good news of Jesus Christ, must be announced to the world. Otherwise, the world would not know the particularities of the gospel message beyond the law that had been engrafted on the soul, as mentioned in the previous chapter. Furthermore, Wesley believed proclamation itself to be critical to the Methodist revival. In the *Minutes* Wesley argues that one of the reasons Methodism "stood still" at times was due to a lack of field preaching and morning preaching.[6] Heitzenrater's conclusion in his helpful essay on Wesley's preaching is certainly correct: "In the end, in spite of all the rules, the questions, the suggestions, the publications on the technique of preaching, it was the message of the gospel communicated to the listener by the voice and life of the preacher that was most important for Wesley himself and his lay preachers."[7] Proclamation is simply essential to the Methodist movement's efforts to "offer Christ."

The Means of Proclamation and the Means of Grace

Wesley is clear that he believes the Spirit communicates God's love and call to holiness in a variety of means. In his appropriately titled sermon "The Means of Grace," Wesley writes that the means of grace are the "outward signs, words, or actions, ordained of God, and appointed for this end, to be the ordinary channels whereby he might convey to men, preventing, justifying or sanctifying grace."[8] He describes the three primary means, namely, prayer, "searching the scriptures," and receiving the Lord's Supper, as "the ordinary channels of conveying his grace to the souls of men."[9] He writes of the means in a number of other places as well. In his sermon "On Zeal" Wesley further defines the means of

[6]*Minutes of Conference*, 1768, Q. 23.2–3, 10:361.

[7]Heitzenrater, 51.

[8]*Sermons I*, Sermon 16, "The Means of Grace," §II.1, 1:381.

[9]Ibid.

grace as both "works of mercy" and "works of piety," the latter of which include "reading and hearing the Word, public, family, private prayer, receiving the Lord's supper, fasting or abstinence."[10] He further clarifies the means of grace in *The Scripture Way of Salvation*, where he lists the works of piety as "public prayer, family prayer, and praying in our closet; receiving the supper of the Lord; searching the Scriptures, by hearing, reading, meditating; and using such a measure of fasting or abstinence as our bodily health allows."[11] Wesley continues, writing that the works of mercy,

> relate to the bodies or souls of men; such as feeding the hungry, clothing the naked, entertaining the stranger, visiting those that are in prison, or sick, or variously afflicted; such as the endeavouring to instruct the ignorant, to awaken the stupid sinner, to quicken the lukewarm, to confirm the wavering, to comfort the feeble-minded, to succour the tempted, or contribute in any manner to the saving of souls from death.[12]

In each of these examples Wesley is clear: God communicates God's grace through some primary "means" that helps people better perceive the depth of God's love. Proclamation is only an element of some of these means.

For instance, God's care and compassion can be communicated through general acts of service and justice that do not specifically narrate the motivation behind those acts. After all, "feeding the hungry, clothing the naked, entertaining the stranger, visiting those that are in prison, or sick, or variously afflicted" does not necessarily include a particular proclamation of the law or gospel.

Yet Wesley is clear the Spirit sometimes miraculously intervenes in a person's life, apart from any specific means of grace. In "The Means of Grace," Wesley notes God's ability to miraculously convey grace apart from any human or scriptural connection; God can convey grace in "an immediate stroke of his convincing Spirit, without any outward means at all," because God "is above all means" and "doeth whatsoever and whensoever it pleaseth him." God conveys grace "either in or out of any of the means which he hath appointed." The Holy Spirit, on these few occasions, spoke to a person's spirit, imparting the gospel apart from a reading of the biblical text. Wesley believed that in such instances the Spirit communicated the heart of the gospel story, but without reference to the Bible and without a human intermediary to communicate the Bible.

[10]*Sermons III*, Sermon 92, "On Zeal," §II.5, 3:313.

[11]*Sermons II*, Sermon 43, "The Scripture Way of Salvation," §III.9, 2:166.

[12]Ibid., §III.10, 2:166.

It was simply the Holy Spirit ministering to a person's spirit. The central ideas of the scriptures, those necessary for salvation, were thus communicated through a direct encounter between an individual and the Holy Spirit.

Yet according to Wesley these highly private and spiritual encounters are not normative ways of engaging God's grace. Rather, the entire Methodist system is built on Wesley's belief that most people encounter grace through a partnership of hearing other people narrate the fundamentals of the faith and their own private prayer life and scripture readings. The normative means of encountering grace are "searching the Scriptures, by hearing, reading, meditating" and "endeavouring to instruct the ignorant, to awaken the stupid sinner, to quicken the lukewarm, to confirm the wavering, to comfort the feeble-minded, to succour the tempted." And these means entail a particular encounter with the fundamentals of the Christian faith.

These encounters do not always necessitate a human mediator to encounter the fundamentals of faith. For instance, Wesley mentions that people often encounter God's grace in their solitary reading of scripture and prayer. Wesley also devoted enormous energy and time to types of proclamation that proved to be means of grace for many, including his journals and written sermons. Wesley was one of the most voluminous writers of his day. In his lifetime he produced numerous volumes of sermons, journals, and letters, which, along with the pamphlets and books he helped write and publish, form an enormous corpus. In each of these mediums, Wesley occasionally, if not regularly, proclaimed biblical passages. This is most evident in the written sermons, but also in numerous tracts, pamphlets, and journal entries. A good example of Wesley's proclamation of the law, or the necessity of following Christ's moral commands, is found in his pamphlet *Thoughts on Slavery* where he criticizes all forms of the buying and selling of human beings.

In his journals Wesley also occasionally proclaims. But proclamation in the journals is minimal compared to his letters and written sermons. Wesley kept up a remarkable correspondence with many people throughout his life. These numerous letters allowed him to carry on spiritual conversations that sometimes lasted for decades. Wesley used some of these correspondences to proclaim the gospel and encourage people to deeper faith.

Wesley's written sermons most clearly included proclamation. This is not surprising since sermons, oral or written, typically focus on expounding on a certain biblical text or biblical theme. Unlike the oral sermons, which were intended to convince people of sin and encourage them to join a Methodist society, written sermons were typically composed for Methodist society members as a way to encourage them to justification and sanctification. They were written primarily for people to read, not for people to hear, though Methodist preachers often read Wesley's sermons from their pulpits. Many commentators note the apparent dullness of the written sermons as compared with the compelling reviews of spoken sermons. As William Doughty writes, "It is not possible to conceive of any powers of oratory or intensity of zeal for the souls of men that could commend these sermons, as they stand."[13]

With a few exceptions, the sermons in these published collections are substantially different from those he presented in public. For example, of his favorite thirty-five preaching texts, only five are the topic of published sermons, and only one before 1760.[14] Furthermore, of the forty-three sermons published by 1760, the sermon register only records his preaching on sixteen of the texts, seven of which were preached only once or twice.[15] Perhaps surprisingly, his second and fourth most common preaching texts (2 Cor 8:9, "[Christ] became poor for our sakes, so that you could become rich through his poverty"; and Isa 55:7, "Let the wicked abandon their ways and the sinful their schemes") are not represented in any written or published form.[16] Sermons that do appear in written form are edited specifically for publication. Written and oral sermons had different purposes and were delivered under different circumstances. Yet both emphasize proclamation of the biblical text and were within the same "theological universe."[17]

In this book I focus only on the means of grace that necessarily include a verbal proclamation. In this way this book is about the verbal "means of Grace," not the means of grace as a whole as Wesley understood them. To these various types of verbal proclamation the discussion now turns.

PREACHING

A dispensation of the gospel is committed to me, and woe is me if I preach not the gospel wherever I am in the world.[18]

For the majority of his life, John Wesley was known as a preacher. Preaching was his passion and the epicenter of his ministry. As he wrote

[13]Doughty, 84.

[14]Heitzenrater, 45.

[15]Ibid., 45–46.

[16]Ibid., 46.

[17]Ibid., 45.

[18]*Journal and Diaries II*, 11 June 1739, 19:67.

in the 1750s, "I do indeed live by preaching."[19] He grew up the son of a preacher who ingrained the preaching life into his children. In a 1706 letter to John's brother Samuel, John's father wrote, "Be very attentive to the sermon, because you know in whose name and by whose commission it is delivered."[20] Wesley pursued his theological education at Oxford University, ultimately becoming a fellow of Lincoln College (1726). While at Oxford he joined a group of men that his brother Charles had helped found, the "Methodists"—a derogatory name given to them by outsiders but ultimately embraced by the group itself. Sensing a call to spread the gospel across the seas, he and Charles traveled to the British colonies in North America, working in Georgia for almost two years with the Society for the Propagation of the Gospel. While in Georgia he preached, but he also experimented further with the ideas of ministry in a small community of people that he had experienced in Oxford. His ministry in Georgia ended in crisis, and his own state of turmoil continued as he ventured back to England in 1737. But in May 1738 he had a transformative religious experience that helped open him to George Whitefield's invitation in 1739 to come see the work that God was doing with the poor through outdoor preaching. From 1739 to his death in 1791, many characteristics defined both Wesley's personal ministry and the movement he helped found, but none more so than preaching.

A common image of early Methodism is that of a preacher speaking to crowds in a field, or Wesley himself preaching from his father's tombstone. In those nascent days Methodism did not have a single proper church and had only a few preaching houses. That this preaching was evangelistic in nature has been noted many times. Skevington Wood comments, "Wesley was first and foremost an evangelist, and as such he was aware that his commission was to preach the gospel."[21] Ron Benefiel writes, "The Methodist movement was to be an evangelistic movement. Above all else, they were to be concerned with preaching the gospel and the salvation of souls."[22]

Wesley himself was known as a good preacher, but not the most dynamic of his age. That title was reserved for George Whitefield. Nevertheless, observers frequently left with positive impressions of Wesley.

[19]*Journal and Diaries IV*, 28 July 1757, 21:118.

[20]George J. Stevenson, *Memorials of the Wesley Family* (London: S. W. Partridge and Co., 1876), 99.

[21]Wood, 147.

[22]Ron Benefiel, "John Wesley's Mission of Evangelism" (paper presented at the Missio Ecclesia, Missio De: A Wesleyan Perspective on the Church in Mission, Point Loma Nazarene University, 12 March 2012, http://www.pointloma.edu/sites/default/files/filemanager/School_of_Theology_Christian_Ministry/Wiley_Lectures/2012/John_Wesley_-_Evangelism.pdf), 3.

Swedish professor Johan Henrik Liden, who visited England in 1769, commented,

> The sermon was short but eminently evangelical. He had no great oratorical gifts, no outward appearance, but he speaks clear and pleasant...He is small, a thin old man, with his own long and straight hair, and looks as the worst country curate in Sweden, but has learning as a Bishop and zeal for the glory of God which is quite extraordinary. His talk is very agreeable, and his mild face and pious manner secure him the love of all rightminded men...He seems to me a living representative of the loving Apostle John.[23]

Thomas Rutherford, an early Methodist preacher, provides a more hagiographical representation:

> In the month of May that year [1770], I, for the first time, saw and heard that extraordinary man, the Rev. Mr. John Wesley, at Morpeth. He was in the pulpit when I went to the chapel. His apostolic and angelic appearance struck me exceedingly. He appeared like one come down from heaven to teach men the way thither. His text was, Heb. viii. 10–12...He opened the words in a concise and easy manner, and spoke from them with such perspicuity and simplicity, and, at the same time, with wisdom and authority, as I never heard before. To me he seemed like one of the apostles going about confirming the churches.[24]

Adam Clarke tells the intriguing story of Dame Summerhill of Bristol's encounter with Wesley's preaching:

> When he [Wesley] first came to Bristol I went to hear him preach; and, having heard him, I said, "This is the truth." I inquired of those around, who and what he was. I was told that he was a man who went everywhere preaching the Gospel. I further inquired, "Is he going to preach here again?" The reply was, "Not at present." "Where is he going to next?" I asked. "To Plymouth," was the answer. "And will he preach there?" "Yes." "Then I will go and hear him. What is the distance?" "One hundred and twenty-five miles." I went, walked it, heard him, and walked back again![25]

Even critics sometimes commented admiringly. For instance, after preaching in the fields on Sunday morning at Peasholm Green, Wesley

[23]Johan H. Liden, "Extract from the Journal of Professor John Henrick Liden," *Proceedings of the Wesleyan Historical Society* 17, no. 1 (1929–30): 1-4.

[24]Thomas Rutherford, "An Account of Mr. Thomas Rutherford," *Methodist Magazine* 31 (1808): 437.

[25]John Wesley Etheridge, *The Life of the Rev. Adam Clarke* (Nashville: Southern Methodist Publishing House, 1859), 182.

went, as usual, to the parish church to attend the service. The parish priest, seeing Wesley dressed in his clerical attire but not knowing who he was, offered him the pulpit. After the service, the priest asked the clerk the name of the preacher. "Sir, he is the vagabond Wesley, against whom you warned us." "Aye, indeed!" said the rector, "we are trapped; but never mind, we have had a good sermon."[26] While people differed in their opinions of Wesley's preaching, there is no doubt that preaching was the most obvious type of verbal proclamation that Wesley engaged in and that in turn he insisted his preachers engage in.

TYPES OF PREACHERS

In general there were three types of Methodist preachers. The first were based in the town in which they lived, preached periodically, and traveled to other towns to preach only on occasion. This first group was "settled" and did not typically itinerate as one of Wesley's traveling preachers. Nevertheless, Wesley believed that most were "zealous for the salvation of men."[27] The second type of preacher itinerated for periods of time, traveling extensively, but then eventually settled back into their regular lives. The third type of preacher Wesley called "assistants" or "helpers"; they were the ones Wesley depended upon the most. After a time of probation as well as inquiry into their character, doctrine, and gifts, they were ultimately admitted into the Methodist connection.

With the exception of a few preachers in Wesley's inner circle, most preachers were laypersons. Few received specific training, other than what Wesley provided. This lack of training for laity was one of the reasons non-Methodists were often critical of Methodist preachers. A "Mr N." complained about Wesley's inclusion of lay preaching, to which Wesley responded, "I do tolerate lay preaching, because I conceive there is an absolute necessity for it; inasmuch as were it not, thousands of souls would perish everlastingly."[28] Lay preaching was "irregular," but along with other irregularities in Methodism—such as field preaching, Methodist societies, and extemporary prayer and preaching—Wesley embraced lay preachers, arguing that he would sooner separate from the church, something he was loath to do, than stop lay preaching.[29] He believed that the laity are called to

[26]Luke Tyerman, *The Life and Times of the Rev. John Wesley*, 2 vols. (London: Hodder and Stoughton, 1870–71), 2:571.

[27]Richard Watson, *The Life of the Rev. John Wesley*, 14th ed. (New York: T. Mason and G. Lane, 1840), 146.

[28]*Letters III: 1756–65*, v. 27 in *The Bicentennial Edition of the Works of John Wesley* (Nashville: Abingdon, 1982). Letter to Nicholas Norton, 3 September 1756, 27:45. Hereafter cited as *Letters III.*

[29]*Letters II*, Letter to the Revd. Thomas Adam, 31 October 1755, 26:609–11. See also ibid., Letter to the Revd. Samuel Walker, 20 November 1755, 26:611–13; *Letters III*, Letter to the Revd. Samuel Walker, 3 September 1756, 27:51–55.

preach as much as the ordained, and indeed that they are often more fruitful than the ordained. But from a more practical standpoint, since there simply were not enough ordained people who responded to Methodism, Wesley looked to laypeople to preach. They helped extend his ministry.[30] As Frank Baker writes, "Neither the spread of the Methodist Societies nor their proliferation into a connected network of evangelical pockets throughout the land would have been possible without the itinerant lay preacher."[31]

TESTING THE CALL TO PREACH

For the Wesley brothers, a person's fitness for preaching does not depend primarily on his or her status as a lay or clergy person. The real question is whether a person can demonstrate a call to preach. The brothers examined and critiqued preachers in order to find out. John emphasized the preacher's spiritual and theological fitness as well as the fruit of his preaching. To the question "How shall we try those who think they are moved by the Holy Ghost to preach?" Wesley responds,

> Inquire, (1.) Do they know God as a pardoning God? Have they the love of God abiding in them? Do they desire and seek nothing but God? And are they holy in all manner of conversation? (2.) Have they gifts (as well as grace) for the work? Have they (in some tolerable degree) a clear, sound understanding? Have they a right judgment in the things of God? Have they a just conception of salvation by faith? And has God given them any degree of utterance? Do they speak justly, readily, clearly? (3.) Have they fruit? Are any truly convinced of sin, and converted to God, by their preaching?[32]

As long as these three marks concur in any one, Wesley says the person is called of God to preach. These three marks he receives as sufficient proof that he is "moved thereto by the Holy Ghost."[33]

Just as important was the fruit of a preacher's sermons, or the grace that flowed from the preacher, changing hearts and lives with the word of God. John was happy to see a preacher of poor external qualities keep preaching if fruit was evident from the preacher's ministry. John writes, "Of the two, I prefer grace before gifts."[34] His emphasis on fruit in determining fitness for preaching is part of what led him to embrace women as preachers.[35]

[30]*Letters II*, Letter to the Revd. Samuel Walker, 20 November 1755, 26:612–13.

[31]Frank Baker, *John Wesley and the Church of England* (London: Epworth, 1970), 81.

[32]*Minutes of Conference, Large Minutes*, 1753–63, §52, 10:861.

[33]Ibid.

[34]*Letters II*, Letter to the Revd. Charles Wesley, 24 July 1751, 26:472.

[35]Paul W. Chilcote offers important insight into the vital role of women preachers in early Methodism. See Paul Wesley Chilcote, *She Offered Them Christ: The Legacy of Women Preachers*

Charles had different criteria for determining one's fitness for preaching, and his requirements were often more stringent than John's. Charles sought gifts at least as much as he did grace. He criticized John on a number of occasions for accepting preachers whom Charles found incoherent. The preacher Joseph Cownley wrote to Charles expressing concern that John was very lenient, allowing virtually anyone to preach as long as "some body or other" would testify that the preacher showed fruit:

> The door to preaching is as wide as our Societies, so that any ignorant or designing man that takes it into his head that he can preach may preach without anymore ado unless to procure some body or other to inform your Bro, which is not always needful, that he is well enough qualified for it. And there is no man that takes this work upon him though never so unfit for it but may find at least some old woman who will abide by it that he is the finest man they ever heard in all their life.[36]

The result was that sometimes Charles found himself trying to undo his brother's work. In 1751, he wrote the following about a preacher he thought his brother had accepted errantly: "[John,] without God's counsel, made a preacher of a tailor; I, with God's help, shall make a tailor of him again."[37]

ITINERANCY

The Methodist movement expanded primarily because of the traveling preachers, including John himself. While Charles traveled in the early days of the revival, he soon "settled," thereby not preaching regularly on one of his brother's preaching circuits. But John and many other preachers traveled extensively. In this way preaching was the work of the Methodist community, not just the Wesley brothers, especially after the first few years of the revival. While John became the best-known Methodist preacher, Methodism ultimately grew into a movement because he was able to recruit others to itinerate. Some of these others include Adam Clarke, Francis Asbury, John Nelson, and Freeborn Garrettson. In the beginning Wesley initiated preaching in new areas, but by the late 1740s he traveled primarily to established preaching points and left the pioneering to others.

in Early Methodism (Eugene, OR: Wipf and Stock, 2001), and *Her Own Story: Autobiographical Portraits of Early Methodist Women* (Nashville: Kingswood, 2001).

[36]*Catalogue of the Early Preachers Collection, Methodist Archives and Research Centre (MARC), John Rylands University Library of Manchester* (Manchester, England), Letter from Joseph Cownley to Charles Wesley (26 April 1760), GB 135 DDPr 2/16. Former Reference: Leather Volume V–Letters of Methodist Preachers, 16. Cited hereafter as *Early Preachers Collection*.

[37]Frank Baker, *Charles Wesley as Revealed by His Letters* (London: Epworth, 1948), 86.

Anglican preachers were for the most part "settled" preachers. They were typically given leadership over one or two churches, often for decades, and therefore spent the entirety of their ministry preaching to or with only a few communities. Early Methodist preachers, on the other hand, rarely stayed longer than a few weeks in any one place; a given preacher would move around a circuit of churches, usually with one or two others. Their constant movement encouraged some preachers to develop only a few sermons that they could reuse time and time again. Until his death Wesley assigned preachers to specific circuits, set up the calendar for preaching, and moved preachers periodically—at least annually—to new circuits. These traveling preachers came to be known as "circuit riders" in the colonies and were marked by their determined commitment to preach despite all odds.

While the circuit rider model of preaching has now disappeared for the most part in the United States, the itinerant nature of pastoral leadership is still evident in many Wesleyan communities where preachers are assigned to certain parishes by a supervising elder. In the British Methodist Church, the original model is still followed to a great degree: preachers are assigned to a circuit with a number of churches and a number of other preachers who rotate through the circuit.

"Borderless" Preachers

The itinerant nature of Methodist preachers put them into immediate conflict with many in the Church of England who were used to parish borders and often insisted that preachers preach only within their parish borders. Both Whitefield and Wesley had to defend their practice of preaching outside a parish on a number of occasions. John always felt that the church's missional imperative outweighed ecclesiastical norms in this case. His famous refrain, "The world is my parish," helped define his insistence that a Methodist preacher had no border. Methodists rarely felt bound by the Anglican concept of a parish with borders, and certainly John never wanted to be hindered by parish boundaries.

Nevertheless, Wesley frequently discouraged field preaching or society meetings on Sunday mornings because he wanted to encourage Methodists to attend the service of their local Anglican parish. The Methodist movement was not intended to replace the Anglican Church, but rather to supplement it and to encourage deeper discipleship. From the 1740s onward there was constant discussion about whether the Methodists would leave the church and become a distinct church. While John seemed to waver at times, Charles was unrelenting in his insistence that Methodists remain within the Church of England. In fact, by the mid-1750s Charles seemed to loosen his close ties with the Methodist movement, at least in part because of John's wavering, though Charles never left the movement completely.

WESLEY'S STYLE OF PREACHING

When it came to public preaching, Wesley was quite clear regarding his expectations. Some were purely stylistic. For example, he says that a preacher must always show up unless a true emergency arises, that he should begin and end on time, and that he should be "serious, weighty, and solemn."[38] Wesley's sermons usually lasted around thirty minutes.[39] Even though Wesley occasionally preached for up to an hour, that does not seem to be his norm, and he certainly does not encourage long sermons.[40] He writes to Mrs. Johnston, "People imagine the longer a sermon is, the more good it will do. This is a grand mistake."[41] He even threatened some with expulsion: "Unless you can and will leave off preaching long, I shall think it my duty to prevent your preaching at all among the Methodists."[42] Wesley's public oral sermons were not academic treatises. They included "excellent stories" and were designed to spark people's imaginations to follow Christ.[43] They were also focused on speaking to the uneducated masses, even though Wesley could and did engage the educated and wealthy.

Wesley encouraged a "plain" style of preacher and sermon. The preacher was to be plain in attire, not calling attention to either himself or the language. For the sermon itself Wesley encouraged a style of rhetoric that was plain, pointed, and accessible to uneducated persons, as opposed to the embellished orations of some Church of England preachers.[44] "Clearness in particular is necessary for you and me," he writes to Samuel Furly, "because we are to instruct people of the lowest understanding... We should constantly use the most common, little, easy word (so they are pure and proper) which our language affords."[45] Samuel Johnson identified the key to Methodist success as: "Their expressing themselves in a plain and familiar manner which is the only way to do good to the

[38]*Minutes of Conference, Large Minutes*, 1753–63, §45, 10:859.

[39]*Societies*, "Thoughts Upon Methodism," §4, 9:528.

[40]Heitzenrater, 36–7.

[41]*Letters* (Telford), Letter to Mrs. Johnston, 16 February 1777, 6:225.

[42]Ibid., Letter to Jeremiah Brettell regarding Nathaniel Ward and Henry Foster, 26 June 1781, 7:70.

[43]James Downey, *The Eighteenth Century Pulpit: A Study of the Sermons of Butler, Berkeley, Secker, Sterne, Whitefield and Wesley* (Oxford: Clarendon Press, 1969), 164 and Doughty, 198.

[44]Albert C. Outler, *John Wesley's Sermons: An Introduction* (Nashville: Abingdon, 1991), 31.

[45]*Letters III*, Letter to Samuel Furley, 16 July 1764, 27:381.

common people, and which clergymen of genius and learning ought to do from a principle of duty, when it is suited to their congregations; a practice for which they will be praised by men of sense."[46]

Indeed, the phrase so often quoted by Wesley rang true. He desired "plain truth for plain people."[47]

EXTEMPORANEOUS PREACHING

A dramatic difference between much Methodist preaching and that which defined typical parishes in the Church of England of the time is that Methodist preaching was typically extemporaneous. While Church of England clerics typically read one of the church's approved homilies, Methodist preachers often preached extempore, or at least with much less formality than their counterparts in the Church of England. Wesley found extemporary preaching that responded to the needs of the congregation was most effective. Francis Asbury describes the effectiveness of extemporaneous preaching in his journal when he tells of his first encounter with Methodist preachers and Methodist worship: "I soon found this was not the church—but it was better. The people were so devout…What was yet more extraordinary, the man took his text, and had no sermon book: thought I, this is wonderful indeed! It is certainly a strange way, but the best way."[48] Wesley himself doesn't appear to have preached without notes until July 11, 1738, a practice that he became "less and less dependent upon" until he gave up notes entirely on February 11, 1739.[49] Charles seems to have begun preaching "ex tempore" sometime in 1738, at least by October 20, 1738, and perhaps as early as July 11 of that year.[50] Throughout the rest of his life, Charles encouraged others to adopt the same practice.[51]

The extemporaneous nature of the public sermons made them

[46]James Boswell, *The Life of Samuel Johnson, LL.D*, 2 vols. (Oxford: Talboys and Wheeler; William Pickering, 1826), 357–58.

[47]*Sermons I*, Preface, §3, 1:104.

[48]Francis Asbury, *The Journal of the Rev. Francis Asbury, Bishop of the Methodist Episcopal Church, from August 7, 1771, to December 7, 1815*, v. 2 (New York: N. Bangs and T. Mason, 1821), 135.

[49]William L. Doughty, "Charles Wesley, Preacher," *The London Quarterly and Holborn Review* 182 October (1957): 264.

[50]Charles Wesley, *The Journal of the Rev. Charles Wesley* (Grand Rapids: Baker, 1980), 11 July 1738, 1:120. See also John R. Tyson, ed., *Charles Wesley: A Reader* (Oxford: Oxford University Press, 1989), 14. Tyson argues that after October 20, 1738, Charles's sermons are increasingly extempore. Charles himself writes of "adding much extempore" to a sermon on July 11, 1738, though it was probably to a sermon of John's he was reading. Newport argues, however, from manuscript references that Charles was preaching extempore by July 11, 1738. Kenneth G. C. Newport, ed. *The Sermons of Charles Wesley: A Critical Edition, with Introduction and Notes* (Oxford: Oxford University Press, 2001), 35.

[51]Ibid., 36.

dramatically different from Wesley's published sermons. The latter, as Outler demonstrates, are primarily theological treatises designed to nurture those committed to the movement, while the former are primarily for proclamation and an invitation to discipleship.[52]

THE METHOD OF PREACHING

Beginning in 1744 Wesley asks the rhetorical question in every annual gathering of Methodist preachers, "What is the best general method of preaching?" His answer: "(1.) To invite. (2.) To convince. (3.) To offer Christ. (4.) To build up; and to do this in some measure in every sermon."[53] These four basic attributes of a sermon are critical. In the first place each sermon was supposed to invite people to the next stage of Christian discipleship. If someone had yet to be "awakened," then that was the goal. Those who had been awakened but had not yet come to faith in Christ were invited to a first experience of faith and repentance leading to justification. If they had been justified, then they were invited to deeper faith and repentance leading to an ongoing growth in holiness.

Each stage of this invitation took convincing, the second aspect of Wesley's method. Wesley argued that God's grace works to convince people of the truth of Christ and the prevalence of sin in their lives but that human efforts are also necessary. This human task of encouraging people to deepen their faith and commitment is discussed in more depth at the end of this chapter as it relates to each of the various types of proclamation. At this point it is enough to reiterate that Wesley understood convincing as critical to the preacher's task.

The third aspect of Wesley's method is "to offer Christ." For Wesley, offering Christ is the initial invitation to faith and repentance leading to conversion and justification. The fourth aspect is "to build up." In Wesley's mind, building up involves the specific task of encouraging those who experience conversion and justification to continue growing in the image of God (i.e., toward holiness). For Wesley these four are important aspects of every sermon and are to be incorporated every time one preaches.

INSTRUCTION

This chapter devotes a significant section to preaching, which is understandable given preaching's role in early Methodism. Preaching was, in Wade Crawford Barclay's words, "Wesley's supreme instrument."[54]

[52]Heitzenrater, 24.

[53]*Minutes of Conference, Large Minutes*, 1753–63, §44, 10:859.

[54]Wade Crawford Barclay, *History of Methodist Missions, Part 1: Early American Methodism: 1769–1844*, v. 1 (New York: The Board of Missions and Church Extension of the Methodist Church, 1949), xvi.

And yet preaching was not the only way in which proclamation occurred. Teaching and exhortation were also critical. At this point I will simply touch upon each subject; I will return to them later in the book, during the discussion of each forum for proclamation.

Wesley believed that instruction in the basics of the Christian faith is critical. A typical example is found in his journal when he visited a man at St. Thomas's Hospital. "O what a harvest might there be," he writes, "if any lover of souls, who has time upon his hands, would constantly attend these places of distress, and, with tenderness and meekness of wisdom, instruct and exhort those on whom God has laid his hands."[55] Instruction is in some ways more personal and pointed than preaching, even though sometimes Wesley seems to use the words *teaching* and *preaching* interchangeably at times. Instruction in the foundations of Christianity allowed Wesley and the early Methodists to have direct conversations regarding a person's questions and to clear up areas of confusion in both the doctrine and practice of Christianity. This personal engagement, Wesley found, was more difficult for many than preaching itself. He makes sure to include in the *Minutes* Richard Baxter's reminder that, "It is far easier to preach a good sermon than to instruct the ignorant in the principles of religion."[56]

EXHORTATION

There was a little town not far from ours, where I sometimes went, got a few poor people together, and talked to them about their souls. I often read the Scriptures to them, and sometimes made remarks thereon. The Lord was pleased to bless my weak endeavours among them.[57]

While preaching is often rightly considered the epicenter of Methodist proclamation, exhortation is a significant type of proclamation as well. Exhortation was not unique to Methodists in eighteenth-century Britain. Both George Whitefield and Howell Harris, for example, refer on occasion to some of their speaking as exhortation and to themselves as exhorters. This is especially true for Harris, who seemed reticent for much of his life to speak of himself as a preacher. Instead, he preferred to call his kind of speaking "exhortation."

Exhortation was, from one perspective, simply preaching without

[55] *Journal and Diaries II*, 17 September 1741, 19:226.

[56] *Minutes of Conference, Large Minutes*, 1770–72, §17.6, 10:881.

[57] Thomas Jackson, *The Lives of Early Methodist Preachers*, 3rd ed., 6 vols. (London: Wesleyan Methodist Book Room, 1865). *The Life of Mr. William Hunter*, 2:244.

"taking a text."[58] The central content of exhortation was a biblical theme, even if a particular text was not "taken." On a number of occasions Wesley used a biblical example upon which to build an exhortation, as when he "exhorted every prodigal to 'arise and go to' his 'Father.'"[59] In another example he writes, "I therefore exhorted the congregation, in the words of our Lord, Luke xxi. 36, 'Watch ye therefore, and pray always, that ye may be accounted worthy to escape all these things that shall come to pass, and to stand before the Son of Man.'"[60] A final example comes from his journal a few days prior when he "exhorted them all, to love their enemies, as Christ hath loved."[61] Exhortation involved someone speaking, in groups large or small, on a biblical theme, the subject of which was often found in sermons on the same theme, but without citing a specific guiding passage, which is so often commonplace in sermons. Most importantly, exhortation was known as a type of speaking where "the word went with power to many hearts."[62]

Exhortation was also much less formal and frequently spontaneous.[63] Wesley provides an example of this in his journal:

> I preached at five to, at least, three hundred hearers. I walked from thence to see a poor woman that was sick, about a mile from the town. About an hundred and fifty people ran after me. After I had prayed with the sick person, being unwilling so many people should go empty away, I chose a smooth, grassy place, near the road, where we all kneeled down to prayer; after which we sung a psalm, and I gave them a short exhortation.[64]

Finally, exhortations were often much more pointed and short, sometimes only four or five minutes long, whereas Wesley recommends twenty to thirty for preaching and himself preached up to an hour on occasion. Perhaps because of the brevity and spontaneity of exhortations, sermons were sometimes better ordered.[65] Often this seems to have been due to the maturity and experience of the preachers, by contrast with the

[58]*Minutes of Conference, Large Minutes*, 1753–63, §45.1, 10:860. Church describes how Wesley clearly believed in a difference between preaching and exhortation. Leslie F. Church, *More About Early Methodist People* (London: Epworth, 1949), 100.

[59]*Journal and Diaries II*, 25 October 1743, 19:350.

[60]*Journal and Diaries III: 1743–54*, v. 20 in *The Bicentennial Edition of the Works of John Wesley* (Nashville: Abingdon, 1991), 15 February 1744, 20:9. Cited hereafter as *Journal and Diaries III.*

[61]Ibid.,10 July 1745, 20:79.

[62]Jackson, *The Lives of Early Methodist Preachers*, The Life of Mr. Thomas Mitchell, 1:246.

[63]Nathan O. Hatch and John H. Wigger, eds., *Methodism and the Shaping of American Culture* (Nashville: Kingswood, 2001), 136.

[64]*Journal and Diaries III*, 3 April 1748, 20:216.

[65]Church, 215.

spontaneous nature of exhortation. Though the differences between the two were sometimes minor, preaching and exhortation were distinct acts in early Methodism and uniquely evangelistic in nature.

Wesley uses the word *exhortation*, as distinct from *preaching*, in two primary ways. The first is purely semantic. Since women and laity were prohibited from preaching in the Church of England (because that was a clerical task), Wesley uses the term *exhort* on a number of occasions as a way to refer to the proclamation of both groups without using the word *preaching*. In the case of women, before Wesley became comfortable with them "preaching" he encouraged them to exhort. There were no ecclesial hindrances on women exhorters, and Wesley clearly observed gifted women sharing their experience of faith in public and even talking about scriptural teachings. So he encouraged them to exhort in ways that resembled preaching in virtually every respect, with the exception of "taking a text." Exhortation becomes a way to encourage women to preach in all but name.

The second way Wesley uses the word *exhortation* is as "encouragement." Wesley exhorted, or encouraged, people in various ways. A typical example is his statement "I concluded my preaching here, by exhorting all" to continue growing in their faith.[66] Sometimes the encouragement is to continue positively in a faithful direction. For example, Wesley records a letter from one of the Masters at the Kingswood School, describing the wonderful atmosphere of prayer there and the corresponding lack of a need to "exhort" the children to pray.[67] Children, like adults, were to be exhorted when necessary.[68] Furthermore, exhortation also entailed comfort as a complement to encouragement.[69] This kind of encouragement through exhortation is often noted in conversations with persons on their deathbed. Frequently, preaching ends with an exhortation to progress in some aspect of discipleship.[70]

Other times exhortation involved correction or reproof. Wesley encouraged people to take on certain practices or doctrines and reproved them for choosing others. Yet Wesley acknowledges that excessive or unfounded reproof can be detrimental:

> I was sorry to find both the society and the congregations smaller than when I was here last. I impute this chiefly to the manner of preaching which has

[66]*Journal and Diaries II*, 20 September 1743, 19:340.

[67]*Journal and Diaries V: 1765–75*, v. 22 in *The Bicentennial Edition of the Works of John Wesley* (Nashville: Abingdon, 1993), 5 May 1768, 22:129. Cited hereafter as *Journal and Diaries V*.

[68]Ibid., 7 October 1770, 22:255; 20 September 1755, 22:466.

[69]*Letters III*, Letter to the Rev. Samuel Walker, 24 September 1756, 27:52.

[70]*Sermons I*, Sermon 19, "The Great Privilege of those that are born of God," 1:433; *Sermons III*, Sermon 77, "Spiritual Worship," 3:97; *Sermons IV*, Sermon 143, "Public Diversions Denounced," 4:328.

been generally used. The people have been told, frequently and strongly, of their coldness, deadness, heaviness, and littleness of faith, but very rarely of any thing that would move thankfulness. Hereby many were driven away, and those that remained were kept cold and dead.[71]

In another entry he writes:

> I made an odd observation here, which I recommend to all our Preachers. The people of Canterbury have been so often reproved, (and frequently without a cause,) for being dead and cold, that it has utterly discouraged them, and made them cold as stones. How delicate a thing is it to reprove! To do it well, requires more than human wisdom.[72]

The point of reproof and encouragement in the form of exhortation was, in the end, to encourage people in their lives of discipleship. As Wesley comments on Matthew 13:45 in his Notes on the New Testament,

> The kingdom of heaven—That is, one who earnestly seeks for it: in Matthew 13:47 it means, the Gospel preached, which is like a net gathering of every kind: just so the Gospel, wherever it is preached, gathers at first both good and bad, who are for a season full of approbation and warm with good desires. But Christian discipline, and strong, close exhortation, begin that separation in this world, which shall be accomplished by the angels of God in the world to come.

Exhortation urged people forward in their Christian discipleship, "to pursue inward religion: the renewal of their souls in righteousness and true holiness,"[73] for it was not just a one-way communication; rather, Methodists could exhort "one another" as they gathered together.[74]

THE OFFICE OF EXHORTER

The importance of exhortation is also evident in the title of Exhorter that many Methodists received. Gifted speakers who had come to faith were identified in class meetings and invited to "exhort" first in their class, then in the society, and eventually "in public" in the fields. Their messages often seemed almost identical to actual preaching, but again, without the formality and authority of taking a text. This process became a way in which to train future preachers. This progression is evident in the *Minutes* where Wesley is asked, "What is the best general method of preaching?"

[71]*Journal and Diaries V,* 2 August 1767, 22:96–7.

[72]Ibid., 1 December 1768, 22:165.

[73]*Journal and Diaries II,* 4 September 1738, 19:12.

[74]Ibid., 24 December 1739, 19:131.

to which he responds, "Frequently read and enlarge upon a portion of the Notes. And let young Preachers often exhort, without taking a text."[75] Exhortation was often seen as a time of trial for men who were not yet approved as preachers. After this time of trial, they were either approved to "preach" or else their ministry of preaching was not affirmed. In his journal Wesley provides an example of this process of testing exhorters and discerning their gifts:

> On Thursday the Stewards of all the societies met. I now diligently inquired what Exhorters there were in each society; whether they had gifts meet for the work; whether their lives were eminently holy; and whether there appeared any fruit of their labour. I found, upon the whole, 1. That there were no less than eighteen Exhorters in the county. 2. That three of these had no gifts at all for the work, neither natural nor supernatural. 3. That a fourth had neither gifts nor grace; but was a dull, empty, self-conceited man. 4. That a fifth had considerable gifts, but had evidently made shipwreck of the grace of God: These therefore I determined immediately to set aside, and advise our societies not to hear them. 6. That J. B., A. L., and J. W. had gifts and grace, and had been much blessed in the work. Lastly, That the rest might be helpful when there was no Preacher in their own or the neighbouring societies, provided they would take no step without the advice of those who had more experience than themselves.[76]

Others exhibit this pattern as well. Richard Rodda writes of his early days exhorting, before preaching: "I exhorted . . . for the first time, which was in my father's house. Soon after I was desired to exhort in the society; and then, by their advice I did it in public. The first time I attempted to preach, I was exceedingly anxious about dividing the word in a proper manner."[77]

Exhortation was a testing ground that Wesley used to discern who would be good Methodist preachers on a circuit.

WOMEN AND THEIR "EXTRAORDINARY CALL"

Wesley wanted anyone to speak whose words encouraged others to maturity in faith, including women. Fruit, not gender, ultimately mattered the most to Wesley. As early as 1742 female class leaders were appointed at the Foundery Chapel in London. People of both genders were encouraged to speak of their spiritual life in public gatherings and to exhort fellow Methodists to faith and repentance. In the early years of the revival Wesley was unwilling to go against church law, which clearly prohibited women and laity from preaching. Through the 1750s and 1760s Wesley

[75] *Minutes of Conference, Large Minutes*, 1753–63, 10:860.

[76] *Journal and Diaries III*, 7 July 1747, 20:182.

[77] Jackson, *The Lives of Early Methodist Preachers*. The Life of Mr. Richard Rodda, 2:307.

began to embrace the idea that Methodism was an "extraordinary" movement and that women preachers were part of its surprising nature.

Sarah Crosby is but one example of how Wesley's encouragement of women as preachers grew over time. After joining the movement around 1750, Crosby gradually grew in her responsibilities in Methodist leadership, her first role being that of class leader. By 1761 she sought to help start a Methodist society. On February 8 of that year she recorded an example of exhorting that sounds remarkably similar to preaching:

> This day my mind has been calmly stayed on God. In the evening I expected to meet about thirty persons in class: but to my great surprise there came near two hundred. I found an awful, loving sense of the Lord's presence, and much love to the people: but was much affected both in body and mind. I was not sure whether it was right for me to exhort in so public a manner, and yet I saw it impracticable to meet all these people by way of speaking particularly to each individual. I, therefore, gave out an hymn, and prayed, and told them part of what the Lord had done for myself, persuading them to flee from all sin.[78]

Evidently fearing she was too close to preaching, she sought Wesley's advice on how to proceed. But five days later, on February 13, and before she heard back from him, she had another opportunity to speak to a larger crowd:

> This day being appointed for a public Fast, I humbled myself in prayer. In the evening I exhorted near two hundred people to forsake their sins, and shewed them the willingness of Christ to save: They flock as doves to the windows, tho' as yet we have no preacher. Surely, Lord, thou hast much people in this place! My soul was much comforted in speaking to the people, as my Lord has removed all my scruples respecting the propriety of my acting thus publicly.[79]

Wesley's February 14 response to her February 8 experience is telling. He acknowledges that she has come close to preaching and the problems that may ensue, but he also clearly expresses his desire for her to keep speaking as she has:

> I think you have not gone too far [in exhorting at a Methodist meeting]. You could not well do less. I apprehend all you can do more is, when you meet

[78]Sarah Crosby, "The Grace of God Manifested in an Account of Mrs. Crosby," *Methodist Magazine* 29 (1806): 8 February 1761, 518.

[79]Ibid., 13 February 1761, 518.

> again, to tell them simply, "You lay me under a great difficulty. The Methodists do not allow of women preachers. Neither do I take upon me any such character. But I will just nakedly tell you what is in my heart." . . . I do not see that you have broken any law. Go on calmly and steadily. If you have time, you may read to them the Notes on any chapter before you speak a few words, or one of the most awakening sermons, as other women have done long ago.[80]

Nevertheless Wesley warns Sarah Crosby in 1769, "Keep as far from preaching as you can; therefore never take a text; never speak in a continued discourse, without some break, above four or five minutes."[81]

In the 1770s Wesley clearly embraces women preachers.[82] In response to a 1771 letter from Mary Bosanquet, Wesley writes:

> I think the strength of the cause rests there, on your having an *Extraordinary Call*. So, I am persuaded, has every one of our Lay Preachers: otherwise I could not countenance his preaching at all. It is plain to me that the whole Work of God termed Methodism is an extraordinary dispensation of His Providence. Therefore I do not wonder if several things occur there in which do not fall under ordinary rules of discipline. St. Paul's ordinary rule was, "I permit not a woman to speak in the congregation." Yet in extraordinary cases he made a few exceptions; at Corinth, in particular.[83]

While the acceptance of female preachers in Methodism was curtailed in both the United States and Great Britain after Wesley's death, by the 1770s Wesley himself encouraged all women with "extraordinary" fruit to preach and exhort.[84]

REPETITIVE PERSUASION

Each type of proclamation, be it preaching, exhortation, or teaching, included aspects of persuasion. Wesley used a number of terms that indicate the persuasive nature of proclamation. He talks about "pressing," "provoking" (especially to love and good works),[85] "speaking closely," "apply-

[80]*Letters III*, Letter to Mrs. Sarah Crosby, 14 February 1761, 27:241–42.

[81]*Letters* (Telford), Letter to Mrs. Sarah Crosby, 18 March 1769, 5:130.

[82]Again see Chilcote's two works mentioned previously.

[83]*Letters* (Telford), Letter to Mary Bosanquet, 13 June 1771, 5:257.

[84]John H. Wigger, *Taking Heaven by Storm: Methodism and the Rise of Popular Christianity in America* (Urbana: University of Illinois Press, 2001), 151–72. Wigger describes the similarity between preaching and exhortation in the United States in the seventeenth and eighteenth centuries and the characteristics common to female exhortation and male preaching.

[85]*Sermons IV*, Sermon 121, "Prophets and Priests," 4:82.

ing the word," or "enforcing the word." A typical example may be found in a journal entry from 1779:

> I spoke as closely as I could, both morning and evening, and made a pointed application to the hearts of all that were present. I am convinced, this is the only way whereby we can do any good in Scotland. This very day [Sunday] I heard many excellent truths delivered in the kirk. But as there was no application, it was likely to do as much good as the singing of a lark.[86]

Two other examples of this concept are also notable:

> At two I explained to an earnest congregation, at Hensingham, the "redemption that is in Jesus Christ;" and at five exhorted a large multitude at Whitehaven, with strong and pressing words, to examine whether they had sufficient grounds for calling either themselves or their neighbours Christians.[87]

> About ten I preached at New-Mills, to as simple a people as those at Chapel. Perceiving they had suffered much by not having the doctrine of Perfection clearly explained, and strongly pressed upon them, I preached expressly on the head; and spoke to the same effect in meeting the society. The spirits of many greatly revived; and they are now "going on unto perfection." I found it needful to press the same thing at Stockport in the evening.[88]

Wesley's preaching was intentionally persuasive. He encouraged people to mature in their faith, and not to "stand still" spiritually. He hoped his sermons were informative and challenging, but persuading people to deepen their faith in Christ was his primary concern.[89]

Yet while the preacher had a role in persuasion, Wesley was convinced that the Spirit was the primary mover in people's hearts and lives. As he writes, "The Spirit applied the Word," or "God made the application," or "The Word of the Lord prevailed." Still, the proclaimer's task was clear. Wesley knew, as Wood observes, "that his main task was to persuade men... The appeal had to be pressed home in a personal manner, so that every hearer was left feeling that the protective covering of neutrality and indifference had been stripped off... the decisive moment had arrived."[90]

Important to Wesley is the idea that persuasion is cumulative, namely

[86]*Journal and Diaries VI*, 13 June 1779, 23:135.

[87]*Journal and Diaries III*, 1 October 1749, 20:306.

[88]*Journal and Diaries VI*, 2 April 1782, 23:234.

[89]Louise Annie Dygoski, "The Journals and Letters of John Wesley on Preaching" (PhD diss., University of Wisconsin, 1961), 157.

[90]Wood, 157.

that most people require multiple conversations, over a period of time, in order to be effectively persuaded to the gospel. The whole point of the Methodist structure of field preaching, societies, classes, and visitation, as is discussed later, was to have ongoing conversations with people regarding the nature of faith, to convince them of faith, invite them to it, and then to continually persuade them to pursue the holy life. Preaching once in a place was almost not worth the effort. For "to preach once in a place, and no more, very seldom does any good; it only alarms the devil and his children, and makes them more upon their guard against a first assault."[91] Wesley, as Francis Gerald Ensley argues,

> Depended less on one grand effort than on the cumulative effect of many sermons...He never cherished the delusion that the war with evil can be won by a blitzkrieg. He knew it is a war of attrition, where victory goes to the force that holds out the longest. He never conceived of evangelism as solitary appearance...Rather, he counted on the power of many successive small blows to bring the citadels of evil down.[92]

Conclusion

Verbal proclamation took place in three primary ways, namely, preaching, teaching, and exhortation. Preaching is often thought of as the primary way in which proclamation occurs, and indeed in some ways it was for Wesley. As he reminds us in his Christian Library, hearing the word preached is "a standing Provision which God has made for the Edification of his Church."[93] And yet preaching was not the only means of proclamation. The reason Wesley embraced other types of proclamation was that he knew people responded in different ways to the biblical narrative and that these responses were encouraged by multiple types of proclamation. So it is to the responses to proclamation this narrative now turns.

---

[91] *Letters* (Telford), Letter to Freeborn Garrettson, 30 November 1786, 7:353–54.

[92] Francis Gerald Ensley, *John Wesley, Evangelist* (Nashville: Methodist Evangelistic Materials, 1958), 45.

[93] John Wesley, "A Christian Library: Consisting of Extracts from and Abridgments of the Choicest Pieces of Practical Divinity Which Have Been Published in the English Tongue," Northwest Nazarene University, http://wesley.nnu.edu/john_wesley/christian_library/index.htm. v. 30, *On Christian Prudence, Extracted from Mr. Norris*, §3.5, http://wesley.nnu.edu/john-wesley/christian-library/a-christian-library-volume-30/on-christian-prudence-extracted-from-mr-norris/.

CHAPTER 3

RESPONSES TO PROCLAMATION

The word of God has had free course among them. Sinners are daily awakened and converted to God; and believers grow in the knowledge of Christ.[1]

On March 28, 1781, Wesley visited Burslem, a city he visited many times previously. But this time was different. Over the previous twenty years the economy had boomed thanks to the success of the potteries, and the population soared in order to meet the ever-growing needs of industry. And yet Wesley noticed not just a thriving economy but also a thriving spirituality. "The country," he writes in his journal, "is not more improved than the people."[2] The cause of the spiritual growth is clear to Welsey: "The word of God has had free course among them;" with the result that "sinners are daily awakened and converted to God; and believers grow in the knowledge of Christ."[3] The previous two chapters discussed the content of proclamation and the critical types of proclamation, namely, preaching, exhortation, and teaching. This chapter explores Wesley's understanding of three primary responses to that proclamation, and in turn the three stages of discipleship to which those responses correlate. As will be demonstrated throughout the remainder of this book, appreciating these responses, their relationship with the word of God proclaimed, and the forums in which proclamation occurred is critical to understanding Wesley's evangelistic vision.

THE WAY OF SALVATION

John Wesley believed there to be a normative path of maturity in the Christian faith. The path is often circuitous and sometimes involves

[1]*Journal and Diaries VI*, 28 March 1781, 23:196.

[2]Ibid.

[3]Ibid.

backtracking, but nevertheless in his view there is a normative path. This path progresses through identifiable stages, whereby people can frequently identify their stage of discipleship. The journey itself is a gift of God, Wesley thought, but each person is responsible for embracing or neglecting their journey. This maturing process Wesley refers to as the "way" of salvation. In Wesley studies, the term "order of salvation" has been a normative term in recent decades. The phrase refers to what many scholars argue is the typical progression through which disciples mature in their Christian faith. With God's grace at work in every stage, people begin discipleship by awakening from the state of nature, experiencing initial repentance and faith in Christ that leads to justification, and then ongoing faith and repentance that results in holiness.

In recent years some have argued that Wesley's view of how people progress though Christian discipleship differs from the Reformed "*ordo salutis*." Maddox, for instance, argues (and I think correctly) that Wesley's view is more of a "way of salvation" than an "order."[4] This shift took place for two primary reasons. First, Wesley himself seems to prefer the language of "way," using it in a number of important writings—for example "The Scripture Way of Salvation," "The More Excellent Way," "The Way to the Kingdom," "The Spirit of Bondage and Adoption," and "The Almost Christian." Second, as is demonstrated in this chapter, while Wesley certainly affirms a general progression of identifiable steps, he understands the progression as a journey as opposed to a mechanical process. In his mind people progress spiritually in fits and starts, taking steps forward, then back, and then forward again, usually not moving in a linear path. Third, the delineation between these states is not always stark, but they are distinct enough to be discernable. Just as importantly, he finds differentiating them helpful in the process of encouraging discipleship. Making the distinction, in other words—imperfect though it may be—helps people know how they are maturing, and in turn gives those who teach a framework by which to motivate people. Maddox, for instance, argues that regeneration, instead of being a single step, is operative throughout the spiritual life.[5] Nevertheless, these different stages—or what are referred to as "stages of discipleship" in this book—are critical to Wesley's understanding of discipleship and how proclamation functions throughout discipleship.

The Stages of Discipleship

I use the term "stage of discipleship" to describe Wesley's understanding of the primary transitions the Spirit desires in each person's spiritual

[4]Randy L. Maddox, *Responsible Grace: John Wesley's Practical Theology* (Nashville: Kingswood, 1994), 157–58.

[5]Ibid., 159–60.

journey. These are similar but not to be confused with Wesley's understanding of the three "states" of people: natural, legal, and evangelical.[6] Contemporary scholars discuss these various stages in different ways. Lester Ruth identifies a progression from "unawakened" to "seeker" to "mourner" to "believer" or "professor."[7] Laura Bartels Felleman argues for five stages of the order of salvation: asleep, almost, awake, abiding, altogether.[8] Tom Albin identifies three different spiritual experiences, namely awakening or convinced, the New Birth, and sanctification.[9] Each scholar is attempting to label the primary spiritual transitions that Wesley identifies, which in turn mark significant different periods of spiritual development.

I argue that Wesley believed each person can mature through three primary stages of discipleship in this life. Each person begins in the state of nature or the natural state. The first stage of discipleship begins as one "awakens" to the idea of God in Christ and becomes aware of the sin in the person's life. During this stage the Spirit works to encourage initial repentance and faith, leading to justification, conversion, and the New Birth. Immediately after the second stage, people begin the third of sanctification (alternatively holiness or Christian perfection) where the Spirit keeps working to encourage a person to further faith and repentance. These three stages mark the primary transitions in Wesley's vision of mature discipleship. Since the transitions have been discussed at length by other scholars, I need mention them only briefly here. I discuss them further in subsequent chapters as we trace the role of proclamation in the various forums, and how Wesley believed the word of God draws people toward the next stage of the spiritual life.

The State of Nature

The first spiritual state of a person, in fact of all people at their birth, is the state of nature. Wesley refers to it as the "wilderness state"; those in this state, whom he calls "natural" people, are asleep. Wesley describes the characteristics of a person in the state of nature, and not yet awake to God, in his sermon titled "Awake, Thou That Sleepest": "By sleep is signified the natural state of man; that deep sleep of the soul, into which the sin of Adam hath cast all who spring from his loins; that supineness,

[6]*Sermons I*, Sermon 9, "The Spirit of Bondage and Adoption," §III.8, 1:263.

[7]Lester Ruth, *Early Methodist Life and Spirituality: A Reader* (Nashville: Kingswood, 2005), 69.

[8]Laura Bartels Felleman, *The Form and Power of Religion: John Wesley on Methodist Vitality* (Eugene: Cascade Books, 2012), 29. Felleman describes Wesley's understanding of grace as follows: Preventing the asleep, convincing the almost, justifying the awake, sanctifying the abiding, perfecting the altogether.

[9]Albin, 277–78.

indolence, and stupidity, that insensibility of his real condition, wherein every man comes into the world, and continues till the voice of God awakes him."[10]

Wesley refers to the "stupidity" of persons in this state on a number of occasions. He does not seem to mean their core intelligence, but rather that they live in a "state of utter darkness; a state wherein 'darkness covers the earth, and gross darkness the people.'"[11] People in this state are "utterly ignorant of God, knowing nothing concerning him as [they] ought to know."[12] They are "alive unto the world, and dead unto God."[13] They live in the "sin of Adam" and are asleep to the ways of God.[14] Furthermore,

> [The unawakened sinner] knows not that he is a fallen spirit, whose only business in the present world is, to recover from his fall, to regain that image of God wherein he was created. He sees *no necessity* for the *one thing needful*, even that inward universal change, that "birth from above," figured out by baptism, which is the beginning of that total renovation, that sanctification of spirit, soul, and body, "without which no man shall see the Lord."[15]

People in the natural state do not know they are dead to God. In fact, Wesley fears that the "one who sleeps" may be a "rational, inoffensive, good-natured professor of the religion of his fathers" and capable of performing some of the outward works of piety.[16] The result is that the natural person is left without a sense of God's goodness, or his or her own sinfulness.[17] While God's grace works preveniently in the natural state, inherited sin still reigns in a person's life, and therefore true discipleship has not yet begun.[18] God's grace works preveniently, stirring up in people the desire to begin seeking God, the desire of which marks the beginning of awakening.

Awakening

Wesley believed that helping people awaken to the truth of God's love in Christ is "the greatest charity" one can perform in this

[10] *Sermons I*, Sermon 3, "Awake, Thou that Sleepest," §I.1, 1:142.

[11] Ibid., §I.2, 1:142–3.

[12] Ibid., Sermon 9, "The Spirit of Bondage and of Adoption," §I.1, 1:251.

[13] Ibid., Sermon 17, "The Circumcision of the Heart," §2, 1:401.

[14] Ibid., Sermon 3, "Awake, Thou that Sleepest," §I.1, 1:142.

[15] Ibid., §I.2, 1:143.

[16] Ibid., §I.5, 1:144.

[17] Ibid., §I.7–12, 1:144–47.

[18] Maddox, *Responsible Grace: John Wesley's Practical Theology*, 81.

life.[19] Awakening, Wesley held, comes about as people became more and more aware of their sinful nature. As people awaken they "are snapped out of their false sense of confidence, recognize that their thoughts, words, and actions do not conform to God's moral law, feel shame, repent of their rebellion, and desire to be obedient."[20] The result is a deep "sorrow and heaviness."[21] People who awaken begin the search for God, at first "darkly feeling after God."[22] They become aware that they are "a child of the devil!"[23] William Dean sums up Wesley's understanding of awakening as "the stirring of a deep religious sense of condemnation and judgment for having broken God's laws."[24] It was a time of "shaking among the dry bones" of faith.[25] Upon awakening, people are not immediately soothed but rather are convicted by their sins. The Spirit, in conjunction with the interactions of others, attempts to convince them of their need for God.

Wesley believed that the Spirit uses a number of catalysts to encourage awakening. In his sermon "The Means of Grace," Wesley describes a number of them. "A stupid, senseless wretch is going on in his own way, not having God in all his thoughts, when God comes upon him unawares, perhaps by an awakening sermon or conversation, perhaps by some awful providence, or, it may be, by an immediate stroke of his convincing Spirit, without any outward means at all."[26]

In Wesley's eyes people usually awaken because of some unusual event that takes them by surprise. Sometimes it is a terrible event, an "awful providence." At other times the Spirit may move mysteriously, with no apparent outside resource, speaking directly to a person's inner spirit.[27] Finally, and perhaps most notably for Methodists, preachers and laity alike, awakening comes through a conversation or sermon in which a person is particularly challenged to consider the gospel story.

In his writings Wesley discusses at length the role sermons play in encouraging awakening. Crowds or congregations often, if not usually, included many who were not awake. Sometimes most of the crowd was not awake. This being the case, he or another Methodist would preach

[19] *Sermons I*, Sermon 3, "Awake, Thou that Sleepest," §I.12, 1:146–47.

[20] Felleman, 30.

[21] *Journal and Diaries IV*, 5 March 1759, 21:179.

[22] *Journal and Diaries V*, 23 April 1768, 22:127.

[23] *Sermons I*, Sermon 3, "Awake, Thou that Sleepest," §1.12, 1:146–47.

[24] Dean, 301.

[25] *Journal and Diaries III*, 7 October 1749, 20:307.

[26] *Sermons I*, Sermon 16, "The Means of Grace," §V.1, 1:393–94.

[27] Ibid., Sermons 10 and 11, "The Witness of the Spirit, Discourses I & II," 1:267–98.

an "awakening sermon."[28] Awakening sermons were designed to move a person spiritually from the natural person to awakening. One of Wesley's most common awakening sermons was his sermon "The Important Question," in which he expounds on Matthew 16:26: "Why would people gain the whole world but lose their lives?" Awakening sermons were designed not to call someone to conversion through justification, but rather to shock a person out of the spiritual lethargy of the natural state. In his journal Wesley describes the importance of preaching about awakening when the crowd needs it: "I preached at St. Ewin's church, but not upon Justification by Faith. I do not find this to be a profitable subject to an unawakened congregation. I explained here, and strongly applied, that awful word, 'It is appointed unto men once to die.'"[29]

Fundamental to Wesley's vision of proclamation, and specifically preaching, is his belief that the first spiritual movement, and therefore a primary goal of preaching, is from the natural state to awakening, not straight from the natural state to justification.[30] Whitefield was better known as an awakening preacher than John, even though Wesley preached countless awakening sermons. Yet Whitefield was aware that Wesley nurtured people in the faith better than he and designed Methodism to help them mature as disciples. Henry D. Rack writes that Whitefield "more or less deliberately left Wesley to consolidate the results in an organized way."[31] Whitefield himself writes in his journal once that his only consolation in departing for Georgia is, "That my dear and honoured Friend Mr. Wesley is left behind to confirm those that are awakened, so that when I return from Georgia, I hope to see many bold Soldiers of Jesus Christ."[32]

Wesley is clear that the content of proclamation that leads to awakening consists in one thing: the law. Of those who preach the gospel only, he writes,

> Their grand plea is this: That preaching the gospel, that is, according to their judgment, the speaking of nothing but the sufferings and merits of Christ, answers all the ends of the law. But this we utterly deny. It does not answer

[28] *Journal and Diaries III*, 12 July 1752, 20:433. In this example Wesley writes, "I took my old stand in the market-place, about seven in the morning, and proclaimed 'the Lord God, gracious and merciful, forgiving iniquity, transgression, and sin.' In the afternoon we had an awakening sermon at the new church, on, 'One thing is needful.'"

[29] Ibid., 14 January 1750, 20:318.

[30] Dean, 301–02.

[31] Henry D. Rack, *Reasonable Enthusiast: John Wesley and the Rise of Methodism*, 3rd ed. (London: Epworth Press, 2002), 194.

[32] George Whitefield, *A Journal of a Voyage from London to Savannah in Georgia*, 5th ed. (London: James Hutton, 1739), 2 April 1739, 66.

the very first end of the law, namely, the convincing men of sin; the awakening those who are still asleep on the brink of hell. There may have been here and there an exempt case. One in a thousand may have been awakened by the gospel: But this is no general rule: The ordinary method of God is, to convict sinners by the law, and that only. The gospel is not the means which God hath ordained, or which our Lord himself used, for this end.[33]

He states even more clearly in a letter to Joseph Cownley dated April 12, 1750, that the law awakens, not the gospel. Of course the gospel is a blessing, Wesley writes,

But yet it would be utterly wrong and unscriptural to preach of *nothing else*. Let the Law always prepare for the Gospel. I scarce ever spoke more earnestly here of the love of God in Christ than last night. But it was after I had been tearing the unawakened in pieces. Go thou and do likewise.

It is true, the love of God in Christ alone *feeds* his children. But even they are to be *guided* as well as fed. Yea, and often *physicked* too. And the bulk of our hearers must be *purged* before they are fed. Else we only feed the disease. Beware of *all honey*. It is the best extreme; but it is an extreme.[34]

Through the law, God's grace works preveniently to call people to awaken to the reality and depth of their sin. The gospel alone will not awaken. In "The Means of Grace," Wesley describes the effect on the sinner of preaching the law:

Having now a desire to flee from the wrath to come, he purposely goes to *hear* how it may be done. If he finds a preacher who speaks to the heart, he is amazed, and begins searching the Scriptures, whether these things are so? The more he *hears* and *reads*, the more convinced he is; and the more he meditates thereon day and night. Perhaps he finds some other book which explains and enforces what he has heard and read in Scripture. And by all these means, the arrows of conviction sink deeper into his soul. He begins also to talk of the things of God, which are ever uppermost in his thoughts; yea, and to talk with God; to pray to him; although, through fear and shame, he scarce knows what to say. But whether he can speak or no, he cannot but pray, were it only in "groans which cannot be uttered." Yet, being in doubt, whether "the high and lofty One that inhabiteth eternity" will regard such a sinner as him, he wants to pray with those who know God, with the faithful, in the great congregation. But here he observes others go up to the table of the Lord. He considers, "Christ has said, 'Do this!' How is it that I do not? I am too great a sinner. I am not fit. I am not worthy." After struggling with these scruples a while, he breaks through. And thus he continues in God's way, in hearing, reading, meditating, praying, and partaking of the Lord's

[33]*Sermons II*, Sermon 35, "The Law Established through Faith, Discourse 1," §I.3, 2:22–23.

[34]*Letters II*, Letter to Joseph Cownley, 21 April 1750, 26:418.

Supper, till God, in the manner that pleases him, speaks to his heart, "Thy faith hath saved thee. Go in peace."[35]

The law shakes people awake; focusing only on God's promises, as many "gospel ministers" do, will not awaken people to their dire state and need for God.[36] Through the preaching of the law, people are awakened to the idea that God is real, God loves them and calls them to discipleship, and that—most important of all—they are broken sinners. Awakening was of utmost importance to Wesley; from his journals and early documents it is evident that he was more concerned about the number of people awakened as a result of field preaching than the number converted.[37] The function of evangelistic proclamation of the gospel is to call people to awakening by making them aware of their sinfulness before God and their need for the gospel, a first response that all too often is overlooked.[38] The natural response of people who become aware of their sinfulness is to seek God's mercy.[39] Indeed, awakening is the first fruit of proclamation.[40] And to wake people up requires close or "sharp" preaching.[41]

Justification

Wesley wrote in his journal, "I fear the Preachers have been more studious to please than to awaken, or there would have been a deeper work."[42] That deeper work is justification. As people begin to encounter the law, the first response is awakening. But awakening is never the end. Wesley argues that stopping there, at awakening, is like "begetting children for the murderer."[43] After awakening, preachers are charged to "follow the blow" and encourage people on toward conversion through

[35]*Sermons I,* Sermon 16, "The Means of Grace," §V.1, 1:394.

[36]*Treatises II,* "Thoughts Concerning Gospel Ministers," 13:568–70.

[37]*Journal and Diaries VII: 1787–91,* v. 24 in *The Bicentennial Edition of the Works of John Wesley* (Nashville: Abingdon, 2003). 30 April 1787, 24:21–22. Cited hereafter as *Journal and Diaries VII.*

[38]Alexander L. Boraine, "The Nature of Evangelism in the Theology and Practice of John Wesley" (PhD diss., Drew University, 1969). Boraine, for instance, cites Wesley's emphasis on conversion and sanctification, but overlooks awakening completely.

[39]Dean, 301–02.

[40]Meadows, "The Journey of Evangelism," 422. Meadows argues that in early Methodism, "the most important fruit of evangelistic preaching and proclamation was not conversion as such, but the awakening of sinners to the need of salvation."

[41]*Journal and Diaries III,* 13 May 1750, 20:336. Wesley recounts, "I strove to shake some of them out of sleep, by preaching as sharply as I could."

[42]*Journal and Diaries V,* 12 October 1774, 22:431.

[43]*Journal and Diaries IV,* 25 August 1763, 21:424.

repentance and faith.[44] As people continue to engage the ideas of the law, Wesley argues, they are confronted with the reality and pervasiveness of their sin. While they may have heard the gospel, the gospel itself is not the central focus of proclamation. The gospel may be preached in an effort to share with people the glory of what is to come, but in Wesley's mind the law is still the focus, for people must then repent of their sin and come to faith in Christ. Thus the next state of discipleship is marked by a person's initial repentance of sin and faith in Christ.

Repentance is a critical response to God's grace in the Methodist understanding of discipleship. Methodist preachers, class leaders, and laity are taught and trained to question people about their spiritual state. Part of the inquiry, Wesley says to his preachers, is to discover whether people are "convinced or unconvinced, converted or unconverted."[45] If someone is unconverted, then the Methodist is supposed to describe what leads to conversion "and then renew and enforce the inquiry."[46] Wesley describes the process:

> They should begin with repentance; the knowledge of themselves; of their sinfulness, guilt, and helplessness. They should be instructed next, to seek peace with God, through our Lord Jesus Christ. Then let them be taught to retain what they have received; to "walk in the light of his countenance;" yea, to "walk in the light as he is in the light," without any darkness at all; till "the blood of Jesus Christ cleanseth" them "from all sin."[47]

This instruction inevitably includes a discussion of the gospel. It is here that the fulfillment of the law is proclaimed in Jesus. The legal part of the gospel leads to awakening, but the fulfillment of the good news leads to faith and repentance. For once people are awakened, God's grace works to convince them not only of their sin but also of God's love and the need for faith and repentance. This initial experience of faith and repentance leads to justification.

Wesley's basic definition of justification is simple: being forgiven of one's sins and being made right for heaven.[48] At this point one is "saved" from their sins. Wesley never underestimates the importance of justification and salvation in the Christian life. As he says to his preachers: "You have nothing to do but to save souls. Therefore spend and be spent in this work; and go always, not only to those who want [or need] you, but

[44] *Journal and Diaries II,* 13 March 1743, 19:318.

[45] *Minutes of Conference, Large Minutes,* 1770–72, §17.6.8, 10:882. In this portion of the *Minutes* Wesley summarizes Richard Baxter's *Gildas Salvianus.*

[46] Ibid., §17.6.8, 10:883.

[47] *Sermons III,* Sermon 79, "On Dissipation," §19–20, 3:123–24.

[48] Maddox, *Responsible Grace: John Wesley's Practical Theology,* 166.

to those who want you most."[49] He writes to Charles, "Your business as well as mine is to save souls."[50] While salvation begins at the moment of justification, justification is neither the goal of discipleship nor the end of proclamation. Rather, proclamation continues in sanctification, which itself marks the completion of salvation.

Sanctification

At the moment of justification one experiences the New Birth which itself marks the entry into a final stage of discipleship—namely, sanctification. Sanctification, also referred to as holiness, is the season of discipleship where the Spirit forms people more and more into the image of God. In "The Circumcision of the Heart," Wesley defines sanctification as,

> That habitual disposition of the soul which, in the sacred writings, is termed holiness; and which directly implies being cleansed from sin, "from all filthiness both of flesh and spirit;" and, by consequence, being endued with those virtues which were in Christ Jesus; being so "renewed in the image of our mind," as to be "perfect as our Father in heaven is perfect."[51]

People are, "inwardly changed by the almighty operation of the Spirit of God; changed from sin to holiness; renewed in the image of him who created us."[52] The relationship between sanctification and the New Birth is seen in Wesley's description of the latter:

> It is that great change which God works in the soul when he brings it into life; when he raises it from the death of sin to the life of righteousness. It is the change wrought in the whole soul by the almighty Spirit of God when it is "created anew in Christ Jesus;" when it is "renewed after the image of God, in righteousness and true holiness;" when the love of the world is changed into the love of God; pride into humility; passion into meekness; hatred, envy, malice, into a sincere, tender, disinterested love for all mankind. In a word, it is that change whereby the earthly, sensual, devilish mind is turned into the "mind which was in Christ Jesus." This is the nature of the new birth. "So is everyone that is born of the Spirit."[53]

During this stage the Spirit's works of regeneration takes place. While Maddox argues that Wesley believed this renewal of the Spirit begins long

[49]*Minutes of Conference, Large Minutes*, 1753–63, §37, 10:854.

[50]Wesley, *Letters* (Telford), Letter to Charles Wesley, 26 April 1772, 5:316.

[51]*Sermons I*, Sermon 17, "The Circumcision of the Heart," §1.1, 1:402–03.

[52]John Wesley, *Doctrinal and Controversial Treatises I*, v. 12 in *The Bicentennial Edition of the Works of John Wesley* (Nashville: Abingdon, 2012). "The Doctrine of Original Sin, Part II," §VI.2, 12:298. Cited hereafter as *Treatises I*.

[53]*Sermons II*, Sermon 45, "The New Birth," §II.5, 2:193–94.

before sanctification, it certainly begins no later than at the New Birth. While justification is typically understood as taking place in a moment, sanctification (like awakening) is best understood as a lifelong process that may conclude with a momentary experience of Christian perfection.

This season of sanctification, which culminates either in this life or the next in Christian perfection, is the conclusion of salvation in Wesley's mind. Souls are saved at justification, but salvation as a whole includes "two general parts, justification and sanctification."[54] Wesley is clear:

> By salvation I mean, not barely (according to the vulgar notion) deliverance from hell, or going to heaven, but a present deliverance from sin, a restoration of the soul to its primitive health, its original purity; a recovery of the divine nature; the renewal of our souls after the image of God in righteousness and true holiness, in justice, mercy, and truth.[55]

True fitness for heaven means more than just affirming a specific creedal statement Rather it means being as holy as the Apostles:

> Can any man be saved if he be not holy, like the Apostles? A follower of them, as they were of Christ? And ought not every Preacher of the gospel to be in a *peculiar* manner like the Apostles, both in holy tempers, in exemplariness of life, and in his indefatigable labours for the good of souls? Woe unto every ambassador of Christ who is not like the Apostles in this: in holiness; in making full proof of his ministry, in spending and being spent for Christ![56]

Therefore sanctification, not justification, is the true end of discipleship for Methodists.

For the purposes of this study we can note at this point Wesley's belief that the Spirit works to facilitate holiness, at least in part, through the proclamation of the story of God in Christ. In his note on John 17:17, Wesley writes that "sanctify" means to "consecrate them by the anointing of the Spirit to their office, and perfect them in holiness, by means of thy word."[57] John would certainly have echoed his father's words to John's brother Samuel that, "Faith and obedience . . . come by hearing [the word]: this being God's ordinance for the conversion of mankind, and the church's edification, or increase in charity and knowledge."[58]

The importance of this relationship between sanctification and the story of God in Christ continued in Methodist circles for many years. For

[54]Ibid., Sermon 43, "The Scripture Way of Salvation," §1.3, 2:157.

[55]Wesley, *Appeals*, "A Farther Appeal to Men of Reason and Religion, Part I," §I.3, 11:106.

[56]Ibid., "A Farther Appeal to Men of Reason and Religion, Part III," §9, 11:295–96.

[57]*Explanatory Notes Upon the New Testament* (New York: J. Soule and T. Mason, 1818), 271.

[58]Stevenson, 99.

example, just a few years after Wesley's death, the *Arminian Magazine* included an extract of Isaac Watts's "An Humble Attempt Towards the Revival of Practical Religion Amoung Christians." In that extract the editors argue only the gospel "is so happily suited to attain these ends [Christian perfection], so it is the only effectual means that God has appointed in the lips of his ministers for this purpose."[59] People respond to the proclamation of the gospel with awakening and conversion, but the great hope is Christian perfection. And in Wesley's understanding, the word of God is what sanctifies.

INITIAL THOUGHTS ON PROCLAMATION THROUGHOUT DISCIPLESHIP

At this point a number of issues are immediately evident that will require further investigation throughout the course of this book, but it would be helpful to touch upon them here.

Proclamation as a Means of Grace

In each stage, barring a miraculous intervention of the Spirit, the message of God has to be particularly engaged through proclamation, a reading of the scriptures, or conversation. In this way proclamation is one of the means of grace, the normative ways in which the Spirit reveals God's love for the world. Wesley describes how proclamation functions as a means of grace in his sermon of the same title. First, proclamation works to awaken through sermons, conversations, unfortunate events, or the miraculous work of the Spirit in one's spirit. Then,

> Having now a desire to flee from the wrath to come, he purposely goes to *hear* how it may be done. If he finds a preacher who speaks to the heart, he is amazed, and begins "searching the Scriptures," whether these things are so. The more he *hears* and *reads*, the more convinced he is; and the more he meditates thereon day and night. Perhaps he finds some other book which explains and enforces what he has heard and read in Scripture. And by all these means, the arrows of conviction sink deeper into his soul.[60]

Wesley continues:

> By observing this order of God, we may learn what means to recommend to any particular soul. If any of these will reach a stupid, careless sinner, it is probably hearing, or conversation. To such, therefore, we might recommend these, if he has ever any thought about salvation. To one who begins to feel

[59] *Arminian Magazine*, 20 (1797): 72.

[60] *Sermons I*, Sermon 16, "The Means of Grace," §V.1, 1:394.

> the weight of his sins, not only hearing the word of God, but reading it too, and perhaps other serious books, may be a means of deeper conviction. May you not advise him also, to meditate on what he reads, that it may have its full force upon his heart? Yea, and to speak thereof, and not be ashamed, particularly among those who walk in the same path. When trouble and heaviness take hold upon him, should you not then earnestly exhort him to pour out his soul before God; "always to pray and not to faint;" and when he feels the worthlessness of his own prayers, are you not to work together with God, and remind him of going up into the house of the Lord, and praying with all them that fear him? But if he does this, the *dying word* of his Lord will soon be brought to his remembrance; a plain intimation that this is the time when we should second the motions of the blessed Spirit. And thus may we lead him, step by step, through all the means which God has ordained; not according to our own will, but just as the Providence and the Spirit of God go before and open the way.[61]

Proclamation allows people to "hear" the gospel and functions as a means of grace. The Spirit works through the word proclaimed to help people mature as disciples of Jesus.

Responding to Grace Proclaimed

Because Wesley believed proclamation to be a means by which the Spirit reveals God's love, he held that Methodists should naturally desire a response to proclamation. Early Methodists sought a response, and they believed that people respond in three normative ways: awakening, faith, and repentance leading to justification, and finally, an ongoing deepening of faith and repentance leading to holiness. While many contemporary Methodists think that there are different kinds of grace, among them prevenient, justifying, sanctifying, convincing, and glorifying, God's grace is singular. God's grace is, as Wesley writes, simply "the love of God."[62] But depending on their stage of discipleship, people experience God's grace differently. Those in the state of nature experience grace preveniently; once awakened, they experience grace in a convincing and justifying manner; and then finally, once they are justified, they experience grace working to sanctify their hearts and minds.

This desire for response explains Wesley's fourfold vision for each sermon: invite, convince, offer Christ, and build up.[63] At other times he expands the list to include six key goals: instructing the ignorant, convicting the "stupid sinner," softening the obstinate, converting the wicked,

[61]Ibid., Sermon 16, "The Means of Grace," §V.2, 1:394–95.

[62]*Sermons III*, Sermon 110, "Free Grace," §1, 3:544.

[63]*Minutes of Conference*, 1744, §70, 10:139.

edifying converts, and admonishing backsliders.[64] Either way, Wesley is clear that proclamation, at least through preaching, leads people to multiple responses. In this way Wesley's evangelistic task must not be seen as ending with justification, but as also working for sanctification.[65]

Both Law and Gospel Preached in Each Stage of Discipleship

As Wesley witnessed people responding to the proclamation of grace, he learned that people do so in different ways. Awakening is the typical response to the preaching of the law, while justification and sanctification flow from the responses of faith and repentance as the gospel is proclaimed. These are the usual responses. Perhaps surprisingly to some, Wesley believed that sometimes the gospel, and not only the law, can awaken and convict people. He records in his journal,

> We came to St. Ives about seven: The Room would nothing near contain the congregation; but they stood in the orchard all round, and could hear perfectly well. I found to-night, that God can wound by the Gospel as well as by the Law; although the instances of this are exceeding rare, nor have we any Scripture-ground to expect them. While I was enforcing, "We pray you in Christ's stead, be ye reconciled to God," a young woman, till then quite unawakened, was cut to the heart, and sunk to the ground; though she could not give a clear, rational account of the manner how the conviction seized upon her.[66]

Thus we see that the gospel, like the law, can "wound" people, making them aware of their sinfulness and their need for Christ.

The role of law and gospel in multiple stages is evident in Wesley's December 20, 1751, letter to Ebenezer Blackwell. Here Wesley writes that in order to encourage initial faith and nurture believers as disciples means preaching both the law and gospel, not ignoring one or the other.[67] An extended citation of Wesley's letter is helpful at this point:

> I think the right method of preaching is this. At our first beginning to preach at any place, after a general declaration of the love of God to sinners, and his willingness that they should be saved, to preach the law in the strongest, the closest, the most searching manner possible, only intermixing the gospel here and there, and showing it, as it were, afar off.
>
> After more and more persons are convinced of sin, we may mix more

---

[64]Isaac Watts, *The Arminian Magazine: Consisting of Extracts and Original Treatises on Universal Redemption*, 21 vols. (London: Fry, J. and Co., 1778), 20; (1797), 69.

[65]Boraine, 18. Boraine writes, "For Wesley, the end of evangelism is not simply a climactic experience but holiness of heart and life."

[66]*Journal and Diaries III*, 25 September 1748, 20:249–50.

[67]*Letters II*, Letter to an Evangelical Layman, 20 December 1751, §4–7, 26:482–83.

> and more of the gospel, in order to "beget faith", to raise into spiritual life those whom the law hath slain—but this is not to be done too hastily, neither. Therefore it is not expedient wholly to omit the law; not only because we may well suppose that many of our hearers are still unconvinced, but because otherwise there is a danger that many who are convinced will heal their own wounds slightly: therefore it is only in private converse with a thoroughly convinced sinner that we should preach nothing but the gospel.
>
> If, indeed, we could suppose a whole congregation to be thus convinced, we should need to preach only the gospel; and the same we might do if our whole congregation were supposed to be newly justified. But when these grow in grace, and in the knowledge of Christ, a wise builder would preach the law to them again, only taking particular to place every part of it in a gospel light, as not only a command but a priveledge also.[68]

Wesley continues:

> Thus would he preach the law even to those who were pressing on to the mark. But to those who were careless or drawing back he would preach it in another manner, nearly as he did before they were convinced of sin. To those meanwhile who were earnest but feeble-minded he would preach the gospel chiefly yet variously intermixing more or less of the law, according to their various necessities.[69]

The gospel and the law together help nurture people as Christian disciples. An unbeliever needs to hear both that God loves her and that she is broken and in need of a savior. Believers also need to hear both gospel and law (though the law with "the love of Christ" as its foundation) to continue maturing as disciples.[70] For the law preached, "both enlightens and strengthens the soul; that it both nourishes and teaches; that it is the guide, 'food, medicine, and stay,' of the believing soul."[71]

Law and gospel are thus not opposing theologial doctrines, but instead intimately linked concepts, neither of which can be understood apart from the other. Therefore while they are properly preached distinctively, they must also be preached "both at once, or both in one."[72] For only as the "law and gospel mixed together" can the promises of God be fully embraced.[73]

[68]Ibid., §8–10, 26:483.

[69]Ibid., §11, 26:484.

[70]Ibid., §10, 26:484.

[71]Ibid., §18, 26:485.

[72]Ibid., §17, 26:485.

[73]Ibid., §17, 26:485.

Multiple Responses in Each Proclamation

While some proclamation is designed to encourage one response over others—perhaps most notably the "awakening sermons" Wesley describes—the reality is that sermons typically are multifunctional. A single act of proclamation might cause various people to respond in different stages of discipleship. An example from Wesley's journal illustrates this phenomenon:

> Last summer, the work of God revived, and gradually increased till the end of November. Then God made bare his arm. Those who were strangers to God felt, as it were, a sword in their bones: those who knew God, were filled with joy unspeakable. The convictions that seized the unawakened were generally exceeding deep; so that their cries drowned every other voice, and no other means could be used than the speaking to the distressed, one by one, and encouraging them to lay hold on Christ. And this was not in vain. Many that were either on their knees, or prostrate on the ground, suddenly started up; and their very countenance showed that the Comforter was come. Immediately, these began to go about from one to another of those that were still in distress, praying to God, and exhorting them without delay to come to so gracious a Saviour. Many who then appeared quite unconcerned were thereby cut to the heart, and suddenly filled with such anguish as extorted loud and bitter cries.[74]

One person might awaken, another might experience the New Birth, while still another might experience Christian perfection. An example of various responses to a single act of proclamation is given in a letter that Hester Ann Rogers wrote to John Wesley regarding the fruit of one sermon. She writes, "On Christmas morning, at four o'clock, the preaching house was well filled, and God was truly present to bless; many were awakened, and some converted... Fourteen souls were that day born of God..."[75] In this case both awakening and conversion are cited as appropriate responses to one sermon. In this way, the proclamation of the gospel simultaneously encourages people in each stage of discipleship.

The Wesleyan understanding that various responses are appropriate in relationship to Christian proclamation is evidenced in Wesley's multiple aims for sermons. In his view, any single act of preaching can accomplish any or all of these evangelistic aims. The preacher, teacher, or exhorter is to proclaim the gospel and then to press people to respond as the Spirit leads them, from natural person to awakening, conversion, or Christian perfection.

[74] *Journal and Diaries V*, 4 June 1772, 22:330–31.

[75] Rogers, 270.

Methodists "Provoke" Responses in Partnership with the Spirit

Wesley is clear that Methodists, preachers as well as laity, need to encourage people to respond to the story of God through the power of the Holy Spirit. The Spirit charges Methodists, when the time is appropriate, "To awaken those that sleep in death; to bring those who are awakened to the atoning blood, that 'being justified by FAITH' they may have peace with God; and to provoke those who have peace with God to about more in love and good works."[76] Methodists themselves do not actually awaken, convert, or sanctify. That power belongs only to the Spirit. Yet the Spirit requires, in many cases, the partnership of a Methodist's proclamation in order to help encourage maturity in people's Christian discipleship.

Responding over Time

Wesley clearly believed that people can respond instantaneously to the Spirit in any stage of discipleship. But while Wesley acknowledges these immediate responses, and even rejoices in them, he does not see them as the norm. Two examples demonstrate the normal pattern. The first is from a letter Margaret Austin penned to Charles Wesley where she describes the different preachers who were significant in her discipleship, "Awakened by the Reverend Mr. Whitefield: Convicted by the Reverend Mr. Jn Wesley: Converted by the Reverend Mr. Charles."[77] The second example is from a letter written by Samuel Hewitt to Charles Wesley, is more typical of the pattern of response: "After two years deep convictions God rebuked the stormy wind and tempest and there was a great calm—I tasted that peace of God which Paseth all understanding of the natural man."[78] Methodists tended to respond to a variety of different people over time who proclaimed the good news.

Thomas Albin documents this reality quite dramatically. His analysis of early Methodist autobiographical accounts indicates that the average length of time between being awakened and being converted was 2.4 years, while the time between conversion and sanctification was 5.8 years.[79] Albin goes on to reflect that the evidence suggests that the process of maturity in discipleship—even toward conversion, much less

[76] *Societies*, "The Character of a Methodist," §16, 9:41.

[77] Margaret Austin to Charles Wesley, 19 May 1740, ms. letter, Early Methodist Volume, John Rylands Library, University of Manchester, U.K.

[78] MARC, Unpublished letter from Samuel Hewit to Charles Wesley, November 1741. Cited in Benefiel, 24.

[79] Albin, 285–86.

sanctification—was a deliberate one that involved much thought and reflection.[80]

Backsliding

Wesley is clear that just as people can grow in grace, they can also revert to an earlier stage of discipleship. In *Farther Thoughts upon Christian Perfection*, Wesley writes that he is "well assured" that people can take a step back in their stage of discipleship, and then mature once again.[81] One cause of falling back, he goes on to write, is an incorrect belief that a person no longer needs to "hear" the word proclaimed, especially in morning preaching.[82] Not only does proclamation initiate people's maturing as disciples, it also helps keep disciples moving forward. This is true in each of the various stages of discipleship. For instance, Wesley exhorts and preaches for people to go on to perfection.[83] The Methodists were constantly reminded to keep proclaiming, especially through preaching, or else all their work would turn to naught.

In numerous places John Wesley writes that when proclamation in its various forms ceases to take place, those who had been awakened often fall asleep again. For example, while commenting on David Taylor's ministry, Wesley records in his journal, "I found he had occasionally exhorted multitudes of people in various parts; but, after that, he had taken no thought about them; so that the greater part were fallen asleep again."[84] Furthermore, in a letter to Adam Clarke, Wesley writes, "I hope those who were then awakened are not all fallen asleep again. Preaching in the morning is one excellent means of keeping their souls awake."[85] In a letter to his brother Charles dated June 28, 1755, John expresses this concern regarding the preachers: "I only fear the Preachers' or the people's leaving, not the Church, but the love of God, and inward or outward holiness. To this I press them forward continually. I dare not, in conscience, spend my time and strength on externals."[86]

This new life of love is the core to which Wesley called himself, his preachers, and his people, and he constantly worried that they would fall away from it. Proclamation was Wesley's solution to the problem of regression in discipleship. The ongoing and consistent verbal proclamation

---

[80]Ibid., 279.

[81]*Treatises II*,"Farther Thoughts upon Christian Perfection," §I.30, 13:110.

[82]Ibid., §I.33, 13:113.

[83]*Journal and Diaries VII*, 20 August 1787, 24:52.

[84]*Journal and Diaries II*, 15 June 1742, 19:278.

[85]*Letters* (Telford), Letter to Adam Clark, 3 January 1787, 7:362.

[86]*Letters II*, Letter to Charles Wesley, 28 June 1755, 26:565.

of the gospel is what startspeople on the journey to Christian perfection, and also what keeps them going.

CONCLUSION

Wesley believed that the best way to encourage people to progress through the stages of discipleship is to establish a process whereby the word of God can have "free recourse" among the people. As they encounter the word in the state of nature, they can become aware of their sin and awaken. Wesley hoped that as they further encounter the word they will come to an initial experience of faith and repentance that will lead to justification and an initial experience of sanctification with the New Birth. Then, as they continue to engage the word, they will experience additional times of faith and repentance leading to deeper sanctification, and perhaps even Christian perfection.

Wesley understood this journey of discipleship as a lifelong journey. While a straight line for some people, for many others the journey takes them back and forth among the three stages of discipleship. The principal means by which people mature as disciples is a hearing of the law and gospel anew, and a call to obey the Spirit's leading. Early Methodists operated under the assumption that many, if not most, people are not converted the first time they hear the gospel. Rather, after hearing the gospel—perhaps once, perhaps many times—people awaken to the good news of God's love for the world and God's call to be part of his work in the world through the community of faith. At some point after awakening and the continued hearing of the gospel, faith and repentance leading to conversion is viewed as the next response necessary. After conversion, Christian perfection follows—sometimes quickly, sometimes after an extended period.

Even at this point, it is clear that if Wesley's vision of evangelism can be discerned, it is much different from many contemporary understandings of it. In the first place, evangelism must include a particular announcement of the law and gospel, in different ways and in different degrees, throughout a person's life. Second, while many contemporary advocates of evangelism understand justification as the primary response to the word, Wesley clearly believed that response is more multifaceted and includes important seasons of awakening and sanctification in a disciple's life. Unlike many contemporary Methodists who underemphasize evangelism out of fear of focusing too much on conversion, Wesley believed conversion was a vital stage of discipleship and a necessary one for people to truly begin a journey of holiness. Furthermore he was not concerned that proclamation and an invitation to discipleship would be overly focused on conversion as he new proclamation played an important part in every stage of discipleship. Proclamation did more than convert people or initiate them into the faith; it called people to increasingly deeper discipleship. In this way, the entire journey of Christian discipleship was enabled through proclamation.

The next four chapters of the book examine the four primary forums in which proclamation took place, namely, field preaching, Methodist society meetings, class meetings, and visitation. Society and class meetings are relatively well understood in contemporary Methodism, and society meetings especially find a parallel today in weekly worship services in almost every Methodist community. Even class meetings are similar in many ways to the contemporary small groups found in many Methodist churches. Field preaching is well understood but rarely practiced by Methodists today. The final forum—visitation—is almost universally misunderstood and ignored. Only when proclamation and the responses it elicits are understood in light of these four forums can Wesley's evangelistic vision be comprehended and perhaps even revived in contemporary settings.

CHAPTER 4

FIELD PREACHING

About seven I preached . . . and the people flocked together from all quarters. The want of field-preaching has been one cause of deadness here. I do not find any great increase of the work of God without it.[1]

In June 1764 Wesley was traveling, as he had so many times before and as he would for the remainder of his years, with the goal of starting new Methodist communities and encouraging those that already existed. He traveled along the west coast of England, passing through Whitehaven. The Methodist society there had been struggling. Attendance numbers were declining, and the society itself was not dealing with the primary issue of helping people mature as disciples. By 1764 the revival that began in the late 1730s in Great Britain had reached its apex in many ways. The Methodist work particularly, while still growing nationally, was stagnant in some areas around the country. The west coast was no exception. On June 24 Wesley records in his journal the passage quoted above. He concludes quite startlingly, "If ever this [field preaching] is laid aside, I expect the whole work [Methodism] will gradually die away."[2]

This was not the only time Wesley placed such responsibility on field preaching. He writes in the *General Rules*, "The want of preaching abroad, and of preaching in new places, has greatly damped the work of God."[3] In a number of letters he communicates similar sentiments. In 1768 Wesley wrote to John Mason, "I would advise to make a longer trial of Kinsale. I am still in hope that good will be done there. And there has been considerable good done at Bandon; and will be more if the Preachers do not coop themselves up in the house. But no great good will be done at any place without field-preaching."[4] Four years later, again writing to John Mason, Wesley echoed the concept: "You cannot expect to do good at Carlisle till

[1]*Journal and Diaries IV*, 24 June 1764, 21:473.

[2]Ibid.

[3]*Minutes of Conference*, 1767, 10:350.

[4]*Letters* (Telford), Letter to John Mason, 6 August 1768, 5:100.

you either procure a more comfortable place, or preach in the open air. For many years Cockermouth has been the same, and will be till you can preach abroad."[5] In a 1774 letter to Joseph Benson, Wesley continues the thought: "The harvest cannot be large till we can preach abroad."[6] Wesley was prone to grand statements, and field preaching was not the only aspect of Methodism that he claims is essential, but here and elsewhere he is clear: Methodism's fate depends, at least in part, on field preaching.

"Field preaching" describes the practice of preaching anywhere other than inside a Church of England parish building. It is synonymous with the phrase "preaching abroad," though in this book I tend to use the term "field preaching." Both terms identify the practice of moving religious services, especially singing, prayer, and preaching, out of parish buildings and into outdoor spaces or indoors in nonchurch buildings. Sometimes that preaching literally took place in fields, often next to mines where workers and their families tended to gather before and after a day's work. But it also took place in market squares, under trees, and on hills; in homes, public buildings, military barracks, and prisons; on street corners, on top of tombstones, in yards, gardens, village greens, and even beaches. To this day, many locales for Methodist preaching can still be identified around England. Names such as "Wesley Steps," "Wesley Stones," "Wesley Field," "Wesley Oak," "Wesley's Tree," "Wesley's Place," "Wesley Lane," and "Wesley's Cross" all indicate places where Methodists preached "abroad." They are all places, as Alexander Mather called them, in "God's chapel under the roof of heaven."[7]

The practice of preaching outside of Church of England church buildings became a familiar, if uncommon, practice in the centuries leading up to the eighteenth century in England. But it became a defining element of the revival of the late 1730s and 1740s. While Methodists were not alone in incorporating field preaching into their ministry, they were unique in how they systematized it into their entire method of ministry. As Heitzenrater argues, field preaching became a defining aspect of the Methodist revival.[8] Wesley began preaching in the open air in 1739, and he wove the practice into the heart of the Methodist movement. He preached abroad thousands of times over the course of his life. The practice became central to Methodism, in general, and Wesley's own ministry, in particular. In fact, his final sermon was delivered "abroad," while preaching under an ash tree in Winchelsea, Sussex, in 1790. Within just a few years of the beginning of the Methodist revival, the entire method of Methodism was built upon the

[5]Ibid., Letter to John Mason, 26 January 1772, 5:301.

[6]Ibid., Letter to Joseph Benson, 4 March 1774, 6:77.

[7]Church, 106.

[8]Heitzenrater, 29. Heitzenrater offers an insightful and brief overview of Wesley's preaching, including field preaching.

proposition that in the mid-eighteenth century in England, many people first engaged the gospel story outside of a parish church.

The words of Donald Soper, one of the great British Methodist preachers of the twentieth century, are most certainly true: "If it is true that Methodism was born in song, it was certainly bred in the open air."[9] This chapter explores the heritage of field preaching in England, the principles and practices of Methodist field preaching specifically, the various types of proclamation that occurred in it, and the corresponding personal responses to gospel proclamation that Methodists sought in people who came to field preaching events.

A Heritage of Field Preaching in Britain

Field preaching was not an invention of Methodism or the eighteenth century. Augustine of Canterbury preached outdoors to King Ethelbert in the seventh century. Saint Aiden was known as a traveling preacher who traversed "both town and country...inviting to embrace the mystery of faith."[10] Thirteenth-century itinerant friars followed Saint Francis's pattern of traveling through the countryside and preaching in towns and to those they passed on their journeys.[11] Scottish Covenanters incorporated the practice, and field preaching helped launch the Quakers.[12] By the seventeenth century, the British religious landscape had embraced, if coolly, the practice of field preaching to the extent that apparently both Wesley's grandfather, John Wesley, and his great-grandfather, Bartholomew Wesley, preached outside parish buildings on at least a few occasions.[13]

In the first few decades of the eighteenth century, four people, in particular, who began preaching outside parish buildings helped shape the religious sphere that Wesley and the early Methodists built upon. The first was Griffith Jones, Rector of Llandowror. He began preaching in Wales, both in the open air and in other ministers' parishes, as early as 1714.[14] Jones came to know both Daniel Rowland and Howell Harris and encouraged them to begin preaching outside parish buildings. Both Rowland and Harris became important figures in the Welsh Calvinistic Methodist movement. These Welsh Calvinist Methodists, especially Rowland and Harris, were noted for their open-air preaching as well as their emphasis

[9]Donald Soper, "Wesley the Outdoor Preacher," in *John Wesley: Contemporary Perspectives*, ed. John Stacey (London: Epworth, 1988), 183.

[10]Bede, *The Ecclesiastical History of the English Nation*, ed. Vida Dutton Scudder, Everyman's Library (London: J.M. Dent & Sons, 1910), 133.

[11]Wood, 108.

[12]William Parkes, "John Wesley: Field Preacher," *Methodist History* 30 (July 1992): 220.

[13]Ibid., 221.

[14]Rack, 164.

on forming societies as a way of encouraging discipleship in those who responded to the gospel message during field preaching events. Harris, a layperson who never received orders to preach from the Church of England, was especially important to Wesley, and the two would later converse on numerous occasions. By the late 1730s, field preaching had long been an aspect of English religious life, even if cultural and ecclesial elites declined to embrace it.

The fourth contemporary figure who influenced Wesley was George Whitefield. Rowland came to know George Whitefield in the early 1730s and was influential in Whitefield's conversion in 1734. Whitefield had long been friends with John and Charles, having been one of the first members of the Holy Club, a small group of Oxford students who began meeting when John and Charles were students there. The three remained friends throughout their lives. Though they drifted apart over theological differences, the relationship between John and George was strong enough that John preached at Whitefield's funeral.

Two years after his 1734 conversion, Whitefield was ordained a deacon in the Church of England. He quickly became known as a powerful preacher, though he was sometimes criticized for his style of preaching, which seemed overly charismatic to many in the church. Whitefield decided to go to Georgia as a missionary, and he encouraged the Wesley brothers to go to Georgia as well. Whitefield returned to London from the colonies before John and Charles, arriving there at the end of 1738. Upon his return he soon began preaching once again in churches, and his reputation as a noted preacher grew even more quickly. Benjamin Franklin commented on his preaching, saying "that every Accent, every Emphasis, every Modulation of Voice, was so perfectly well turn'd and well plac'd, that without being interested in the Subject, one could not help being pleas'd with the Discourse."[15]

Whitefield had been ordained to serve in Georgia by the bishop of London, and upon his return to London he assumed that this authority carried over to the London parishes as well. But a number of characteristics of his preaching soon led to his banishment from many Church of England pulpits. First, his preaching was quite "enthusiastic." He was very oratorical and verged on acting. His preaching emphasized faith alone as the necessary precursor to salvation. Even more problematic in the eyes of many clergy were the enormous crowds that filled chapels when he preached. The result was that by early 1739 Whitefield was, for all practical purposes, barred from preaching in virtually all Church of England parish buildings and worship services.

Within a few weeks of his banishment, Whitefield visited Howell

[15] J. A. Leo Lemay, *The Life of Benjamin Franklin*, 3 vols. (Philadelphia: University of Pennsylvania Press, 2013), 2:450.

Harris in Wales. Whitefield later referred to Harris as a "burning and shining light," and the two connected immediately.[16] In light of Whitefield's gifts, and given the barriers the church put up to his preaching, Harris encouraged Whitefield to venture out of the chapel to preach. Before preaching abroad himself, Whitefield observed Harris in action. Watching Harris seemed to light the spark of field preaching in Whitefield's life.[17] On February 17, 1739, Whitefield "broke the ice" and preached outdoors for the first time. In his journal from that day Whitefield remarked, "I believe that I was never more acceptable to my Master than when I was standing to teach those hearers in the open fields."[18] Not only was he acceptable to his master, but Whitefield also thought field preaching made his ministry similar to his master's. "I thought," Whitefield wrote on a manuscript for his first sermon, "it might be doing the service of my Creator, who had a mountain for his pulpit and the heavens for a sounding board, and who, when his Gospel was refused by the Jews, sent his servants into the highways and hedges."[19] Soon Whitefield was preaching to large crowds, sometimes tens of thousands, and multitudes responded in ways he had never observed, at least not in those numbers, when he preached in local parish buildings.

The general public became increasingly interested in Whitefield as he grew more and more alienated from the Church of England hierarchy. Whitefield was first challenged by ecclesial authorities for field preaching in 1739, being asked why he was preaching in Bristol, both in homes and in public, without a license. But Whitefield refused to relinquish his authority to preach outside parish buildings, arguing that the law only applied to Dissenters. Since he was a deacon in the Church of England, he argued that the law did not refer to him. Furthermore, he argued that his license to preach in Savannah, being authorized by the bishop of London, gave him permission to preach in London. When asked by what authority he preached in the fields, his response was straightforward: "By the authority of Jesus Christ, conveyed to me by the (now) Archbishop of Canterbury, when he laid hands upon me, and said, 'Take thou authority to preach the Gospel.'"[20]

[16]George Whitefield, *George Whitefield's Journals* (Edinburgh: Banner of Truth, 1960), 246.

[17]*Journal and Diaries II*, 18 June 1739, 19:72. Harris also encouraged Wesley's field preaching. The two met Wesley in Bristol in 1739, though both had already heard of each other. As Harris immediately connected with Whitefield, Harris and Wesley also were kindred spirits. Wesley quotes one time in which Harris heard Wesley preach. "He [Harris] said, he had been much dissuaded from either hearing or seeing me, by many who said all manner of evil of me. 'But,' said he, 'as soon as I heard you preach, I quickly found what spirit you was of. And before you had done, I was so overpowered with joy and love, that I had much ado to walk home.'"

[18]Whitefield, *George Whitefield's Journals*, 216.

[19]Luke Tyerman, *The Life of the Rev. George Whitefield*, 2 vols. (New York: Anson D. F. Randolph, 1877), note 1, 1:180.

[20]*Journal and Diaries II*, 19:64.

He also argued that his style, while often criticized as being too similar to some of the charismatic preachers, was an important part of engaging people who would not otherwise attend services in a parish building. While some disparaged his charisma, that same charisma engaged others:

> My Curiosity lately led me, to hear Mr. Whitefield preach. I own I went with no other View than to see the Itinerant Preacher, as he is generally call'd, and to hear a confused heap of Nonsense, the Effect, as I imagin'd, of an ignorant Enthusiast. He had just began his Sermon, when I arrived at Kennington Common; at the Sight of such a prodigious Number of People to hear a young ignorant Upstart babble, I began to make myself merry, and be somewhat ludicrous on the Account; but I was immediately oblig'd to be silent. I then listened attentively to his Discourse, and soon found he had been very grossly misrepresented. His Doctrine was good, his Reasoning just; and I am now thoroughly convinc'd that we must either follow the Doctrine of Mr. Whitefield, or be profess'd Deists; for I can find no other Medium.[21]

Finally, Whitefield justified his field preaching by the fruit of his ministry, particularly the frequent awakenings and conversions. These demonstrated in his mind that God "sealed" field preaching "in an extraordinary manner."[22] Whitefield embraced the criticism that field preaching is a vile practice that violates ecclesial order and turned it into the motivation to keep pursuing this ministry, which bore such noticeable fruit in his mind. He recorded in his journal just a few months after he had first preached abroad that if field preaching "is to be vile, Lord grant that I may be more vile. I know this foolishness of preaching is made instrumental to the conversion and edification of numbers."[23] Wesley echoed this same sentiment regarding the "vile" nature of field preaching and his belief that the true "seal" of approval for the ministry by Christ is the fruit of the work.[24]

Methodist Field Preaching Develops[25]

Wesley and Whitefield had what is for all practical purposes a joint ministry of field preaching for a number of years. In the 1740s they had

[21]Deist in London, *The True Character of the Rev. Mr. Whitefield* (London: Mrs. Dodd, Nutt, Cook, Bartlett, 1739), 3.

[22]George Whitefield, *Letters of George Whitefield: For the Period 1734–1742* (Edinburgh: Banner of Truth Trust, 1976). Letter to James Hervey, 10 November 1739, 95.

[23]*George Whitefield's Journals*, 13 May 1739, 265.

[24]*Letters* (Telford), Letter to James Hervey, 20 March 1739, 1:287.

[25]Wesley discusses field preaching throughout his writings, but three sources are especially important. First are various editions of the *Minutes*. Second is Wesley's 1745 justification of the practice as found in *Appeals, A Farther Appeal to Men of Reason and Religion*, Parts I (§VI.4–10, 11:178–85) and III (§III.22–24, 11:305–07). The third is Wesley's *Societies*, "Short History of the People Called Methodist," 9:425–503, which he wrote later in life, in November 1781.

a parting of ways over theological issues, but early on they experienced deep personal and spiritual kinship. Indeed, in the early years of the revival they were both seen as leaders, if not founders, of the movement. While both theological and methodological differences later led to separate ministries, in the early days of the revival the two were partners in ministry. Perhaps the greatest evidence of their partnership was their mutual embrace and practice of field preaching, a practice that over time would engage hundreds of thousands, if not millions, of people.

On March 3, 1739, Whitefield wrote to his friend John from Bristol. Whitefield's ministry among the colliers had begun, and he was already preaching abroad to many thousands. He wrote to Wesley of the "glorious door" that had opened, saying that Wesley "must come and water what God has enabled me to plant."[26] Since Wesley did not respond immediately, in the middle of March Whitefield wrote again, this time all but begging Wesley to join him: "If the brethren after prayer for direction think proper, I wish you would be here the latter end of next week [for] many are ripe for bands. I leave that entirely to you—I am but a novice; you are acquainted with the great things of God. Come, I beseech you; come quickly."[27]

John still hesitated, unsure if he should accept the invitation. He remained unconvinced of the ecclesial justification for the practice. He knew field preaching was "irregular," but he also recognized that many priests were closing their pulpits to him, as they were doing to Whitefield. Wesley was concerned that he might be soon, for all practical purposes, completely banned from preaching to Church of England congregations in England, yet still he hesitated. The churches were closing to Wesley for two reasons. First, some clergy opposed the content of his preaching, namely, what they claimed was the "new doctrine" of salvation by faith alone.[28] The second reason, at least according to Wesley, was the large crowds. The crowds that gathered often filled parishes with the people from lower classes, exactly those Wesley wanted to attend. Unfortunately, often the result was that, in the eyes of critics within the Church of England, the crowds left little room for the "best of the parish" to attend.[29]

Initially, Charles shared John's reluctance, but soon he sensed the Spirit calling John to preach outdoors and encouraged him to submit. Still unsure, John put Whitefield's invitation to come to Bristol in the hands of the leaders of the Fetter Lane Society. They, like Wesley, failed

---

[26] John Wesley, *Letters I: 1721–1739*, v. 25 in *The Bicentennial Edition of the Works of John Wesley* (Oxford: Clarendon Press, 1980). Letter from George Whitefield to John Wesley, 3 March 1739, 25:605. Cited hereafter as *Letters I*.

[27] Ibid., Letter from George Whitefield to John Wesley, 22 March 1739, 25:612.

[28] *Societies*, "Short History of People Called Methodists," §11, 9:431.

[29] Ibid., §110, 9:431.

to discern a firm conviction of the Spirit leading one way or another. Wesley, therefore, left the fateful decision of whether to go to Bristol and help Whitefield to a casting of lots.[30] The lots indicated that Wesley should go to Bristol.

Wesley arrived in Bristol on Saturday, March 31, 1739, just in time to hear Whitefield preach. The following day he accompanied Whitefield as Whitefield preached to about thirty thousand people at Bowling Green, Rose Green, and Hanham Mount. Of that experience Wesley writes in his journal, "I could scarce reconcile myself to this strange way of preaching in the fields, of which he [Whitefield] set me an example on Sunday; having been all my life till very lately so tenacious of every point relating to decency and order, that I should have thought the saving of souls almost a sin if it had not been done in a church."[31]

Wesley faced a stark choice. He could continue to search for the few remaining pulpits open to him, with crowds that could never rival those Whitefield was now preaching to every day. Or he could preach abroad and speak to many thousands who would never otherwise hear his orderly and decent preaching on a Sunday morning. Wesley, like Whitefield, had come face to face with the ecclesial reality of embracing a practice that was questionable in the eyes of the church hierarchy but that was also deeply meaningful to many thousands of people, especially poor ones, who never went (and who, Wesley believed, never would go) inside a proper Church of England parish building for worship. The next day Wesley made his decision.

Wesley records in his journal, "At four in the afternoon, I submitted to 'be more vile,' and proclaimed in the highways the glad tidings of salvation, speaking from a little eminence in a ground adjoining to the city, to about three thousand people."[32] On the following Sunday he twice preached outdoors, first to a crowd of about three thousand, and later, in the afternoon, to about fifteen hundred in Rosewood, near Kingswood. Within a month of beginning, Wesley estimated that he preached to about 47,500 people, with an average attendance of about 3,000.[33] Over the next eight months Wesley preached about five hundred times, only eight or so of which were sermons delivered inside churches.[34]

Charles abandoned his own hesitancy a few months later. On June 24,

[30]*Journal and Diaries II*, 10 March 1739, 19:38.

[31]Ibid., 29 March 1739, 19:46.

[32]Ibid., 2 April 1739, 19:46.

[33]Richard P. Heitzenrater, *Wesley and the People Called Methodists* (Nashville: Abingdon, 1995), 100.

[34]Luke Tyerman, *The Life and Times of the Rev. John Wesley, M.A., Founder of the Methodists* (New York: Harper & Brothers, 1872), 1:234.

1739, he abandoned his "doubts and scruples" and preached outside to a crowd of approximately ten thousand people. He records in his journal,

> I found near ten thousand helpless sinners waiting for the Word in Moorfields. I invited them in my Master's words, as well as name: "Come unto me all ye that travail, and are heavy laden, and I will give you rest." The Lord was with me, even me his meanest messenger according to his promise...God shone upon my path; and I knew this was his will concerning me.[35]

Charles preached abroad for many years, but not for the rest of his life, as his brother did. Charles found field preaching difficult. It was, as Frank Baker notes, "a heavy cross, an affront to [Charles's] health, his temperament, and to his ecclesiastical propriety."[36] Charles himself reflects this sentiment in a letter to Whitefield:

> I am continually tempted to leave off preaching, and hide myself like J. Hutchings. I should then be freer from temptation, and at leisure to attend my own improvement, God continues to work *by* me, but not *in* me, that I can perceive. Do not reckon upon me, my brother, in the work God is doing; for I cannot expect he should long employ one who is ever longing and murmuring to be discharged. I rejoice in your success, and pray for its increase a thousand fold.[37]

And yet Charles was seen as an effective field preacher. As the Congregationalist Joseph Williams observed, "I found [Charles Wesley] standing upon a table, in an erect posture, with his Hands and Eyes lifted up to Heaven in Prayer, surrounded with (I guess) more than a thousand People; some few of them Persons of Fashion, both men and women, but most of them of the lower Rank of Mankind."[38] Charles eventually "settled" and centered his ministry in and around London, but in the early days of the revival, field preaching was as central to his ministry as it was to John's.

THE FORMAT OF FIELD PREACHING

The specifics of proclamation in field preaching are dealt with in more detail later in this chapter, but I mention the basic format for field

[35]Tyson, 24 June 1739, 137.

[36]Baker, *Charles Wesley as Revealed by His Letters*, 33.

[37]Charles Wesley, *The Letters of Charles Wesley: A Critical Edition, with Introduction and Notes*, v. 1, 1728–56, ed. Kenneth G. C. Newport and Gareth Lloyd (Oxford: Oxford University Press, 2013). Letter from Charles Wesley to George Whitefield, 10 August 1739, 1:75.

[38]*Early Preachers Collection*, Letter from Joseph Williams to Charles Wesley, 19 October 1739, 1/92.

preaching at this point. The format was at once flexible and standardized. It was flexible in that the location could be almost any place. It was standardized in that the preaching followed a typical, though not mandated, format. People gathered in a location other than parish sanctuary. Sometimes the location was another building, such as a person's home, but the location could be just about anywhere. For example, the Methodist preacher Christopher Hopper over just a few days describes preaching next to a castle wall, an ale-house, and even a cock-pit.[39] Many times, however, the location was outside. Sometimes it was outside in a small, confined area, such as the front door stoop of a home. But most of the time, the location was a broad open space either in a town or on the outskirts, such as those mentioned earlier—town squares, the yard outside a home, even beaches. Sometimes the location was an actual field. Frequently, fields outside of mines were used in coal-producing parts of the country. Field preaching events were typically organized before or after a day's work so that both workers and their families could be part of the service.

Other large gathering spaces, such as town squares or yards, were also sites that allowed large numbers of people to gather. People often provided large, privately owned spaces for field preaching. Williams, in the same letter to Charles cited previously, expresses his desire for John or Charles to come preach and offers a location, if necessary:

> I now humbly desire to let you know when we may expect you or Mr. John Wesley here. I have provided you a Close, or Field, larger than any Bowling green, and enclosed by a high wall to preach in: and cannot but greatly hope, if you could continue a while with us, you and our Lord might reap a plentiful Harvest here and hereabout: and that a wide and effectual Door would be opened to you—[40]

On another occasion a previously scheduled location was closed to John, but someone offered another location on the spot:

> I was informed his name was Harcourt. He was talking very loud, and tolerably fast, when a gentleman came and said, "Sir, if you are not allowed to preach here, you are welcome to preach in Mr. M'Gough's avenue." Mr. M'Gough, one of the chief merchants in the town, himself showed us the way. I suppose thrice as many people flocked together there, as would have heard me in the market-house. So did the wise providence of God draw good out of evil! And his word had indeed free course.[41]

[39]Telford, 129.

[40]*Early Preachers Collection.* Letter from Joseph Williams to Charles Wesley, 19 October 1739, 1/92.

[41]*Journal and Diaries V,* 15 April 1767, 22:77–78.

Sometimes friendly Church of England clerics allowed Methodists to use parish buildings in unique situations—for instance, if it was raining too hard to meet outside.[42]

Many aspects of field preaching were, however, standardized. The actual field preaching event often started with the singing of some of Charles's hymns. Hymns were sung until a sufficient crowd had gathered or until the announced time had come. Sometimes singing would begin at one end of town and continue while the congregation was moving through the town, adding to the group as people heard the music and came out and then followed the congregation to the field preaching. Sometimes preachers and others would raise awareness of the upcoming preaching by walking "down the village street singing hymns, stopping here and there for a word of exhortation, and then at some suitable place, proclaiming his message."[43] Other times preachers would simply climb the nearest structure, begin singing, and then preach when the crowd gathered and was ready.[44] Methodists used singing to draw a crowd and set the spiritual tone. Once the preacher set the tone, he would begin to preach. Sometimes field preaching would be located at the opposite end of town from a preaching house in order to reach out to people who might not come to the regular service.[45] Wesley's portable pulpit of wood and canvas was set up and he would then preach.[46] He specifically liked to preach in various parts of the city and thus encounter more people than if he always preached in only one place. Wesley describes the growth of the society at Cork because of this pattern:

> They set up meetings for prayer in several places, and preached abroad at both ends of the city. Hearers swiftly increased; the society increased; so did the number both of the convinced and the converted. I went when the flame was at the height; and preached abroad at both ends of the city. More and more were stirred up; and there was a greater awakening here than in any part of the kingdom.[47]

---

[42]*Journal and Diaries VI*, 15 April 1776, 23:9. Wesley recounts one rainy afternoon, "As we were considering in the afternoon what we should do, the rain not suffering us to be abroad, one asked the Vicar for the use of the church; to which he readily consented."

[43]Bernard Crosby, "Methodist Evangelism, 1800–1820," *The London Quarterly and Holborn Review* 6, no. 13 (1944): 298.

[44]Church, 106.

[45]*Minutes of Conference*, 1767, 10:350. In Q. 28 Wesley asks, "How may our preaching be more extensively useful?" His answer, "Wherever we have a large preaching-house at one end of a great town, let us preach abroad at the other end of it, every Sunday morning, at least, if it be fair."

[46]*Journal and Diaries III*, 19 April 1753, 20:454, and 2 June 1752, 20:426. By the early 1750s Wesley had a portable pulpit for field preaching.

[47]*Societies*, "Short History of People Called Methodists," §110, 9:488.

Sometimes services began early if the crowd reached the maximum number of people a space could accommodate before the set service time. After singing there was usually a time of prayer. Testimonies or exhortations then came either before or after the sermon. Often the service was followed with a Methodist society meeting or a prayer meeting.

Field preaching was not a one-time event. Rather Methodist preachers often preached in the same town year after year, and in large urban areas they often preached monthly or even weekly. The result was that people had the opportunity to encounter field preachers on a regular basis, even in smaller towns and villages. The consistent nature of repeated field preaching was not accidental; Wesley built it into his methodology because he knew the repetition mattered:

> My preaching has so rarely made any impression at all, till the novelty of it was over. When I had preached more than sixscore times at this town, I found scarce any effect; only that abundance of people heard, and gaped and stared, and went away much as they came. And it was one evening, while I was in doubt if I had not laboured in vain, that such a blessing, of God was given, as has continued ever since, and I trust will be remembered unto many generations.[48]

Field preaching facilitated a repetitive encounter between the word of God and people who rarely if ever attended Christian worship in a parish building. The result was that many people had multiple opportunities to respond to the good news of God in Christ who might otherwise have never heard.

DEFENDING FIELD PREACHING

For much of the rest of his ministry Wesley found himself defending field preaching. One pointed defense is found in *A Farther Appeal*:

> Be pleased to observe: (1.) That I was forbidden, as by a general consent, to preach in any church, (though not by any judicial sentence,) "for preaching such doctrine." This was the open, avowed cause; there was at that time no other, either real or pretended, except that the people crowded so. (2.) That I had no desire or design to preach in the open air, till after this prohibition. (3.) That when I did, as it was no matter of choice, so neither of premeditation. There was no scheme at all previously formed, which was to be supported thereby; nor had I any other end in view than this,—to save as many souls as I could. (4.) Field-preaching was therefore a sudden expedient, a thing submitted to, rather than chosen; and therefore submitted to, because I thought preaching even thus, better than not preaching at all: First, in regard to my

[48]*Letters II*, Letter to John Smith, 25 March 1747, 26:237.

> own soul, because, "a dispensation of the gospel being committed to me," I did not dare "not to preach the gospel:" Secondly, in regard to the souls of others, whom I everywhere saw "seeking death in the error of their life."[49]

Critics challenged Methodist field preaching on a number of fronts, primarily its social propriety, its ecclesial/civil legality, and its general uncommonness or "irregular" nature. In the first case some critics charged that field preaching encouraged uncivil behavior among those who came to hear. Certainly, some of the people who came to the fields were often quite rough, rambunctious, and even violent; at one point Charles refers to some in the fields as "wild colts."[50] Charles records an instance in Shoreham of onlookers "roaring, stamping, blaspheming, ringing the bells, and turning the church into a bear-garden."[51] Wesley was also warned on a number of occasions that he might have some enemies in a crowd—including an occasional vicar![52] The crowds, he argued, were being egged on, especially by ecclesial leaders, to "knock these mad dogs [Methodist field preachers] on the head."[53] Some accused Methodists of forming "private cabals against the state," but Wesley insisted that preaching was the purpose.[54]

That said, the crowds clearly were violent at times. Indeed, one Methodist martyr, William Seward, died a few days after he was struck on the head in 1740 at an outdoor field preaching event.[55] John and Charles's brother Samuel understood the danger, writing that he would rather see John and Charles "picking straws within the walls than preaching [outside] in Moorfields."[56] Preaching to these crowds took great courage and fortitude at times. A critic of Methodism, Isaac Taylor, writes,

> The men who commenced and achieved this arduous service, and they were scholars and gentlemen, displayed a courage far surpassing that which carries the soldier through the hailstorm of the battlefield. Ten thousand might more easily be found who would confront a battery than two who, with the sensitiveness of education about them, could mount a table by the roadside, give out a psalm, and gather a mob.[57]

[49]Wesley, *Appeals, A Farther Appeal to Men of Reason and Religion,* Part I, §VI.3, 11:178.

[50]*Journal and Diaries IV,* 11 August 1761, 21:341.

[51]Wesley, *The Journal of the Rev. Charles Wesley,* 16 September 1746, 1:428.

[52]*Early Preachers Collection,* Letter from Joseph Williams to Charles Wesley, 19 October 1739, 1/92.

[53]Tyerman, *The Life and Times of the Rev. John Wesley, M.A., Founder of the Methodists,* 1:236.

[54]Wesley, *Appeals, A Farther Appeal to Men of Reason and Religion,* Part I, §VI.6, 11:180.

[55]*Journal and Diaries II,* 27 October 1740, 19:172.

[56]Joseph Priestley, *Original Letters by the Rev. John Wesley and His Friends* (1791): 109. Letter from Samuel Wesley (Jr.) to Susanna Wesley, 20 October 1739, 109. Cf Parkes, 233.

[57]Isaac Taylor, *Wesley and Methodism* (New York: Harper and Brothers, 1852), 432.

But most of the time the violence was minimal. One commentator, an experienced circuit rider offering counsel to a novice, gives perhaps a typical response:

> The majority of any crowd will be bad throwers, and so only a few will hit you with their missiles. And of those that do hit you, most will strike your legs or body, which are protected by your clothes. The only ones that can damage you will be the few that strike your face, and most of these will be soft. And I have never received more damage from heavy or jagged missiles, than what a day or two in bed has easily repaired.[58]

In a similar vein, Wesley notes on one occasion, "One or two only were angry, and threw a few stones; but it was labour lost; for none regarded them."[59] On still a different occasion, Wesley tells of a man who tried to cause harm but failed:

> I preached in the morning at Newport, on, "What must I do to be saved?" to the most insensible, ill-behaved people I have ever seen in Wales. One ancient man, during a great part of the sermon, cursed and swore almost incessantly; and, towards the conclusion, took up a great stone, which he many times attempted to throw. But that he could not do.—Such the champions, such the arms, against field-preaching![60]

For Wesley, the benefits of field preaching were worth the risks. Instead of encouraging violence, Wesley believed that field preaching actually stimulates peaceful behavior. Many events ended quite peacefully:

> About noon we reached Stokesley, where I found none had ever yet preached abroad. Samuel Larwood had attempted it, but in vain: And so had Mr. Roberts, some time after; but a Clergyman came at the head of a large mob, and obliged him to desist. About one, the person in whose house we were came in trembling, and told us what threatenings were breathed out. I answered, "Then there is no time to lose;" and went out immediately. I suppose the mob expected to hear us sing; but they were disappointed; for I began preaching without delay. By this means, missing their signal, they came, not in a body, but two or three at a time; and as fast as they came their minds were changed; so that all were quiet, from the beginning to the end.[61]

The role of field preaching in rough communities is perhaps best demonstrated in the interaction between Methodists and colliers in various

[58]Reginald Kissack, "Two Hundred Years of Methodist Field Preaching," *The London Quarterly and Holborn Review* (April 1939): 152.

[59]*Journal and Diaries IV*, 5 July 1761, 21:333.

[60]*Journal and Diaries II*, 19 October 1739, 19:107.

[61]*Journal and Diaries III*, 28 April 1752, 20:421–22.

places around the country. Colliers were known as a rough and often violent group of men, especially in Kingswood. Yet Wesley reports that field preachers brought about peace, not additional turmoil. He records in his journal a letter to one Mr. D. that he includes in his *Short History* as well:

> Few persons have lived long in the West of England, who have not heard of the colliers of Kingswood; a people famous, from the beginning hitherto, for neither fearing God nor regarding man: So ignorant of the things of God, that they seemed but one remove from the beasts that perish; and therefore utterly without desire of instruction, as well as without the means of it.
>
> Many last winter used tauntingly to say of Mr. Whitefield, "If he will convert Heathens, why does not he go to the colliers of Kingswood?" In spring he did so. And as there were thousands who resorted to no place of public worship, he went after them into their own wilderness, "to seek and save that which was lost." When he was called away, others went into "the highways and hedges, to compel them to come in." And, by the grace of God, their labour was not in vain. The scene is already changed. Kingswood does not now, as a year ago, resound with cursing and blasphemy. It is no more filled with drunkenness and uncleanness, and the idle diversions that naturally lead thereto. It is no longer full of wars and fightings, of clamour and bitterness, of wrath and envyings. Peace and love are there. Great numbers of the people are mild, gentle, and easy to be entreated. They "do not cry, neither strive," and hardly is their "voice heard in the streets;" or indeed in their own wood; unless when they are at their usual evening diversion, singing praise unto God their Saviour.[62]

Some critics of field preaching, especially wealthy patrons of the Church of England and some of their clergy, insisted that the practice encouraged a bawdiness and uncouthness in the crowds. One critic wrote to Wesley that field preaching was a "fanatical manner of preaching," doing "more harm to society" than good, and "reviving some old heresies" and "inventing new" ones, all the while spreading "disorder and confusion through the whole community." Wesley's response was that field preaching "has no such effect, even among the wildest of men. This [field preaching] has not 'bewildered the imagination' even of the Kingswood colliers, or 'inflamed their passions.' It has not spread disorder or confusion among them, but just the contrary."[63] While Wesley certainly notes the wild character of many gatherings, he also observes on numerous occasions the well-behaved nature of the crowds and their eagerness to be part of the service. For example, he writes: "In the calm, sunshiny evening I preached near King's Square. I know nothing more solemn than such a congregation, praising God with one heart and one voice. Surely

[62]*Societies*, "Short History of People Called Methodists," §15, 9:432–33.

[63]Wesley, *Appeals*, Letter to the Right Reverend the Lord Bishop of Gloucester, 26 November 1762, §17, 11:482.

they who talk of the indecency of field-preaching never saw such a sight as this."[64]

In Wesley's mind the greatest impropriety in eighteenth-century English religious life was not field preaching. Rather, it was the lackadaisical attitude of many Church of England members and their clergy:

> I wonder at those who still talk so loud of the indecency of field-preaching. The highest indecency is in St. Paul's church, when a considerable part of the congregation are asleep, or talking, or looking about, not minding a word the Preacher says. On the other hand, there is the highest decency in a churchyard or field, when the whole congregation behave and look as if they saw the Judge of all, and heard him speaking from heaven.[65]

Wesley was less concerned with a practice's politeness, especially when the critique came from the rich and was directed at the poor. He wanted to offer Christ to all, especially the poor, and he was willing to violate social decorum, even as he insisted that the practice builds the Christian community instead of tearing it down.

While Wesley always advocated for field preaching's "decency," he also acknowledged that it was an uncommon practice. Some criticized field preaching because it was an unusual practice before the 1730's. Most British Christians were familiar with preaching by a cleric in a parish building. Wesley not only opened field preaching to "assistants," who more often than not were laity, but encouraged their preaching outside the parish walls. And yet for Wesley the fact that it was unfamiliar to most British citizens was part of its strength, not its weakness: "It is hard to conceive anything else which could have reached them. Had it not been for field-preaching, the uncommonness of which was the very circumstance that recommended it, they must have run on in the error of their way, and perished in their blood."[66]

Wesley believed that people came to field preaching in the early years precisely "because of the uncommonness of the thing, who would otherwise not have heard at all."[67] Even toward the end of his ministry Wesley marveled that people still came to hear preaching abroad: "Although the novelty of this preaching is over, yet the people flock to hear it in every place far more than when it was a new thing."[68] Yet long after field preaching had lost its "newness," Wesley continued encouraging the practice:

[64] *Journal and Diaries VI*, 9 September 1781, 23:222–23.

[65] *Journal and Diaries III*, 28 August 1748, 20:245.

[66] *Appeals, A Farther Appeal to Men of Reason and Religion*, Part III, §III.24, 11:307.

[67] *Letters* (Telford), Letter to Bishop Lavington, 1 February 1750, 3:260.

[68] *Journal and Diaries IV*, 12 June 1755, 21:18.

"It is plain (notwithstanding what some affirm) that the time of field-preaching is not past, while the people flock to it from every quarter."[69]

Finally, Wesley was required during much of his ministry to defend field preaching's ecclesial and civil legality. Rack writes that field preaching "seemed to violate the rights of the regular clergy...and arguably violated civil as well as canon law."[70] While field preaching was certainly "irregular," Wesley insisted that field preaching was legal. In the *Large Minutes*, for example, he asks, "Is field-preaching unlawful?" To which he responds, "We conceive not. We do not know that it is contrary to any law either of God or man."[71]

Wesley defends field preaching's legality on a number of grounds. First, he argues that any field preaching prohibited by the Act of Toleration refers to Dissenters, not Church of England priests.[72] He also defends the legality of his own field preaching. Similarly to Whitefield, he argued that his appointment as a Fellow of Lincoln College, Oxford, gave him freedom to preach in any part of the Church of England. He understood his ordination as a commission to the church universal, not just members of the Church of England, and claimed that authority allowed him to preach anywhere. Indeed, the world was his parish.

Furthermore, Wesley defends the practice in light of the blessings that came from it and the corresponding call those blessings must entail. Similarly to Whitefield, Wesley saw the success of his ministry as evidence of God's blessing upon it. Perhaps this is best seen in a letter addressed to a John Smith, who was perhaps in reality Thomas Secker, bishop of Oxford and later Canterbury:

> But you "know no call I have to preach up and down; to play the part of an itinerant Evangelist." Perhaps you do not. But I do: I know God hath required this at my hands. To me, his blessing my work is an abundant proof; although such a proof as often makes me tremble. But "is there not pride or vanity in my heart?" There is; yet this is not my motive to preaching. I know and feel that the spring of this is a deep conviction, that it is the will of God, and that were I to refrain, I should never hear that word, "Well done, good and faithful servant;" but, "Cast ye the unprofitable servant into outer darkness, where is weeping, and wailing, and gnashing of teeth."[73]

[69]*Journal and Diaries VI*, 18 September 1776, 23:35.

[70]Rack, 208.

[71]*Minutes of Conference, Large Minutes*, 1753–63, §8, 10:846.

[72]Wesley, *Appeals, A Farther Appeal to Men of Reason and Religion*, Part I, §VI.4, 11:179.

[73]*Letters II*, Letter to John Smith, 25 March 1747, 26:237.

For Wesley the great defense was not a legal one, be it civil or ecclesial; rather, the defense was the fruit of the ministry itself. The results of the ministry are the "abundant proof" that God has called him to this ministry and authorizes it.

His final defense is essentially an act of ecclesial disobedience. Namely, if field preaching is illegal, either because of its irregularity or the incorporation of laity, then the ecclesial and/or civil law needs to be changed. After all, the biblical witness, especially the life of Jesus, offers many examples of field preaching. First and foremost is Jesus's Sermon on the Mount, which Wesley calls "one pretty remarkable precedent of field preaching."[74] Therefore human laws that prohibit field preaching must be changed. The same goes for lay preaching. Wesley denies the illegality of lay preaching, but then usually explains that even if it is illegal, he cannot accept that law. He writes to one critic of lay preaching, "We are not clear that this [lay preaching] is contrary to any such law. But if it is, this is one of the exempt cases; one wherein we cannot obey with a safe conscience. Therefore, be it right or wrong on other accounts, it is, however, no just exception against our sincerity.[75] Furthermore, even if it was illegal, Wesley was willing to face the consequences if the only alternative was not preaching at all. Perhaps Wesley sums up his defense of field preaching, as well as a number of other practices, best in a letter to Thomas Adams:

> With regard to the steps we have hitherto taken, we have used all the caution which was possible. We have done nothing rashly, nothing without deep and long consideration, hearing and weighing all objections, and much prayer. Nor have we taken one deliberate step, of which we, as yet, see reason to repent. It is true, in some things we vary from the rules of our Church; but no further than we apprehend is our bounden duty. It is from a full conviction of this, that we preach abroad, use extemporary prayer, form those who appear to be awakened into societies, and permit laymen, whom we believe God has called, to preach.[76]

Charles felt similarly. While Charles tended to lean toward ecclesial adherence more fervently than either his brother or Whitefield, he ultimately agreed with John's notion that "doing good unto all" people required prioritizing God's "extraordinary call" to preach in the fields over the bishop's "ordinary call" at ordination "to preach the Word of God."[77] Field preaching was legal, John argued, at least in the eyes of God. And if the rules of God

[74]*Journal and Diaries II,* 1 April 1739, 19:46.

[75]*Journal and Diaries III,* 27 December 1746, 20:111.

[76]*Letters II,* Letter to Thomas Adams, 31 October 1755, 26:609.

[77]*Letters I,* Letter to Charles Wesley, 23 June 1739, 25:660.

differ from those of the church and/or state, then the latter must be incorrect. Wesley believed God's call on his life to preach gospel to all people, especially the poor, while "irregular" was also "extraordinary" and overrode any potential ecclesial, civil, or social barriers.

MOTIVATIONS FOR FIELD PREACHING

In light of his initial hesitancy, as well as field preaching's questionable ecclesial propriety, one might wonder about Wesley's motivation to begin field preaching in the first place. What drove Wesley, and the first community of people who gathered around him, to begin preaching outside parish pulpits? Why did he declare that "the work of God seems to stand still" without field preaching? What led him to claim that "more field-preaching" was the solution if Methodism stalled in any place?[78]

Practical Motivations

The first two motivations are practical. He discusses them together in a short addendum to the 1786 *Minutes*: "I began 'preaching in the fields'; and that for two reasons, — first, I was not suffered to preach in the churches; secondly, no parish-church in London or Westminster could contain the congregation."[79] The first motivation was simple—Church of England pulpits were increasingly closed to him: "Being thus excluded from the churches, and not daring to be silent, it remained only to preach in the open air—which I did at first, not out of choice, but necessity."[80] If he wanted to preach, on any kind of regular basis, he had to preach outside parish buildings. Second, those pulpits that were still open to him were frequently filled to capacity. Open spaces held many more people than churches or homes. Houses can only hold as many as can come to a house, but not, Wesley points out, "all that would come to the field."[81] After a particularly meaningful time preaching in the fields outside Moorfield, Wesley reflects,

> A vast majority of the immense congregation in Moorfields were deeply serious. One such hour might convince any impartial man of the expediency of field-preaching. What building, except St. Paul's church, would contain such a congregation? And if it would, what human voice could have reached them there? By repeated observations I find I can command thrice the number in the open air, that I can under a roof.[82]

[78]*Minutes of Conference*, 1768, 10:360–61.

[79]Ibid., "On Separation from the Church," 10:615.

[80]*Societies*, "Short History of the People Called Methodists," §11, 9:431.

[81]*Minutes of Conference, Large Minutes*, 1753–63, §9, 10:846.

[82]*Journal and Diaries IV*, 23 September 1759, 21:230.

Another time Wesley records,

> We had a mild, delightful day, and a pleasant ride to Colchester. In the evening, and on Sunday morning, the House contained the congregation tolerably well; but in the afternoon I was obliged to go out; and I suppose we had on St. John's Green five or six times as many as the Room would contain. Such is the advantage of field-preaching.[83]

The number of people who responded to Whitefield's preaching, and who soon showed up for Wesley's preaching, was extraordinary. Wesley was astounded at the throngs of people who would come hear Whitefield and others like him, and at their apparent openness to hearing and engaging the gospel story at these events.

Theological Motivations

Two additional motivations were primarily theological in nature. First, Wesley wanted to share the gospel with anyone who had not embraced Christ. For him the call to preach to those who had not believed the gospel was a personal call that he was unwilling to relinquish. As he writes in *A Farther Appeal*, he had to preach "in regard to my own soul, because 'a dispensation of the gospel being committed to me,' I did not dare 'not to preach the gospel.'"[84] For some this meant encountering Christ for the first time and coming into a saving relationship through faith and repentance. Salvation through faith in Christ was the primary motivation in all that he did, and submitting to field preaching was no different. Wesley continues in *A Farther Appeal*, "nor had I any other end in view than this, — to save as many souls as I could."[85] In the *Large Minutes* of 1753–63 Wesley tells the preachers they use field preaching "too sparingly... Because our call is, to save that which is lost."[86] Field preaching was the principal method of making a first point of contact with the unconverted masses. The goal of field preaching is to help people who are not otherwise looking for Christ to come to know him: "In field-preaching, more than any other means, God is found of them that sought him not. By this, death, heaven, and hell, come to the ears, if not the hearts, of them that 'care for none of these things.'"[87] Wesley was amazed by the multitudes who would come and "look as if they saw the Judge of all, and heard him speaking from

[83]Ibid., 3 March 1759, 21:178.

[84]Wesley, *Appeals, A Farther Appeal to Men of Reason and Religion*, Part I, §VI.3, 11:178.

[85]Ibid.

[86]*Minutes of Conference, Large Minutes*, 1753–63, §9, 10:846.

[87]*Journal and Diaries V*, 30 September 1767, 22:106.

heaven,"[88] as if they had never encountered God in a significant way before, and in ways or numbers that Wesley had never observed in parish church settings. Wesley clearly states his belief that field preaching is the best tool for taking the gospel to those who have never heard:

> I preached on the Green at Bedminster. I am apt to think many of the hearers scarce ever heard a Methodist before, or perhaps any other Preacher. What but field-preaching could reach these poor sinners? And are not their souls also precious in the sight of God?[89]

> At nine I preached in the Royal Square at the Barracks, on the dead, small and great, standing before God. An huge multitude soon gathered together and listened with deep attention. Many of the soldiers were among them. By what means but field-preaching could we have reached these poor souls?[90]

> Thousands of hearers, rich and poor, received the word, near the new Square, with the deepest attention. This is the way to shake the trembling gates of hell. Still I see nothing can do this so effectually as field-preaching.[91]

Field preaching, Wesley believed, is the most effective way in which great multitudes could hear the gospel who had never really heard, or at least never truly engaged. It allowed Methodist preaching to speak directly to people outside the faith in an evangelistic capacity. Through field preaching the church goes to the people it hopes to reach, instead of waiting for those people to come to the church. Wesley sums up this sentiment in a letter to James Rea: "Preach abroad at Newry, Newtown, Lisburn, and Carrick, if ever you would do good. It is the cooping yourselves up in rooms that has damped the work of God, which never was and never will be carried out to any purpose without going out into the highways and hedges compelling poor sinners to come in."[92] Heitzenrater expresses Wesley's conviction succinctly, writing that field preaching, for Wesley, is the method by which "the gospel could be brought to the people where they were, to the people who could not or would not go to a church at the appointed hour for services."[93]

In Wesley's mind, field preaching was a unique tool to wield against the powers of the devil. Wesley writes to Zechariah Yewdall, "If you desire

[88]*Journal and Diaries III,* 28 August 1748, 20:245.

[89]*Journal and Diaries IV,* 17 September 1763, 21:428.

[90]*Journal and Diaries V,* 23 July 1769, 22:196.

[91]Ibid., 14 August 1768, 22:153. Wesley writes, "Thousands of hearers, rich and poor, received the word, near the new Square, with the deepest attention. This is the way to shake the trembling gates of hell. Still I see nothing can do this so effectually as field-preaching."

[92]*Letters* (Telford), Letter to James Rea, 21 July 1766, 5:23.

[93]Heitzenrater, *Wesley and the People Called Methodists,* 110.

to promote the work of God, you should preach abroad as often as possible. Nothing destroys the devil's kingdom like this."[94] It was plain to Wesley that "field-preaching is the most effectual way of overturning Satan's kingdom."[95] Nothing shook the "trembling gates of hell" as "effectually as field-preaching."[96] "O what a victory would Satan gain," Wesley writes, "if he could put an end to field-preaching! But that, I trust, he never will: At least not till my head is laid."[97]

Wesley's insistence regarding field preaching was due in part to his conviction that many Church of England clergy would not make the sacrifices entailed in taking the gospel to the people:

> Who is there among you, brethren, that is willing (examine your own hearts) even to save souls from death at this price? Would not *you* let a thousand souls perish, rather than you would be the instruments of rescuing them thus? I do not speak now with regard to conscience, but to the inconveniences that must accompany it. Can you sustain them, if you *would*? Can you bear the summer sun to beat upon your naked head? Can you suffer the wintry rain or wind, from whatever quarter it blows? Are you able to stand in the open air without any covering or defence when God casteth abroad his snow like wool, or scattereth his hoar-frost like ashes? And yet these are some of the smallest inconveniences which accompany *field-preaching*. Far beyond all these, are the contradiction of sinners, the scoffs both of the great vulgar and the small; contempt and reproach of every kind; often more than verbal affronts, stupid, brutal violence, sometimes to the hazard of health, or limbs, or life. Brethren, do you envy us *this honour*? What, I pray, would buy you to be a field-preacher? Or what, think you, could induce any man of common sense to continue therein one year, unless he had a full conviction in himself that it was the will of God concerning him?
>
> Upon this conviction it is (were we to submit to these things on any other motive whatsoever, it would furnish you with a better proof of our *distraction* than any that has yet been found) that we now do, for the good of poor souls, what you cannot, will not, dare not do.[98]

Therefore "God was moved to jealousy, and went *out of the usual way* to save the souls which he had made."[99] In other words, God called Methodists to the task the Church of England should have embraced.

[94]*Letters* (Telford), Letter to Zechariah Yewdall, 1 May 1782, 7:122.

[95]*Journal and Diaries V,* 18 June 1765, 22:8.

[96]Ibid., 21 August 1768, 22:153.

[97]*Journal and Diaries IV,* 20 May 1759, 21:193.

[98]Wesley, *Appeals, A Farther Appeal to Men of Reason and Religion,* Part III, §III.24, 11:307. Italics in original. Wesley knew some in the church did take the gospel to the people, but not in sufficient numbers. See also ibid., Part III, §III.20–22, 11:304–05.

[99]Ibid., §III.22, 11:306.

Some in the Church of England simply did not believe there was need for more thorough ministry with those who did not attend congregational worship, but Wesley insisted the need was great:

> "But what need is there," say even some of a milder spirit, "of this preaching in fields and streets? Are there not churches enough to preach in?" No, my friend, there are not; not for us to preach in. You forget; we are not suffered to preach there, else we should prefer them to any places whatever. "Well, there are Ministers enough without you." Ministers enough, and churches enough! for what? to reclaim all the sinners within the four seas? If there were, they would all be reclaimed. But they are not reclaimed: Therefore, it is evident that there are not churches enough.[100]

Wesley begged clergypersons who themselves did not see a need for Methodist field preaching, or who were unwilling to embrace the sacrifices entailed in field preaching, to at least "not increase the difficulties, which are already so great, that, without the mighty power of God, we must sink under them. Do not assist in trampling down a little handful of men, who, for the present, stand in the gap between ten thousand poor wretches and destruction, till you find some others to take their places."[101]

This motivation of taking the gospel to those who did not embrace the Christian faith remained central for the rest of Wesley's life. In 1756 he wrote, "It is field preaching which does the execution still. For usefulness there is none comparable to it."[102] Three years later Wesley expressed a similar sentiment: "What marvel the devil does not love field preaching? Neither do I: I love a commodious room, a soft cushion, an handsome pulpit. But where is my zeal if I do not trample all these under foot in order to save one more soul?"[103] Even into the 1770's his conviction remained, "To this day field-preaching is a cross to me. But I know my commission and see no other way of 'preaching the gospel to every creature.'"[104] The final example noted here is from 1772 where he notes, "The season for field preaching is not yet over. It cannot, while so many are in their sins and in their blood."[105] The primary motivation of field preaching was to take the gospel to those who were not committed Christians, either because they had never heard the gospel, had never responded to it, or had responded

[100]Ibid., §III.22, 11:305.

[101]Ibid., §III.24, 11:307.

[102]*Journal and Diaries IV*, 10 October 1756, 21:79.

[103]Ibid., 26 June 1759, 21:203.

[104]*Journal and Diaries V*, 6 September 1772, 22:348.

[105]Ibid., 5 July 1773, 22:384.

to it but given up on their faith. Most of those people were outside the Church of England, and they were not going to come in without encouragement. The call to take the gospel to the lost was for Wesley a fire that must constantly be relit.

The second theological motivation was Wesley's conviction that the church is called to serve all people and especially those on the margins of the church and of society. Unfortunately, the Church of England struggled to minister effectively with the poor in the eighteenth century. As J. H. Plumb describes it, the Church of England neglected to provide a Christian witness in many industrializing areas, most of which were poor:

> The industrial revolution paid no attention to parish boundaries...the mine ignored the parson...there were scores of industrial villages and suburbs...without any church or priest. Ignorance of the most elementary facts of the Christian religion was astonishingly widespread...Only a fundamental constitutional reform of the Established Church could have coped...but such reform was unthinkable...It was left to Wesley and his disciples to reap the harvest of neglected souls.[106]

Many communities of poor industrial workers simply lacked a close local parish, and the Church of England seemed either unwilling or unable to meet their spiritual needs.

Wesley believed the church must serve in a particular way to share the gospel with the working poor and the outcasts who did not fit the mold of the Church of England elite. So when the poor started showing up for proclamation that took place outside the sanctuaries, Wesley felt called to embrace the ministry, as is demonstrated in this extended quotation from *A Farther Appeal*:

> Behold the amazing love of God to the outcasts of men! His tender condescension to their folly! They would regard nothing done *in the usual way* [e.g. indoor preaching]. All this was lost upon them. The *ordinary* [in a parish building] preaching of the word of God, they would not even deign to hear...[The poor sinners] were utterly inaccessible every other way! And what numbers of these [sinners] are still to be found, even in or near our most populous cities? What multitudes of them were some years since both in Kingswood and the Fells about Newcastle, who, week after week, spent the Lord's day, either in the ale-house, or in idle diversions, and never troubled themselves about going to church, or to any public worship at all. Now would you really have desired that these poor wretches should have sinned on till they dropped into hell? Surely you would not. But by what other means was it possible they should have been plucked out of the fire?

[106]J. H. Plumb, *England in the Eighteenth Century,* v. 7, Pelican History of England (London: Penguin Books, 1963), 89–90.

> Had the Minister of the parish preached like an angel, it had profited them nothing; for they heard him not. But when one came and said, "Yonder is a man preaching on the top of the mountain," they ran in droves to hear what he would say; and God spoke to their hearts. It is hard to conceive anything else which could have reached them. Had it not been for *field-preaching*, the uncommonness of which was the very circumstance that recommended it, they must have run on in the error of their way, and perished in their blood.[107]

The "best" of the parish, as Wesley referred to the rich, had a place to worship—any parish in all of England.[108] But the poor, he thought, would never be fully welcomed by the church. The poor needed something different because regular worship was not truly open to them. The reality is that many poor people simply did not have a Christian community in which they felt welcome and by which they had been embraced.

These motivations helped Wesley accept his "extraordinary" call. Field preaching was neither premeditated nor part of a grand master plan for Methodism. There "was no scheme at all previously formed."[109] Rather field preaching became a "sudden expedient" when parish buildings were closed to him. Yet this "novelty" became a critical component of Methodism.[110] It became part of "the wise providence of God," which made "a way for myriads of people, who never troubled any church, nor were likely so to do, to hear that word which they soon found to be the power of God unto salvation."[111] Field preaching became, as Outler describes, the "threshold of [John Wesley's] true vocation."[112]

Over the next fifty years field preaching became a defining aspect of the early Methodist movement. While the practice cooled in subsequent decades, it remained part of Methodism through the end of Wesley's life. Its heritage continued in the legacy of the circuit riders in the colonies and helped lay the groundwork for the tremendous expansion of Methodism in the United States in the nineteenth century. But it all began almost by happenstance. Had the parishes remained open to Wesley, he may never have ventured into the fields. Yet when they did close Wesley patiently designed a system of ministry around the circumstances in which he found himself. The result, as one of Wesley's preachers, Christopher Hopper, put

[107]Wesley, *Appeals, A Farther Appeal to Men of Reason and Religion*, Part III, §III.22–23, 11:306–07.

[108]*Societies*, "Short History of the People Called Methodists," §11, 9:431.

[109]Wesley, *Appeals, A Farther Appeal to Men of Reason and Religion*, §VI.3, 11:178.

[110]*Journal and Diaries III*, 8 October 1749, 20:307.

[111]Wesley believed field preaching was a way to reach those "who never did and never would come to [regular preaching]." *Societies*, "Short History of the People Called Methodists," §11, 9:431.

[112]Albert Cook Outler, ed. *John Wesley* (New York: Oxford University Press, 1964), 17.

it, was that the "fire [of God's love] spread from heart to heart, and God was glorified."[113]

PROCLAMATION IN FIELD PREACHING

The practices associated with "field preaching" and "preaching abroad" were clear. Preaching was the central act, of course, and is noted in previous citations. Teaching is rarely, if ever, associated with field preaching. Exhortation, on the other hand, is referenced on numerous occasions as a type of proclamation that occurred in the fields. Just a few examples suffice:

> In the afternoon I was obliged to be abroad, thousands upon thousands flocking together. I stood in a convenient place, almost over against the Infirmary, and exhorted a listening multitude to "live unto Him who died for them and rose again."[114]

> In the evening we were obliged to be abroad, and I used great plainness of speech. All suffered the word of exhortation; some seemed to be a little affected.[115]

> We marched to the camp, near Brussels. There a few of us joined into a society, being sensible, where two or three are gathered together in his name, there is our Lord in the midst of them. Our place of meeting was a small wood near the camp. We remained in this camp eight days, and then removed to a place called Ask. Here I began to speak openly, at a small distance from the camp, just in the middle of the English army: And here it pleased God to give me some evidences that my labour was not in vain. We sung an hymn, which drew about two hundred soldiers together, and they all behaved decently. After I had prayed, I begun to exhort them; and though it rained very hard, yet very few went away. Many acknowledged the truth, in particular a young man, John Greenwood, by name, who has kept with me ever since, and whom God has lately been pleased to give me for a fellow labourer.[116]

> In the afternoon I exhorted four or five thousand people at Bristol, neither to neglect nor rest in the means of grace.[117]

[113]Jackson, *The Life of Mr. Christopher Hopper*, 1:199.

[114]*Journal and Diaries VI*, 4 April 1776, 23:8.

[115]*Journal and Diaries IV*, 24 May 1759, 21:194.

[116]*Journal and Diaries III*, Letter from John Haime, recorded in Wesley's journal 4 November 1744, 20:42.

[117]*Journal and Diaries II*, 15 November 1739, 19:122.

So, like other forums for proclamation discussed in subsequent chapters, multiple types of proclamation are important. In the case of field preaching, preaching itself and exhortation are the most important.

Content of Proclamation in Field Preaching

Unlike those who attended parish worship services, those who came to field preaching often had little if any involvement with parish life. They were often remarkably ignorant of the meaning and consequences of faith. The hearers were typically unawakened and still in the natural state. Therefore the content of Wesley's preaching was not the Bible as a whole but rather the particular aspects that deal with the law. Two examples from the late 1760s and one from 1770 demonstrate Wesley's awareness of how his sermon topic met the need of the crowd:

> I rode to Axminster. The rain prevented my preaching abroad, though the Room would ill contain the congregation. Observing many there who seemed quite unawakened, I opened and strongly applied Ezekiel's vision of the dry bones. Lord, "breathe upon these slain, that they may live!"[118]

> I rode to Towcester, and preached to a heavy, unawakened people, on what they did not seem at all to think of, namely, that they were to die. I believe it suited them: They appeared to be more affected than with any discourse I had ever preached.[119]

> Judging most of the congregation here to be unawakened, I preached on the story of Dives and Lazarus. God gave me to speak strong words, so that I trust some were pricked to the heart.[120]

> [Wesley preached in] An open place...I declared, to a large, wild company, "There is no difference; for all have sinned, and come short of the glory of God."[121]

Preaching in the fields was the best way to engage the unawakened with the word of God. Field preaching, Wesley believed, "is the way to shake the trembling gates of hell."[122] While field preaching often included a variety of texts and themes, including the "plain, old Methodist doctrine, laid down in the Minutes of the Conference"[123] of repentance, faith,

[118] *Journal and Diaries V*, 22 October 1768, 22:159.

[119] Ibid., 23 November 1769, 22:208.

[120] Ibid., 11 December 1769, 22:212.

[121] *Journal and Diaries III*, 4 October 1746, 20:144.

[122] *Journal and Diaries V*, August 1768, 22:153.

[123] *Letters* (Telford). Letter from John Wesley to Joseph Benson, 10 September 1773, 6:40.

and holiness, the reality is that in field preaching not all themes were emphasized equally.

The content of Charles's field preaching was similar to his brother's. Joseph Williams commented on Charles's preaching in 1739:

> I scarce ever heard any minister discover such evident signs of a most vehement desire, or labour so earnestly, to convince his hearers that they were all by nature in a state of enmity against God, consequently in a damnable state, and needed reconciliation to God; that God is willing to be reconciled to all, even the worst of sinners, and for that end laid all our guilt on Christ, hath imputed it to him, and Christ hath fulfilled all righteousness and punishment due to our sins in our nature and stead; that on the other hand the righteousness and merits of Christ are, and shall be, imputed to as many as believe on him; that it is faith alone, exclusive entirely of any works of ours, which applys to us the righteousness of Christ, and justifies us in the light of God, that none are excluded but those who refuse to come to him, as lost, undone, yea as damned sinners, and trust in him alone, i.e. his meritorious righteousness, and atoning sacrifice, for pardon and salvation.[124]

Especially at the beginning of the revival, the focus of field preaching was the announcement that all people had broken God's law, that they were sinful. He seemed to touch on the importance of faith, but the real emphasis was the thoroughness in which sin is entrenched in every soul. As the revival matured, Wesley began to include more and more of the theme of "salvation by faith" in field preaching, but in the early days faith was not the focus; rather it was sinfulness and the need to awaken. God's grace operated preveniently in the fields, Wesley believed, and preaching the law helped awaken people to their sinfulness.[125] Wesley's emphasis in the fields was on each person's sin—not the inherited sin of Adam, but rather the darkness in each person's soul for which they were responsible:

> It was neither needful nor proper for an Apostle, in his first sermon to a congregation wholly unawakened, to descant upon original sin. No man of common sense would do it now. Were I to preach to a certain congregation at Norwich, I should not say one word of Adam, but endeavour to show them that their lives, and therefore their hearts, were corrupt and abominable before God.[126]

[124]*Early Preachers Collection*, Letter from Joseph Williams to Charles Wesley, 19 October 1739, 1/92.

[125]Thomas R. Albin, "'Inwardly Persuaded': Religion of the Heart in Early British Methodism," in *"Heart Religion" in the Methodist Tradition and Related Movements*, ed. Richard B. Steele (Lanham, MD: Scarecrow, 2001), 39.

[126]*Treatises I*, Part II, §VI.1, 12:297.

Wesley hoped that people would awaken and then respond at a future point with faith and repentance.

The theme of field preaching was then quite different from what was emphasized in most Church of England sermons, in which faith and repentance would be the subject periodically, as found in the Homilies of the Church. Because of this "there was not the same influence or blessing from Him."[127]

Responses to Proclamation in Field Preaching

In light of the fact that many if not most who attended field preaching, especially in the revival's early days, rarely attended worship services at their local Church of England parish, it should come as no surprise that the primary goal of Methodist field preachers was to elicit an awakening on the part of the hearers. Indeed, as the quotations in the previous section indicate, awakening was the principal outcome Methodists sought in field preaching. John Pawson's observation was not unique: "As we now had regular preaching in my father's house, many of our neighbours came to hear, and several were awakened, and joined the society."[128] In fact, so many began to see awakening as the goal of some sermons that a unique type of sermon, the "awakening sermon" developed. Wesley describes the need for this type of sermons in his own sermon "The Means of Grace."[129] As Alexander Boraine argues, the awakening sermon is Wesley's first tool for reaching the unawakened with the gospel.[130]

Yet awakening was not the only response of people who heard the call to faith and repentance in the fields. Occasionally, awakened people also converted as a result of field preaching.[131] Wesley notes on one occasion,

> I preached on the righteousness of the Law and the righteousness of faith. While I was speaking, several dropped down as dead; and among the rest, such a cry was heard, of sinners groaning for the righteousness of faith, as almost drowned my voice. But many of these soon lifted up their heads with joy, and broke out into thanksgiving; being assured they now had the desire of their soul, —the forgiveness of their sins.[132]

He also notes long after the revival had waned that during field preaching "the converting, as well as convincing, power of God is

[127]*Letters II*, Letter to John Smith, 10 July 1747, §5, 26:246.

[128]Jackson, *The Life of Mr. John Pawson*, 4:16.

[129]*Sermons I*, Sermon 16, "The Means of Grace," §V.1, 1:393.

[130]Boraine, 197.

[131]*Journal and Diaries IV*, 23 September 1759, 21:230.

[132]*Journal and Diaries II*, 12 June 1742, 19:276.

eminently present."[133] Preaching abroad, along with prayer meetings, was "the means of awakening many gross sinners, of recovering many backsliders, of confirming many that were weak and wavering."[134] Hearing the law, even when it was accompanied by only a portion of encouragement to have faith, sometimes was the catalyst for people actually coming to faith, especially when they had heard the law preached many times before.

Occasionally, there are examples of people maturing in sanctification while in the fields. Wesley notes one conversation with a woman at a field preaching event who had clearly already come to a place of faith and repentance:

> At five in the morning I was obliged to preach abroad . . . A little after preaching, one came to me who believed God had just set her soul at full liberty. She had been clearly justified long before; but said, the change she now experienced was extremely different from what she experienced then; as different as the noon-day light from that of day-break: That she now felt her soul all love, and quite swallowed up in God.[135]

In another place Wesley notes that at one field preaching event people already "holy" attended who had grown wealthier without decreasing in holiness.[136] Even in 1739 Wesley writes how he hopes those who hear the message in the fields will respond with "wisdom, righteousness, sanctification, and redemption."[137] But the primary response he sought was awakening.

In his important research on the spiritual biographies of early Methodists, Tom Albin demonstrates that the vast majority did not come to faith and repentance in the fields. Only 10–20 percent of Methodists experienced the New Birth at a field preaching event.[138] The rest experienced it in the societies, classes, bands, or in their own room or home.[139] As long as Wesley lived, awakening to the reality of a loving God from whom humanity has been separated because of sin, not conversion through

[133]*Journal and Diaries IV*, 23 September 1759, 21:230.

[134]*Journal and Diaries V*, 23 June 1765, 22:8. In his "Short History of People Called Methodists," instead of "confirming many that were weak and wavering," Wesley substitutes "and bringing many that never thought of [attending preaching] before, to attend the preaching at the new room." *Societies*, §106, 9:487.

[135]*Journal and Diaries IV*, 6 June 1763, 21:414–15.

[136]*Journal and Diaries VI*, 27 August 1776, 23:30.

[137]*Journal and Diaries II*, 6 May 1739, 19:55.

[138]Albin, "An Empirical Study of Early Methodist Spirituality," 289.

[139]Ibid., 289. Unfortunately Albin does not include the category of visitation in his study.

repentance and faith, was the primary point of field preaching.[140] People who responded with awakening to the evangelistic message were then invited to join a society and class meeting where the deeper work of justification and sanctification was nurtured.

CONCLUSION

Field preaching was not Wesley's invention. Rather, it had been a cultural phenomenon for many centuries that waxed and waned, based on the religious temperature of the country at any given time. By the late 1730s many yearned to engage the Christian story, but the normal ecclesial life of the Church of England tended to exclude many people. The result, as Heitzenrater writes, is that a significant segment of the British population was ripe for an "irregular" encounter with the gospel story:

> Wesley was speaking by and large to people who were the castoffs of society—they lived a hard, sad, and lonely life, had low self-esteem, very little hope, and few friends that could help. When Wesley told these people the scriptural truths that God loved them, that they too could become children of God, could leave the guilt and misery of their sinful lives behind, and that in the face of death, they could enjoy the happiness and holiness that are marks of the Kingdom of God, he not only spoke from his own experience, he also spoke to the anxieties that many of them felt and he spoke of the certainties that many desired.[141]

So Wesley ventured into the fields to reach those who would not come to the sanctuary. Wesley retooled preaching, something he understood as essential to every Christian movement, and gave it a form that was uniquely effective in eighteenth-century England.[142] In this fortuitous embrace of field preaching—a practice Wesley certainly did not know ahead of time would be so influential—he started the spiritual engine that drove the Methodist revival. Lord Soper sums up the importance of field preaching well: "The Methodist Revival could not have happened without the ingredient of field preaching as a vital constituent. The moral and spiritual revival which is the hope, indeed the requirement of man's future on this planet requires a similar evangelical excursion into the open air today."[143]

And yet Wesley became convinced that field preaching alone was not

[140]George Hunter, "John Wesley as Church Growth Strategist," *Wesleyan Theological Journal* 21, no. 1–2 (1986), http://wesley.nnu.edu/fileadmin/imported_site/wesleyjournal/1986-wtj-21.pdf.

[141]Heitzenrater, "John Wesley's Principles and Practice of Preaching," 50–51.

[142]Boraine, 231. Boraine writes, "Field-preaching is an instituted means of evangelism having a prudential form."

[143]Soper, 189.

enough to sustain a revival, either personally or culturally. Wesley records in his journal entry of August 25, 1763,

> I was more convinced than ever that the preaching like an apostle, without joining together those that are awakened and training them up in the ways of God, is only begetting children for the murderer. How much preaching has there been for these twenty years all over Pembrokeshire! But no regular societies, no discipline, no order or connection. And the consequence is that nine in ten of those once awakened are now faster asleep than ever.[144]

Despite the amazing impact of field preaching, from the late 1740s to the end of his life, Wesley, almost without exception, would not send field preachers to an area unless a Methodist society had been established there. The next chapter explores why.

[144]*Journal and Diaries IV,* 25 August 1763, 21:424.

CHAPTER 5

SOCIETY MEETINGS

We had a heaven amongst us; a paradise within us! The Lord poured such peace and joy into our hearts, and we were often so happy, that we did not know how to part. We lived as brethren, and strove together for "the hope of the gospel." We were of one heart and of one mind, in the presence of God. And is this not the communion of saints?[1]

By 1745 the Methodist movement was growing fast in parts of England. Tens of thousands attended field-preaching events annually. Many responded to the preaching abroad with the awakening Wesley desired, and a few even came to repentance and faith after hearing the gospel proclaimed. Of those who awakened, many wanted to hear more about the Christian faith they heard proclaimed in the fields. They wanted to talk about the call of Christ in their lives and perhaps grow in their faith. So many responded that Wesley had trouble staffing the follow-up ministry that helped nurture those who responded with awakening. This follow-up ministry, which is the focus of this chapter, was what Wesley came to call "Methodist societies."

Methodist societies were a gathering of people in a geographic area who committed to follow Christ, or at least to consider following Christ, within the framework of discipleship laid out by John Wesley and the other leaders. Societies tended to range in size from as small as twenty or so to as large as a few hundred. Members met together for mutual support through prayer, worship, fellowship, and spiritual direction.

The importance of Methodist societies in Wesley's method and structure of ministry has been well known since the beginning of the movement. The society became the foundation of Methodist identity. Only after Methodism became an official church in the colonies, and then later in Great Britain, did congregations displace societies as the primary community. What is less emphasized in contemporary conversations, but which was clear in the

[1]Jackson, *The Life of Mr. Thomas Walsh,* 3:71. Walsh is commenting on his experience of a Methodist society.

beginning, is the continuity of proclamation from the fields to societies and ultimately to classes and visitation. Proclamation in the society meetings helped cultivate people awakened in field preaching so they could experience both initial and subsequent times of faith and repentance, resulting in justification and sanctification. Societies became the primary community of Methodists, out of which flowed classes and band meetings.

Their importance, however, was not immediately obvious to Wesley. By the mid–1740s there was tremendous need for both field preachers and society leaders. Wesley had to make a decision: would he continue sending field preachers only to the places where he could also start societies or would he begin to offer field preaching even when he knew he could not launch a society at the same place? So Wesley decided to do an experiment. He records in the *Minutes* of 1745, "May we not make a trial, especially in Wales and Cornwall, or preaching without settling any societies? It might be well: and by this means we may preach in every large town where a door is open."[2] In 1747 Wesley continued the practice, arguing that due to a lack of leadership field preaching without starting a corresponding society needed to continue because, "We have found a greater blessing in field preaching than in any other preaching whatever."[3]

By 1748 he brought the experiment to an abrupt halt. When he asks that year if the three-year-old trial should continue, his response is striking: "By no means. We have made the trial already. We have preached for more than a year without forming societies in a large tract of land from Newcastle to Berwick-upon-Tweed; and almost all the seed has fallen by the wayside. There is scarce any fruit of it remaining."[4]

For the remainder of his life, Wesley encouraged field preaching only in places where societies were already formed or new ones could be launched. Years later he reflected on this 1745 experiment: "I was more convinced than ever that the preaching like an Apostle, without joining together those that are awakened and training them up in the ways of God, is only begetting children for the murderer."[5]

This chapter examines the historical precedents of religious societies in the Church of England, Wesley's encounter with societies in other traditions, the development of distinctly Methodist societies, the role of proclamation in them, and Wesley's understanding of their critical connection with field preaching. For Methodist societies ultimately came to form the framework in which Methodists were nurtured and disciplined—and integral to that nurture was proclamation.

[2]*Minutes of Conference*, 1745, §62, 10:158.

[3]Ibid., 1747, §58, 10:203.

[4]Ibid., 1748, §3, 10:210.

[5]*Journal and Diaries IV*, 25 August 1763, 21:424.

A HERITAGE OF RELIGIOUS SOCIETIES IN BRITAIN

By the 1670s a spiritual vacuum in the Church of England was developing. While today the spiritual vitality of the Church of England in the late seventeenth century is often debated, some people of the period saw a need for renewal. Many people in and around London were concerned that religious fervor in the church was on the wane, that morality in general was in decline, and that they themselves needed personal spiritual renewal.[6] In 1698 Josiah Woodward wrote that those "touch'd with a very affecting sense of their sins, and began to apply themselves, in a very serious manner, to religious thoughts and purposes."[7] Many of these groups that formed in and around London quickly became known as "religious societies." The stated aim of these societies was to provide a Christian community in which people could "apply themselves to good discourse and to things wherein they might edify one another."[8] They met together for devotional purposes, for mutual edification, and in some cases to serve as informants to local authorities regarding "swearers, drunkards and profaners of the Lord's day."[9]

Two people were especially important in the development of religious societies in this time period. The first was Reverend Anthony Horneck. Though he was only one of many society leaders, by 1668 he was among the most influential, helping to nurture a number of societies in and around London. He published a list of "rules" for societies that guided his own and soon became the model for others. The second person of note is Josiah Woodward. His 1698 *Account of the Rise and Progress of the Religious Societies in the City of London* examines the history and development of societies over the previous two decades.[10] His list of "rules" is more extensive than Horneck's, reflecting the development and institutionalization of societies over the thirty years between accounts. The rules are remarkably similar in theme and emphasis, and are especially pertinent in their differences and similarities to the Methodist societies that developed in 1740.[11]

Horneck's and Woodward's rules are quite similar, some being virtually identical. Below is a selection of rules from Horneck's list that are

[6]See especially William Gibson, *The Church of England, 1688–1832: Unity and Accord* (London: Routledge, 2001), 28–69.

[7]Josiah Woodward, *An Account of the Societies for Reformation of Manners in London and Westminster, and Other Parts of the Kingdom* (London: RA Simpson, 1698), 17.

[8]*An Account of the Rise and Progress of the Religious Societies in the City of London*, 4th ed. (London: M. Downing, 1712), 22.

[9]Richard Brindley Hone, *Lives of Eminent Christians* (London: John W. Parker, 1843), 2:308.

[10]Scott Thomas Kisker, *Foundation for Revival: Anthony Horneck, the Religious Societies, and the Construction of Anglican Pietism* (Lanham, MD: Scarecrow, 2008), 143–64. In this book Kisker offers a helpful discussion of the Anglican societies.

[11]Woodward, *An Account of the Societies for Reformation of Manners in London and Westminster, and Other Parts of the Kingdom*, 118. Woodward documents that most of the societies were working off similar "rules."

especially pertinent to the Methodist societies that developed a few decades later:

1. All that enter the Society shall resolve upon a holy and serious life.

2. No person shall be admitted... until... first confirmed by the bishop, and solemnly taken upon himself his baptismal vow.

3. They shall choose a minister of the Church of England to direct them.

4. They shall not be allowed, in their meetings, to discourse of any controverted point of divinity.

5. Neither shall they discourse of the government of Church or State.

6. In their meetings they shall use no prayers but those of the Church...

7. The minister... shall direct what practical divinity shall be read at these meetings.

8. They may have liberty, after prayer and reading, to sing a psalm.

9. After all is done, if there be time left, they may discourse with each other about their spiritual concerns; but this shall not be a standing exercise which any shall be obliged to attend unto.

10. One day in the week shall be appointed for this meeting, for such as cannot come on the Lord's day...

...

18. The following rules are more especially recommended to the members of this society, viz. To love one another. When reviled, not to revile again. To speak evil of no man. To wrong no man. To pray, if possible, seven times a day. To keep close to the Church of England. To transact all things peaceably and gently. To be helpful to each other. To use themselves to holy thoughts in their coming in and going out. To examine themselves every night. To give every one their due. To obey superiors, both spiritual and temporal.[12]

Woodward's rules are similar. He also starts with holiness as the primary goal of the group but phrases it a bit differently. With "real holiness of heart and life" the "sole design of this society," he writes of the absolute necessity "that the persons who enter into it [the society] do seriously resolve to apply themselves in good earnest to all means proper to make them wise unto salvation."[13] As Woodward recounts, "These *Young Men* soon found the benefit of their *Conferences* one with one another, by which (as some have told me with Joy) they better discover'd

[12]Richard Kidder, *The Life of the Reverend Anthony Horneck, D.D., Late Preacher at the Savoy* (London: J. H. for B. Aylmer, 1698), 13–16.

[13]Woodward, *An Account of the Societies for Reformation of Manners in London and Westminster, and Other Parts of the Kingdom*, 120.

their own Corruptions, the Devil's Temptations, and how to countermine his subtle devices; as to which each person communicated his *Experiences* to the rest."[14] Similarly, glorifying God and edifying one another is the point of meeting together. Disputed "controversial points, State-affairs, or Concerns of Trade and worldly Things" discourage the proper "bent of discourse."[15] Both lists of rules emphasize attending prescribed Church of England prayers and "practical" readings, often of approved sermons.

The leaders of the Church of England regulated membership in societies, and members were expected to be members of the church. Because of this expectation, the weekly meetings of the societies could take place any day but Sunday. Similarly, clergy played a central role in each society. Sometimes leaders of a society were laypersons, but clergy often led societies, and if the leader was a layperson then a cleric still oversaw the society. Each of these rules is an effort to encourage holiness of heart and life. This encouragement, both argue, was found best when Christians gather to pursue holiness together. Furthermore, holiness is not individualistic; rather, it is a "broad and practical" spirituality that included caring for the poor and making education more accessible to the population where the love of God was "united" with the love of man.[16] Furthermore in both cases, lay leadership was encouraged. These earlier societies seem organized around clerical leadership, but there were clear allowances, and even a design by which laity were encouraged to step in and lead the societies.[17]

Both Horneck and Woodward understood proclamation as part of the religious societies. In some cases the scripture lesson is read slowly so that members can comment on each verse. Alternatively, stewards can read expositions approved by the Church of England or read portions of the catechism based on certain subjects with the aim that over the course of a year the forty most important biblical topics are addressed, including "the duty of self-examination; faith in our Lord Jesus Christ; Evangelical repentance; effectual conversion to God; [and] Christian charity."[18] These forty, plus twelve weeks on the Lord's Supper, provided the topics for an entire year of society meetings. There was one significant difference between these first societies and the future Methodist societies, namely that these first societies were clearly only for members of the Church of England, a limit that Methodist societies specifically rejected.

The religious societies that Woodward and Horneck described are

[14]Ibid., 37 (emphasis original).

[15]Ibid., 122.

[16]John S. Simon, *John Wesley and the Religious Societies* (London: Epworth, 1921), 20.

[17]Ibid., 15.

[18]Ibid., 16.

quite different from the religious societies that formed in the last decade of the seventeenth century: the Society for the Reformation of Manners (circa 1691), the Society for the Propagation of Christian Knowledge (1698), and the Society for the Propagation of the Gospel in Foreign Parts (1701). These three societies were founded by members of the Church of England but were much more focused on specific perceived social needs as opposed to individual pursuits of holiness of heart and mind. Therefore they did not have the emphasis on weekly meetings and the particular rules that helped define the first religious societies as described by Horneck and Woodward. Nevertheless, the need many felt to "reform" the nation through these societies seems related to the need many felt to reform their own lives by holy living.[19]

While these societies were significant for their focus on personal holiness, their influence seems to have declined after a couple of decades. Daniel Betham, a Moravian, notes that at least some Anglican societies of the time:

> Had so settled down into lifelessness, that the majority of the members were altogether slumbering or dead souls, who cared for nothing but their comfort in this world, and as they had once joined this connection, they were willing to continue in this respectable pastime on Sunday evenings, by which at small expense, they could enjoy pleasure, and fancy themselves better than the rest of the world who did not do the like.[20]

Nevertheless they continued to influence many in the Church of England, including John Wesley's parents, Samuel and Susanna Wesley. Samuel is described as "among their warmest supporters" by John Henry Overton.[21] He actively engaged the societies, writing at least two pieces about them: "Letter concerning Religious Societies" (1699) and "Sermon preached to one of the Religious Societies" (1698). Susanna was also aware of the work of religious societies and their role as smaller gatherings of members of a congregation. For this reason she refers to the group of almost two hundred of Samuel's parishioners who met with her in the Epworth parsonage for prayer and exhortation during a time when Samuel was away as "our society."

Societies were also part of the Welsh revival and especially important to the two Welshmen, Rowland and Harris, who helped launch Whitefield and Wesley into their ministries of field preaching. By the time Wesley met

[19]John Henry Overton, *Life in the English Church, 1660–1714* (London: Longmans, 1885), 216.

[20]Daniel Bentham, *Memoirs of James Hutton: Compromising the Annals of His Life, and Connection with the United Brethren* (London: Hamilton, Adams, and Company, 1856), 9. See also Dean, 121.

[21]Overton, 212.

Harris in 1739, for instance, the latter had organized almost thirty societies, each of which emphasized Bible-reading, hymns, prayers, exhortations, and spiritual conversation.[22]

METHODIST SOCIETIES DEVELOP

In 1760 Wesley described the origins and motivations of a group that he said was the "first rise" of Methodism, namely, that small group of men who came to be known as the Holy Club:

> About thirty years since [ago], I met with a book written in King William's time, called *The Country Parson's Advice to his Parishioners*. There I read these words: "If good men of the Church will unite together in the several parts of the kingdom, disposing themselves into friendly societies, and engaging each other in their respective combinations to be helpful to each other in all good, Christian ways, it will be the most effectual means for restoring our decaying Christianity to its primitive life and vigour and the supporting of our tottering and sinking Church." A few young gentlemen then at Oxford approved of and followed the advice. They were all zealous Churchmen, and both orthodox and regular to the highest degree. For their exact regularity they were soon nicknamed Methodists... Nine or ten years after, many others "united together in the several parts of the kingdom, engaging in like manner to be helpful to each other in all good, Christian ways"... Their one design was to forward each other in true, scriptural Christianity.[23]

The book Wesley refers to was published in 1680, and the similarities with the religious societies discussed earlier are evident. The "few young gentlemen" Wesley refers to are the original members of the Holy Club, or as Wesley sometimes called them, "our little company," which began meeting in 1729 in Oxford. The Holy Club was the small group of students that Charles helped start but that John soon began to lead after he returned to Oxford from Epworth. This small group focused on mutual encouragement, prayer, scripture reading, and visiting the poor and those in prison. John refers to this small group as a society, and he was not alone. Others linked the Holy Club specifically with societies, sometimes referring to the group as a "little society" or a "religious society" and occasionally as the "ridiculous society."[24] By the end of the 1720s Wesley was familiar with the concept that Christian formation took place best in small communities that gathered apart from the Sunday congregation, as had many Anglicans of

---

[22]Rack, 225.

[23]*Letters III*, Letter to Mr. T. H., 12 December 1760, 27:225–26; see note 149 on p. 226 for further description of who Wesley writes in this letter.

[24]Frank Baker, "The People Called Methodists: 3. Polity," in *A History of the Methodist Church in Great Britain*, ed. Gordon Rupp Rupert Davies (London: Epworth, 1965), 216.

the time. Societies had become the normative channel for highly committed members of the Church of England to grow further in their faith beyond what their local parish offered.[25] So by the time Wesley went to Georgia, he was prepared for a community he would encounter on the way.

The group he met on board the *Simmonds* as he sailed to Georgia were Moravians. As they sailed, Wesley writes that this group of Moravians gathered for preaching, singing, and support. He referred to the group as the "little society."[26] He later learned that Moravians emphasized gathering serious congregants in "societies" for more devoted study and prayer.

Soon after landing in Savannah, Wesley incorporated societies into his ministry. Wesley proceeded to establish three societies, one in Savannah and then two in Frederica:

> We considered in what manner we might be most useful to the little flock at Savannah. And we agreed, 1. To advise the more serious among them to form themselves into a sort of little society, and to meet once or twice a week, in order to reprove, instruct, and exhort one another. 2. To select out of these a smaller number for a more intimate union with each other, which might be forwarded, partly by our conversing singly with each, and partly by inviting them all together to our house; and this, accordingly, we determined to do every Sunday in the afternoon.[27]

These societies were designed for the "more serious" of the congregation as a way to meet at least weekly outside of worship for reproof, instruction, and exhortation. Furthermore Wesley recognized even at this point that discipleship necessitated a smaller gathering where Methodists might have a spiritually "more intimate union with each other," a subject I will treat in the next chapter. While his time as a missionary in Georgia is often seen correctly as a low point in his life and ministry, it also laid the foundation for his later incorporations of societies into Methodism.[28] Indeed societies became Methodism's primary community and the epicenter of discipleship formation as long as Wesley lived.

Upon Wesley's dejected return from Georgia to England, he quickly began meeting with various "societies" for fellowship and spiritual growth. First he met in "Mr. Fox's Society" in Oxford, and then also with a group of about seventy people who gathered at John Hutton's house for prayer,

[25]Dean, 109. Dean argues the Wesley brothers, "Adopted, or perhaps absorbed, the society approach from their religious environment. Religious Societies had been a recognized part of English religious life for sixty years and were accepted as the normal outlet for religious interests. Methodism was the direct outgrowth of that movement."

[26]Baker, "The People Called Methodists: 3. Polity," 216.

[27]*Journal and Diaries I: 1735–38*, v. 18 in *The Bicentennial Edition of the Works of John Wesley* (Nashville: Abingdon, 1998), 17 April 1736, 18:157. Cited hereafter as *Journal and Diaries I.*

[28]Ibid.

singing, and Bible study. On May 1, 1738, Peter Böhler invited Hutton and Wesley, the three of whom "were of the same mind and who seek closer fellowship with each other," to start a "band" meeting, which ultimately became known as the Fetter Lane Society.

The Fetter Lane Society, the formation of which Wesley later referred to as the "third rise" of Methodism, was initially a group of between forty and fifty Christians, most of whom were German, who began meeting for prayer and encouragement in the life of faith.[29] Frank Baker argues that this society was originally for members of the Church of England only, citing the removal of two persons because they "disowned themselves of the Church of England" and because the society went as a group to communion at St. Paul's.[30] The members were, however, quite friendly to both the Methodist and Moravian movements and quickly made clear that the society was open to all. Two rules guided the group:

> 1. That they will meet together once in a week to confess their faults one to another and to pray for one another that they may be healed [James 5:16].
>
> 2. That any others, of whose sincerity they are well assumed, may, if they desire it, meet with them for that purpose.[31]

These two rules were noticeably different from the rules of the earlier religious societies. They were much simpler and more clearly focused on the pursuit of holiness. The means by which the group pursued holiness were also simple: they met weekly to confess any sins and to pray for one another. Furthermore, the rules clearly established that membership was open to anyone who was sincere in their desire to meet, thereby opening the door to people from outside the Church of England.

Encouragement in the society came in part through preaching and exhortation at the weekly society meeting. Wesley, Böhler, or a visiting clergyperson would lead the service and the preaching or teaching. This large group format necessitated a lecture model of teaching instead of small-group discussion. In fact, group discussion was not encouraged. Rather, affirmative nods or periodic "amens" were the primary responses members made.[32]

---

[29]*Societies*, "Short History of the People Called Methodists," §9, 9:430. Wesley writes, "But it may be observed, the first rise of Methodism (so called) was in November 1729, when four of us met together at Oxford; the second was at Savannah, in April, 1736, when twenty or thirty persons met at my house; the last was at London, on this day, when forty or fifty of us agreed to meet together every Wednesday evening, in order to a free conversation, begun and ended with singing and prayer."

[30]Baker, "The People Called Methodists: 3. Polity," 217.

[31]David Lowes Watson, *The Early Methodist Class Meeting: Its Origins and Significance* (Nashville: Discipleship Resources, 1992), 197.

[32]David Michael Henderson, *John Wesley's Class Meeting: A Model for Making Disciples* (Nappanee, IN: Evangel, 1997), 66.

A few weeks after forming this band/society, both John and Charles had spiritual experiences that helped define the rest of their lives and ministries. Charles's was first. On May 21, 1738, Charles reported in his journal that he felt a new or renewed faith in Christ. "I believe, I believe!" he wrote, and then continued:

> I now found myself at peace with God, and rejoiced in hope of loving Christ…I saw that by faith I stood; by the continual support of faith, which kept me from falling, though of myself I am ever sinking into sin. I went to bed still sensible of my own weakness, (I humbly hope to be more and more so,) yet confident of Christ's protection.[33]

His brother followed three days later with his famous description of his heart being "strangely warmed." Both were to look back on those days throughout their lives. Whether it was their conversion or a deeper reflection of holiness and commitment is a matter for debate. What is certain is that after they had joined these small group of committed Christians for regular reflection, study, prayer, and encouragement, as they had joined with other groups previously, they both had definitive spiritual experiences. John quickly came to associate the transformative experience with the Moravian emphasis on discipleship through smaller communities.

Therefore Wesley set out for Germany to learn from the Moravians firsthand how they structured their discipleship. Wesley wrote to his brother Samuel that in Herrnhut he was "with a Church whose conversation is in heaven."[34] In Marienborn and Herrnhut he observed longstanding communities of Moravians up close. Wesley noted that the Moravians at Herrnhut were divided into "classes" by geography, gender, and age with the goal of providing spiritual oversight and regular religious community in order to determine what "hinders or furthers the work of God in the souls" of the members."[35] The community was divided even further into ninety "bands" that met multiple times each week for confession and prayer. The bands included times of singing, prayer, and instruction.[36]

Upon Wesley's return from Germany, he began visiting a number of religious societies in and around Oxford once again. During Wesley's absence, Hutton remained involved with the group that became the Fetter Lane Society, referring to it as the "new society." Wesley soon understood this gathering as a society as well, referring to the group as "our little

[33]Wesley, *The Journal of the Rev. Charles Wesley*, 21 May 1738, 2:90–92.

[34]*Letters I*, Letter to Samuel Wesley, 7 July 1738, 25:558.

[35]Wesley, *Works* (Jackson), from Wesley's journal of August 1738, "An Extract of the Constitution of the Church of the Moravian Brethren at Hernhuth, Laid before the Theological order at Wirtemberg, in the year 1733," §9, 1:144.

[36]Ibid., §9, 11–12, 14–21, 1:145–47.

society." As Wesley reengaged that community, he began more clearly incorporating some of the Moravian model and language. For instance, as the group grew through the fall Wesley subdivided it into eight "bands" of men and two of women.

By late December 1738 the society outgrew Hutton's home and moved to a new space in Fetter Lane, thereupon taking the name "Fetter Lane Society." During the same month Wesley wrote his first "Rules of the Band Societies," a somewhat confusing title considering that "band meetings" later became the designation for one of two types of groups formed out of the Methodist societies. But the title demonstrates the link between the two groups that was evident from the late 1730s through the end of Wesley's life. Later he came to describe this time period as the third and final "rise" of Methodism. It was the last stage before the Methodist movement truly became its own distinct community.

In January 1739 Wesley went to Bristol. As in London, a number of societies had already been meeting there, including those on Baldwin and Nicholas streets. George Whitefield's preaching drew in many converts who desired to connect with a community of Christians. Whitefield wrote to Wesley that "many are ripe for bands," and Wesley proceeded to start a number of bands within existing societies in the first half of the year.[37] By summertime Wesley recognized the need for a more permanent space for the societies, especially the two mentioned previously. On July 11, 1739, Wesley purchased a plot of land in which these two societies could meet as one "United Society." From this point on he would continually refer to the movement he helped launch as the "United Societies" of "the people called Methodists."

At the same time that Wesley started the United Society in Bristol, he traveled back and forth to London, helping lead the Fetter Lane Society. But a growing theological gap emerged with Peter Böhler, who had taken the lead of the society while Wesley was in Germany. Böhler encouraged "stillness," a practice of waiting for the Holy Spirit to move in one's life without engaging in any of the means of grace (i.e., prayer, Bible study, taking the Lord's Supper). Wesley believed that those who desired the Spirit's work should participate in these "means of grace" even if they were not Christians, because Wesley understood these means of grace to be the normal way in which the Spirit reveals God's love. Unbeknownst to him, an offer would soon come his way that would provide options for a new direction in his ministry.

In November 1739 Wesley took out a loan to purchase the Foundery, near Moorfields. This was a rapidly growing part of the city, and many in the area had responded to field preaching events nearby. Permanent

[37]*Letters I*, Letter from George Whitefield to John Wesley, 22 March 1738/39, 25:612.

access to this property allowed for both field preaching and society meetings. During this time it seems that Wesley started meeting with a number of members of the Fetter Lane Society who sought his direction. Wesley summarizes this group's development in the *General Rules*:

> In the latter end of the year 1739, eight or ten persons came to me in London, who appeared to be deeply convinced of sin, and earnestly groaning for redemption. They desired (as did two or three more the next day) that I would spend some time with them in prayer, and advise them how to flee from the wrath to come; which they saw continually hanging over their heads. That we might have more time for this great work, I appointed a day when they might all come together, which from thenceforward they did every week, namely, on Thursday, in the evening. To these, and as many more as desired to join with them, (for their number increased daily,) I gave those advices, from time to time, which I judged most needful for them; and we always concluded our meeting with prayer suited to their several necessities. This was the rise of the United Society, first in London, and then in other places.[38]

By July of the next year it was clear that Böhler and Wesley needed to part ways. Wesley resigned from his leadership of Fetter Lane, and the Foundery became the focus of his work in London. Seventy-five members of Fetter Lane joined Wesley at the Foundery, forming the foundation for the new "United Society" or "Foundery Society" in London. "Thus arose," Wesley writes in "A Plain Account of the People Called Methodists," "without any previous design on either side, what was afterwards called a Society; a very innocent name, and very common in London, for any number of people associating themselves together."[39] Just a few paragraphs later he writes, "Upon reflection, I could not but observe, This is the very thing which was from the beginning of Christianity."[40]

The Foundery Society in London and the United Society in Bristol were the first societies that looked to Wesley alone for leadership. In these two he put into action the "Rules of the Band Societies" that he wrote in 1738 and modified for two years. This period marks the beginning of Wesleyan Methodism as a distinct movement. For the rest of Wesley's life Methodism was structured around societies.

Wesley adopted ideas and practices from the religious societies of the late seventeenth century to create a new format that served his own day and his own understanding of the purposes of Christian discipleship.[41] Methodist societies differed from their predecessors in that instead of being

[38]*Societies, The Nature, Design, and General Rules of the United Societies*, §1–2, 9:69.

[39]Ibid., "A Plain Account of the People Called Methodists," §I.7, 9:256.

[40]Ibid., "A Plain Account of the People Called Methodists," §I.10, 9:258.

[41]Dean, 109.

on the fringe of Christian ministry, as they were in the Church of England, societies became the very heart of Methodism. Wesley took the structure of societies from the religious societies of the Church of England, blended them with the soul of the Moravian societies, and created a distinctly Wesleyan community.[42]

THE PURPOSE OF METHODIST SOCIETIES

Wesley describes the general purpose of societies in "A Plain Account of the People called Methodists":

> The thing proposed in their associating themselves together was obvious to every one. They wanted to "flee from the wrath to come," and to assist each other in so doing. They therefore united themselves "in order to pray together, to receive the word of exhortation, and to watch over one another in love, that they might help each other to work out their salvation."[43]

This passage encapsulates the basic purposes and design of the societies. They were for those who sought to grow in the Christian life, in a community of like-minded people who supported one another, while undergirded by proclamation.

Nurture People as Disciples

The societies were multifaceted and had manifold purposes. The first was simply to nurture people as disciples. In the wake of field preaching events many desired to know more about following Christ. A few people responded with repentance and faith in Christ; many more were simply awakened, and perhaps even convinced, but not yet converted. The people who responded were often at different places of maturity. Sometimes people were simply awakened. Other times people were justified. Many times it was a mix of both. Wesley records an occasion when he talked to "seventeen or eighteen [who] then desired to join a society . . . [I] was well pleased to find that near half of them knew the pardoning love of God." The rest were ready to join a society even though they were only awakened.[44] Evidently, that specific society was perceived as being spiritually dead, but Wesley was happy to report that "near one half of the sixty . . . I judged to be real believers."[45] The inference is that Wesley was not surprised that only some were justified and many only awakened. And

[42]Julia Wedgwood, *John Wesley and the Evangelical Reaction of the Eighteenth Century* (London: MacMillan and Co., 1870), 156–57.

[43]Wesley, *Societies*, "A Plain Account of the People Called Methodists," §I.7, 9:256.

[44]*Journal and Diaries IV*, 8 April 1755, 21:5.

[45]*Journal and Diaries V*, 13 June 1771, 22:279.

yet sometimes members of a society were not even awakened. Rather, they had heard the preaching or been to a prayer service and simply wanted to investigate further. They still had to agree to "attend upon the ordinances of God," but it was not necessary for them to have matured beyond the "natural state." Wesley refers once to this reality when, regarding the remarkable growth of a society in Wales, he records in his journal,

> I preached at Brecon the next day, and on Saturday 19 went on to Carmarthen. How is this wilderness become a fruitful field! A year ago I knew no one in this town who had any desire of fleeing from the wrath to come, and now we have eighty persons in society. It is true not many of them are awakened, but they have broke off their outward sins. Now let us try whether it be not possible to prevent the greater part of these from drawing back.[46]

Societies became the larger community of people who strove together in their discipleship as Methodists. Many people came to Wesley, "asking what they should do, being distressed on every side; as every one strove to weaken and none to strengthen their hands in God."[47] They wanted to grow in grace but they found the process a difficult one. Societies became the community for "those who appear to be awakened" in the fields to come together for further nurture.[48] In societies Methodists, having been convinced of sin, wrestled "with God for his love"; those who were justified spent their time "rejoicing therein."[49] The only requirement was the desire to "'flee from the wrath to come,' and to assist each other in so doing."[50]

Watching Over Each Other in Love

Methodists soon discovered that discipleship was not easy. The best way to nurture discipleship, they discovered, was to work together in a community of like-minded people who loved each other and who encouraged each other in the life of faith. "To assist each other," to "watch over one another in love," to "Strengthen you one another," all become common phrases to Methodism in the life of discipleship was an overarching purpose of Methodism. The point, as Wesley describes, was to meet together and "Talk together as often as you can. And pray

[46]Ibid., 17 August 1775, 22:461.

[47]*Societies,* "A Plain Account of the People Called Methodists," §I.5, 9:256.

[48]*Letters II,* Letter to Thomas Adams, 31 October 1755, 26:609.

[49]*Journal and Diaries IV,* 24 July 1762, 21:379.

[50]*Societies,*"A Plain Account of the People Called Methodists," §I.7, 9:256.

earnestly with and for one another, that you may 'endure to the end and be saved.'"[51]

These communal effort fall under a broader category of spiritual care. Societies were the first forum in which Methodists could "care" for the souls that responded to field preaching. Wesley discusses this function in the 1744 *Minutes*. He asks: "How are the people divided who desire to be under your care?" His answer: "Into the United Societies, the Bands, the Select Societies, and the Penitents."[52] Societies were the largest gathering of care, and each society was in turn divided into other groups, as described later in this book, each of which provided even more personal care.

The need for this kind of care is evident from the very beginnings of the Foundery Society. People were coming to Wesley asking for his assistance, but he found there were too many for him to watch over. When Wesley advised them to care for each other, they still asked for his guidance. As Wesley recounts, their response was, "But we want you likewise to talk with us often, to direct and quicken us in our way, to give us the advices which you well know we need, and to pray with us as well as for us."[53] The "advice" Wesley mentions is one way in which people were cared for, and I discuss it at length below.

Providing this care, Wesley believed, was best accomplished in community. He believed that corporate pursuit of holiness was essential for ongoing discipleship. "Solitary religion"—the idea that faith is an individualistic pursuit that people can pursue successfully on their own—was nonsensical to Wesley. He found that people typically matured best as disciples when they were part of a community of people who covenanted together to seek Christ.

John Telford writes of a "serious" person Wesley visited as Methodism began in Oxford who advised Wesley on the importance of the corporate body of Christ in personal discipleship: "Sir, you are to serve God and go to heaven. Remember you cannot serve Him alone; you must, therefore, find companions, or make them; the Bible knows nothing of solitary religion."[54] Christianity, Wesley believed, was "social" in that it requires a community of people gathering with the same intention of becoming more like Christ. To try to be a disciple on one's own is to destroy Christianity itself. "I mean not only that it [Christianity] cannot subsist so well," Wesley writes, "but that it cannot subsist at all, without society,

[51]Ibid., §I.5, 9:256.

[52]*Minutes of Conference*, 1744, §58, 10:136.

[53]*Societies*, "A Plain Account of the People Called Methodists," §I.6, 9:256.

[54]John Telford, *The Life of John Wesley* (London: Epworth, 1924), 147.

—without living and conversing with other men."[55] In another place he writes to Frances Godfrey, "I hope you find satisfaction . . . in some of your Christian companions. It is a blessed thing to have fellow-travellers to the New Jerusalem. If you cannot find any, you must make them; for none can travel that road alone. Then labour to help each other on, that you may be altogether Christians."[56] Charles believed likewise, as shown by a verse from one of his "Hymns for Christian Friends":

> Then let us ever bear
> The blessed end in view,
> And join with mutual care,
> To fight our passage through:
> And kindly help each other on
> Till all receive the starry crown.[57]

The Wesley brothers came to believe quite deeply that Christians need Christian friendships that provide nurture and encouragement on the journey of discipleship. So membership in a society required prioritizing the community, and the mutual encouragement of each other in the society. Therefore failure to attend society meetings or class meetings, even if just a few meetings, sometimes resulted in removal from the society. Societies became the larger community, "a company" of people gathering together for mutual encouragement and direction.

Joining together in an identifiable community helped strengthen and encourage not only the individual who joined but also those already in a society. Wesley makes this clear in a letter, worth quoting at length, where Wesley encourages someone on the periphery of a society to become a full member:

> Dear Sir, There was one thing, when I was with you, that gave me pain: You are not in the society. But why not? Are there not sufficient arguments for it to move any reasonable man? Do you not hereby make an open confession of Christ, of what you really believe to be his work, and of those whom you judge to be, in a proper sense, his people and his messengers? By this means do not you encourage his people, and strengthen the hands of his messengers? And is not this the way to enter into the spirit, and share the blessing, of a Christian community?
>
> The ordinary objections to such an union are of little weight with you. You are not afraid of the expense. You already give unto the Lord as much

[55]*Sermons I*, Sermon 24, "Sermon on the Mount 4," §1.1, 1:533–34.

[56]*Letters* (Telford), Letter to Frances Godfrey, 2 August 1789, 8:158.

[57]*A Collection of Hymns*, Hymn 496, verse 5, 7:685.

> as you need do then: And you are not ashamed of the Gospel of Christ, even in the midst of a crooked and perverse generation. Perhaps you will say, "I am joined in affection." True; but not to so good effect. This joining half-way, this being a friend to, but not a member of, the society, is by no means so open a confession of the work and servants of God. Many go thus far who dare not go farther, who are ashamed to bear the reproach of an entire union. Either you are ashamed, or you are not. If you are, break through at once; if you are not, come into the light, and do what those well-meaning cowards dare not do. This imperfect union is not so encouraging to the people, not so strengthening to the Preachers. Rather it is weakening their hands, hindering their work, and laying a stumbling block in the way of others; for what can any man think, who knows you are so well acquainted with them, and yet do not join in their society? What can he think, but that you know them too well to come any nearer to them; that you know that kind of union to be useless, if not hurtful? And yet by this very union is the whole (external) work of God upheld throughout the nation; besides all the spiritual good which accrues to each member. O delay no longer, for the sake of the work, for the sake of the world, for the sake of your brethren! Join them inwardly and outwardly, heart and hand, for the sake of your own soul. There is something not easily explained in the fellowship of the Spirit, which we enjoy with a society of living Christians. You have no need to give up your share therein, and in the various blessings that result from it.[58]

Being "joined in affection" refers to the task of "watching over" each other spiritually.

This idea of "watching over one another" is a perennial one for Wesley. He discusses it in his sermon "The Late Work of God in North America." Here he criticizes Whitefield for his failure to provide a framework for ongoing discipleship in a Christian community. The result, Wesley argues, is that those who responded to Whitefield's field preaching,

> had no discipline at all. They had no shadow of discipline; nothing of the kind. They were formed into no societies: They had no Christian connexion with each other, nor were ever taught to watch over each other's souls. So that if any fell into lukewarmness, or even into sin, he had none to lift him up: He might fall lower and lower, yea, into hell, if he would; for who regarded it?[59]

Indeed, Wesley saw part of his ministry as "gleaning" into societies those who had responded to Whitefield's field preaching but for whom Whitefield had failed to provide ongoing spiritual support.[60] Whitefield

[58]Ibid., 13 July 1764, 21:478–79.

[59]*Sermons III*, Sermon 113, "The Late Work of God in North America," §I.7, 3:598.

[60]*Letters II*, Letter to Charles Wesley, 21 April 1741, 26:55. John writes to Charles, "I must go

emphasized the call to conversion in field preaching events. Wesley, however, sought to help people mature beyond justification and, if they reverted in their discipleship, even to help them awaken and experience justification again. Wesley is concerned that if people don't start meeting together for spiritual nurture, then many of them may fall away. He writes,

> The far greater part of those who had begun to "fear God, and work righteousness," but were not united together, grew faint in their minds, and fell back into what they were before. Meanwhile the far greater part of those who were thus united together continued "striving to enter in at the strait gate," and to "lay hold on eternal life."[61]

Growing spiritually required being part of a community in which people could care for one another and encourage maturity in discipleship.[62]

Part of Spiritual care and "watching over" one another is spiritual examination. Throughout Wesley's journals he mentions examining people in groups:

> I found the spirit of the people while I was preaching, but much more in examining the society. Four or five times I was stopped short, and could not go on, being not able to speak; particularly when I was talking with a child, about nine years old, whose words astonished all that heard. The same spirit we found in prayer; so that my voice was well-nigh lost among the various cries of the people.[63]

> After preaching I met as many as desired it, of the members of the praying societies. I earnestly advised them to meet Mr. Gillies every week, and at their other meetings not to talk loosely and in general (as their manner had been) on some head of religion, but to examine each others' hearts and lives.[64]

These communal spaces allowed Wesley and, later, other preachers to examine people in their spiritual life and to determine how and where they needed to progress.

---

round and glean after G. Whitefield."

[61] *Societies*, "A Plain Account of the People Called Methodists," §I.9, 9:257–58.

[62] Andrew C. Thompson, "'To Stir Them up to Believe, Love, Obey'—Soteriological Dimensions of the Class Meeting in Early Methodism," *Methodist History* 48, no. 3 (2010): 160–78. Thompson successfully argues that Wesley's understanding of "social religion" is rooted in this understanding of the community as a necessary means through which most people mature in their faith, not in reference to social justice.

[63] *Journal and Diaries III*, 4 June 1750, 20:343.

[64] *Journal and Diaries IV*, 5 June 1757, 21:106.

The task of "watching over" defines both Wesley's ministry and his central understanding of the purpose of the societies. As he wrote in his journal, "My business now lay chiefly with the society. Those who had been scattered I laboured to gather up; those who were drowsy, to awaken; those that were dead, to quicken; and to unite all together in following after peace and holiness."[65] Critical to this care and "watching over" is proclamation, as discussed at great length below.

DESIGN OF THE SOCIETIES

In order to care and watch over each other in a communal setting, societies were designed in a specific manner. Becoming a member of a Methodist society was remarkably simple. The first requirement was an overarching spiritual trajectory, "a desire to flee from the wrath to come, and to be saved from their sins."[66] There was no creedal requirement for membership into a Methodist society. Assumed in this desire to flee from God's wrath was a general "awakening" to the spiritual life, but faith and repentance were not assumed or expected at this first step. But the simple "desire to flee" was not adequate in itself; Wesley required "fruit" of this desire as evidenced in a person "doing no harm," "doing good," and "attending upon all the ordinances of God."[67]

This evidence came in two primary ways. The first was a general commitment to Christian goals and disciplines, namely, doing no harm and doing good. Wesley writes of these in the *General Rules*:

> Doing no harm, by avoiding evil in every kind...Secondly, by doing good, by being in every kind merciful after their power; as they have opportunity doing good of every possible sort, and as far as it is possible to all men...Thirdly: by attending upon all the ordinances of God: such as, the public worship of God, the Supper of the Lord, private prayer, searching the Scriptures, and fasting or abstinence.[68]

Second was a commitment to attend meetings of the society as a whole as well as one's own particular class meeting.

Large Gatherings of the Society

The society as a whole gathered in a number of ways, most importantly in the regular society meetings. These were the regular large

[65]*Journal and Diaries V*, 30 April 1771, 22:272.

[66]*Societies, General Rules*, §4, 9:70.

[67]Ibid., §4–6, 9:70–73.

[68]Ibid.,"A Plain Account of the People Called Methodists," §I.8, 9:257.

group gatherings of everyone within a particular society. These meetings typically took place at least monthly, but sometimes two or three times per week. In the beginning these gatherings took place on Thursday and Friday evenings, but eventually they might meet any time of the week except Sunday mornings. The prohibition against Sunday morning gatherings reflects the Wesley brothers' desire that Methodist gatherings not compete with or substitute for regular worship in a Church of England parish.

In these meetings, which looked similar to many contemporary Methodist Sunday worship services, there were prayers, singing, preaching, testimony, and so on. The society also had periodic special gatherings of the society. Love feasts, for instance, were quite common by 1749 and included times of prayer, praise, thanksgivings, and testimonies. Select societies were for those who had experienced full salvation, or at least sought the sanctification of full salvation. Letter Days started in 1744 and were times of reading people's written testimonies. Watch nights consisted mostly of singing and prayer and were introduced in 1742; initially, they occurred weekly, on Saturday evenings. Over time they met less frequently, usually on the first Friday after a full moon. By 1755, they had become an annual gathering at the New Year that was known as the covenant renewal service. Each of these gatherings brought together members of the society for encouragement and support, with occasional proclamation through testimonies and preaching.

Groups within Societies

As mentioned above, as early as 1744 a variety of smaller groups formed out of the society membership, namely, bands, select societies, penitent bands, and classes. Wesley differentiates the first three as follows:

> The United Societies (which are the largest of all) consist of awakened persons. Part of these, who are supposed to have remission of sins, are more closely united in the Bands. Those of the Bands who seem to walk in the light of God compose the Select Societies. Those of them who have made shipwreck of the faith meet apart as penitents.[69]

"Bands," which are addressed in greater depth in a subsequent chapter, were smaller gatherings of the society, usually four to six people. Groups were formed according to gender and marital status, as well as spiritual state. Specifically, bands were only for those who had experienced remission of their sins and were on the journey toward Christian perfection. "Select societies" were made up of people in bands who

[69]*Minutes of Conference*, 1744, §59, 10:136–37.

"walk in the light of God," having experienced significant progression in holiness. They were people on the journey toward Christian perfection whom Wesley trusted to help guide each society and to advise him. They held each other accountable, serving as conversation partners for Wesley and the other leaders. "Penitents" or penitent bands were smaller gatherings of those in a society who fell short in their faith in specific ways and needed spiritual rehabilitation.

Classes, which also are mentioned in great detail later in the book, were smaller gatherings of the society that ultimately became critical to the method of growth in holiness that Wesley espoused. They became another layer of care, as Wesley describes in the *General Rules*: "That it may the more easily be discerned, whether they are indeed working out their own salvation, each Society is divided into smaller companies, called Classes, according to their respective places of abode. There are about twelve persons in every class; one of whom is styled *the Leader*."[70]

Most classes were larger than bands, usually having between ten and twelve members. Unlike bands, which were divided by gender and marital status, all classes were open to men and women alike, as well as both single and married persons. Members of classes were mixed by gender and marital status and included persons who were in each of the three primary states of grace. Membership in a class was expected of all society members, regardless of their spiritual state. Therefore, as was the case with the bands, many had experienced remission of sins. Unlike the situation in the bands, however, many in classes were only awakened. As Wesley writes, classes were for those who experienced justification by faith and who "wanted some means of closer union" in order to confess their sins and seek healing.[71] While Wesley encouraged bands throughout his lifetime, he never mandated them for all Methodists as he did classes, and therefore bands have been seen as less central to Methodists than classes.[72]

The various groups that made up a Methodist society—including the meetings themselves, the classes, bands, and love feasts—all worked together so that Methodists could make real Wesley's constant refrain to "increase our union with God and each other." But before the introduction of classes in 1743, the primary groups that encouraged this "watching

[70]*Societies, General Rules*, §3, 9:69–70.

[71]Ibid.,"A Plain Account of the People Called Methodists," §6.2, 9:266–68.

[72]Kevin M. Watson, *Pursuing Social Holiness: The Band Meeting in Wesley's Thought and Popular Methodist Practice* (Oxford: Oxford University Press, 2014), 72–98. Watson argues correctly that the importance of bands is often downplayed, especially their role in encouraging holiness within a community of Christians. Nevertheless, I propose here that classes were the primary small group gathering of Methodist societies, if only because of the fact that almost from their inception classes, and not bands, were mandated for membership in a Methodist society.

over" in love were the societies and bands. Once introduced, classes joined bands as the primary small group gatherings of Methodist Societies.

Proclamation in Methodist Society Meetings

In the *Large Minutes* Wesley asks a rhetorical question: "But what particular inconveniences do you observe when Societies are not formed?"[73] His response, year after year, is essentially the same. Without societies, Wesley continues in the *Minutes*, Methodists can neither "watch over one another in love" nor "bear one another's burdens, and build up each other in faith and holiness." But neither of these is the first "inconvenience" Wesley mentions that results from not forming societies. The first problem he mentions is that without society meetings "the Preacher cannot give proper instructions and exhortations to them that are convinced of sin."[74] Similar to the *General Rules*, where Wesley mentions "giving advices" and "exhortation," here he clearly describes the importance of teaching and exhortation. Society meetings were places of proclamation.

On numerous occasions Wesley refers to the role of proclamation in society meetings. Exhortation was common. Wesley writes in his journal, for example, "At eight I exhorted the society to wait upon God in all his ordinances; and in so doing to be still, and suffer God to carry."[75] Indeed, at first the purpose of gathering was so that Wesley could, in essence, exhort by his "giving of advice" to those who sought it.[76] While exhortation sometimes refers to encouragement, at times it also has the connotation of preaching. Walsh provides an example of exhortation's similarity to preaching in society meetings when he writes that in society meetings "there was always a word of exhortation preached or read."[77]

Wesley's recommendation for proclamation in societies is not only for adults. In 1748 Wesley encouraged children to be gathered into societies of their own in which preachers are to meet "them apart, and [give] them

[73]*Minutes of Conference, Large Minutes*, 1753–63, §6, 10:846.

[74]Ibid. In the 1748 *Minutes* (§4, 10:210) Wesley answers more completely, "The Preacher cannot give proper instructions and exhortations to them that are convinced of sin unless he has opportunities of meeting them apart from the mixed, unawakened multitudes." Early in the Methodist revival most of those who heard field preaching had not awakened. As the movement expanded, more and more who attended field preaching had previously experienced awakening or even repentance and faith leading to justification. It is not surprising then that this phrase was cut in later editions because the crowds were not so "unawakened."

[75]*Journal and Diaries II*, 19 November 1739, 19:122.

[76]*Societies*, "A Plain Account of the People Called Methodists," §1.6, 9:256.

[77]Jackson, *The Life of Mr. Thomas Walsh*, 3:71.

suitable exhortations."[78] While "exhortation" sometimes referred to encouragement, the term was also used to describe lay preachers' "extraordinary" but ecclesially frowned-upon preaching. In other words it was a term to describe their speaking that was in all practical ways preaching, just not officially called that most of the time by Methodists.[79]

But proclamation was not limited to exhortation. Wesley specifically saw society meetings as a way to give spiritual "advices and exhortations."[80] People sought his "advices" and therefore wanted to "pray together, to receive the word of exhortation, and to watch over one another in love, that they might help each other to work out their salvation."[81] Wesley believed that people needed and wanted spiritual direction. Society meetings became a place where Methodists then could receive particular instruction based on their spiritual needs. While the proclamation was still of a general nature compared to what would take place in class meetings, the proclamation was more focused on the law and gospel so those who had awakened in the fields could seek faith, repentance, and holiness.

Not only did Wesley understand proclamation as central to the societies, he also understood the role of instruction and exhortation in them as particularly linked to the early church pattern of life and ministry:

> In the earliest times, those whom God had sent forth "preached the gospel to every creature." And the οἱ ἀκροαταὶ, "the body of hearers," were mostly either Jews or Heathens. But as soon as any of these were so convinced of the truth, as to forsake sin and seek the gospel salvation, they immediately joined them together, took an account of their names, advised them to watch over each other, and met these κατηχουμένοι, "catechumens," (as they were then called,) apart from the great congregation, that they might instruct, rebuke, exhort, and pray with them, and for them, according to their several necessities.[82]

Instruction is the first task. Through instruction people were given guidance on the basics of the Christian life. Society meetings provided an opportunity for religious conversation, but typically it was the preacher or leader who did most of the talking and directing; the meeting was typically a place for preaching.[83]

[78] *Minutes of Conference*, 1748, §62, 10:226.

[79] Heitzenrater, *Wesley and the People Called Methodists*, 113.

[80] *Journal and Diaries IV*, 13 July 1763, 21:478.

[81] *Societies, General Rules*, §2, 9:69.

[82] Ibid.,"A Plain Account of the People called Methodists," §1.10, 9:258.

[83] Heitzenrater, *Wesley and the People Called Methodists*, 111.

Preaching was the most common type of proclamation in society meetings. In fact, it seems that most of Wesley's preaching after the revival cooled occurred in society meetings.[84] The content of preaching in society meetings shifted from an almost total focus on the law to a gradual mixing in of grace. Wesley reflects at one point on the critical importance of preaching perfection to believers in a society:

> The more I converse with the believers in Cornwall, the more I am convinced that they have sustained great loss for want of hearing the doctrine of Christian Perfection clearly and strongly enforced. I see, wherever this is not done, the believers grow dead and cold. Nor can this be prevented, but by keeping up in them an hourly expectation of being perfected in love. I say an hourly expectation; for to expect it at death, or some time hence, is much the same as not expecting it at all.[85]

Morning and evening preaching services quickly became integral to the regular society meetings. These preaching services typically consisted of an opening prayer, a hymn, a sermon, another hymn, and a final prayer. As Heitzenrater notes, these services were not society meetings per se but were gatherings that were associated with societies. For people who committed to the Methodist movement after a field preaching event, they became a regular place for growth that worked in partnership with the society meetings. For those intrigued by field preaching, but not to the point of committing to the Methodist movement, morning and evening preaching became a way to listen regularly to preachers and be part of a worship experience.

Wesley especially encouraged morning preaching, a phenomenon he associated with keeping people spiritually awake. In a letter to Adam Clarke, Wesley writes, "I hope those who were then awakened are not all fallen asleep again. Preaching in the morning is one excellent means of keeping their souls awake."[86] Similarly, he writes to Mr. Merryweather, "It is strange that the number of hearers should decrease, if you have regular preaching. I hope the morning preaching is never omitted. If it be, everything will droop."[87] In 1784 Wesley expressed frustration in his journal upon learning that morning preaching was discontinued in a number of places. Each instance, in Wesley's mind, provided another "proof"

[84]"John Wesley's Principles and Practice of Preaching," 33. Heitzenrater cites the work of Wanda Smith, but does not provide a specific reference.

[85]*Journal and Diaries IV*, 15 September 1762, 21:389.

[86]*Letters* (Telford), Letter to Adam Clarke, 3 January 1787, 7:362.

[87]*Letters III*, Letter to Mr. Merryweather, 5 October 1763, 27:343.

that "Methodists are a fallen people."[88] Without it, "Methodism too will degenerate into a mere sect, only distinguished by some opinions and modes of worship."[89]

Responses to Proclamation in Society Meetings

Wesley's clear expectation is that people would mature in their faith, at every level, in society meetings. And proclamation was central to the meetings. When Wesley preached at societies, he taught people to expect pardon of sin or holiness.[90] He emphasized justification and sanctification within the society because the vast majority of people who joined a Methodist society had not experienced either when they joined. In his study of early Methodist testimonies from the *Methodist Magazine*, Thomas Albin discovered that over half (56.6 percent) of Methodists had only awakened at the time they joined a society.[91]

Wesley recognized this reality. On a number of occasions he notes that only some of the society had awakened before joining, and even fewer had come to repentance and faith or sanctification before joining. He tells of meeting with a society once where he "spoke severally to the members of the society. I found far more life among them than I expected. Near one half of the sixty . . . I judged to be real believers."[92] He writes of another occasion in 1750:

> When the society met, some sinners, whom I knew not, were convicted in their own consciences, so that they could not refrain from confessing their faults in the face of all their brethren. One of these I had but just received in, another I had declared to be excluded; but he pleaded so earnestly to be tried a little longer, that there was no refusing; and we wrestled with God on his behalf that sin might no more have dominion over him.[93]

Others recognized the central role of societies in moving toward faith and conversion. One example is found in a letter from William Seward to probably the first Black Methodist, Scipio Africanus: "I keep your kind and duty full [*sic*] letter and desire continuance of your correspondence and to know how your societies go on and whether you feel your self a sinner yet, if you do you will mourn for a while but you shall

[88] *Journal and Diaries VI*, 4 April 1784, 23:301.

[89] Ibid., 5 April 1784, 23:301.

[90] Ibid., 20 May 1783, 23:269.

[91] Albin, "An Empirical Study of Early Methodist Spirituality," 278.

[92] *Journal and Diaries V*, 13 June 1771, 22:280.

[93] *Journal and Diaries III*, 19 July 1750, 20:352.

soon find comfort such comfort which will fill you with true joy tho not with levity."[94]

Much more than in field preaching, Methodist societies were the place where people encountered the work of the Spirit calling them to faith in Christ and to repent of their sins if they had not done so previously.

Various gatherings of societies encouraged Methodists to embrace the Spirit's calling them to faith and holiness. For instance, some matured during love feasts. Margaret Johnston records in a letter to John Pritchard of conversions during a love feast on Christmas Eve 1778. Early in the evening some attended a class, then evening preaching, and "afterwards a love feast was held at which two deeply convinced of sin received a sense of being pardoned."[95] Wesley records an example of Elizabeth Harper's conversion as she received the Lord's Supper. Wesley records that she became quite fearful of dying from an illness, but nevertheless,

> She soon recovered her health, and from that time sought the Lord with her whole heart, till, on Easter-day, (having joined the society before,) as she was receiving the Lord's supper, these words were strongly applied to her soul: "It is God that justifieth: Who is he that condemneth?" She went home, called her husband, and said, "Now all my sins are forgiven. I am not afraid to die now; for I love God, and I know He loves me."[96]

These various gatherings provided a spiritual environment whereby the Spirit encouraged people, over time, to mature from awakening to a place of repentance and faith. The average time it took early Methodists to mature to the next stage of discipleship, Albin discovered, was two years and four months.[97]

Some people experienced further repentance and faith in society meetings that led to sanctification. Albin's research indicates that around 20 percent claimed an initial experience of sanctification during a society gathering.[98] But the primary response identified in societies is repentance and faith leading to justification.

---

[94]William Seward Letter Book, *MARC*, Letter from William Seward to Scipio Africanus, 26 February 1739, GB 135 DDSe 14, http://archives.li.man.ac.uk/ead/html/gb135ddse-p2.shtml#id3159964. See Lloyd's helpful article on Africanus in Gareth Lloyd, "Scipio Africanus: The First Black Methodist," *Wesley and Methodist Studies* 3 (2011): 87–95.

[95]*Catalogue of the Wesley Family Letters, MARC*. Letter from Margaret Johnston to John Pritchard, 28 January 1779, 9/75.

[96]Wesley, *Works* (Jackson), An Extract from the Journal of Elizabeth Harper, §4, 14:263.

[97]Albin, "An Empirical Study of Early Methodist Spirituality," 278. Albin documents that the median time from awakening to justification was one year and the mean was 2.4 years.

[98]Ibid., 278.

The Relationship between Field Preaching and Societies

Wesley always understood field preaching and society meetings as working in tandem. Wesley was aware of the relationship between the two contexts of field preaching and society meetings. He discusses this relationship on a number of occasions:

> I rode to Ennis, but found the preaching had been discontinued, and the society was vanished away. So having no business there, I left it in the morning.[99]

> Through the continual neglect of the Preachers, the congregation was reduced almost to nothing; and so was the society.[100]

> I found a little increase in the society: But there cannot be much without more field-preaching. Wherever this is intermitted, the work of God stands still, if it does not go back.[101]

> I set out, and on Tuesday reached Bristol. After spending two days there, on Friday, 27, I set out for the west; and having preached at Shepton and Middlesey in the way, came on Saturday to Exeter. When I began the service there, the congregation (beside ourselves) were two women, and one man. Before I had done, the Room was about half full. This comes of omitting field-preaching.[102]

> Q. 55. How can we account for the decrease of the work of God in some Circuits, both this year and the last?
>
> A. It may be owing either, (1.) To the want of zeal and exactness in the Assistant, occasioning want of discipline throughout: Or (2.) To want of life and diligence in the Preachers: Or (3.) To our people's losing the life of God, and sinking into the spirit of the world. It may be owing, farther, to the want of more field-preaching, and of trying more new places.[103]

In Wesley's mind field preaching and society meetings had a symbiotic relationship. As noted at the beginning of the chapter, field preaching without a corresponding link to a smaller community where people could watch over one another in love was considered by Wesley to be a waste of time. As Wesley asked in 1753, "Is it advisable for us to preach [in the

[99] *Journal and Diaries V*, 9 May 1767, 22:80.

[100] Ibid., 8 June 1769, 22:186.

[101] Ibid., 26 June 1769, 22:190.

[102] *Journal and Diaries IV*, 23 August 1762, 21:386.

[103] *Minutes of Conference, Large Minutes*, 1780–89, §55, 10:926–27.

fields] in as many places as we can, without forming any societies? [Answer]. By no means. We have made the trial in various places; and that for a considerable time. But all the seed has fallen as by the highway side. There is scarce any fruit remaining."[104]

The correlation was clear. Preaching to large crowds was not an end in itself. Rather, the goal was to encourage people to join a society so that they could mature in their faith. The work of the fields must be followed with the work of the society; otherwise, those who awaken often, and perhaps usually, fall asleep again.[105] As Wesley recounts in his journal,

> I went in the morning in order to speak severally with the members of the society at Tanfield. From the terrible instances I met with here, (and indeed in all parts of England,) I am more and more convinced, that the devil himself desires nothing more than this, that the people of any place should be half-awakened, and then left to themselves to fall asleep again. Therefore I determine, by the grace of God, not to strike one stroke in any place where I cannot follow the blow.[106]

From 1748 to the end of Wesley's life, he understood the symbiotic relationship between field preaching and Methodist societies. The heart of the relationship was proclamation. Any good done through proclamation in the fields was undone if it was not reinforced and elaborated upon in society meetings.

CONCLUSION

Had John Wesley not been willing to take the "vile" step of field preaching the Methodist movement would never have awakened so many people and would never have taken off as it did. But field preaching as an isolated ministry was ineffective in helping people mature from the state of nature and awakening to a faith and repentance that led to justification, followed by a sanctification marked by deeper faith and repentance. Yet keeping them awake and helping them mature was impossible through field preaching alone. Therefore Wesley adopted a common practice in England and modified it according to his particular understanding of the ends of discipleship and the process by which most people mature as

[104]Ibid., *Large Minutes*, 1753–63, §5, 10:845.

[105]Laceye C. Warner, "Spreading Scriptural Holiness: Theology and Practices of Early Methodism for the Contemporary Church," *The Asbury Journal* 63, no. 1 (2008): 119. She writes, "The results of the experiment were unequivocal. Christian formation provided by the Methodist small groups normalized by John Wesley allowed a significant number of those moved by the revival's preaching to be nurtured and maintained in the faith. When these groups were not accessible, those moved by the preaching were often lost."

[106]*Journal and Diaries II*, 13 March 1743, 19:318.

disciples. The result was a framework for ministry in which people came into societies, typically through field preaching events, and then watched over one another's spiritual life with the hope of maturing in holiness of heart and life. They were the forum in which most Methodists made their true commitment to Christ—not the fields. Integral to each society were the regular society meetings, and one of the engines that in turn drove those meetings was proclamation. But proclamation in societies was not limited to the regular meetings of the society as a whole. Proclamation also played an important role in smaller gatherings of society members, an understanding of which is critical to any description of Wesley's vision of evangelism. To these smaller gatherings, the Methodist class meeting, the conversation now turns.

CHAPTER 6

CLASS MEETINGS

From long experience I know the propriety of Mr. Wesley's advice, "Establish class-meetings and form societies wherever you preach [in the fields] and have attentive hearers: for, wherever we have preached without doing so, the word has been like seed by the way-side."[1]

Wesley's 1745 experiment of field preaching in an area without also starting corresponding societies was a failure. But societies were just one element of Methodism that Wesley thought needed to be linked intimately with field preaching. Another element, this one a new addition to British religious life, also needed to be linked—the class meeting. In order for the word to take root in people's souls, it had to be proclaimed and then nurtured in societies and classes.

Since the 1980s the class meeting has been revived as a topic worthy of study both in the academy and in the local church. The work of David Lowes Watson, Tom Albin, D. Michael Henderson, and others has served to call the church to reclaim this central Wesleyan practice. More recent explorations of another important small group—Methodist band meetings—especially by Kevin Watson and Andrew Thompson, have offered compelling visions of early Methodist bands and called the church to reexamine the importance of regularly gathering Methodists who have experienced the New Birth and seek perfect love of God and people. Both classes and bands played a vital role in the movement:

> Never omit meeting your class or band; never absent yourself from any public meeting. These are the very sinews of our Society. And whatever weakens or tends to weaken our regard for these, or our exactness in attending them, strikes at the very root of our community. As one saith, "God only could have been the Author of that part of our economy, the private weekly meetings for prayer, examination, and particular exhortation. It was above the

[1]John Wesley Etheridge, *The Life of the Rev. Adam Clarke* (London: John Mason, 1858), 165. Adam Clarke commenting on Wesley's understanding of the relationships among field preaching, society meetings, and class meetings.

> reach of mere human thought, and been the greatest means of deepening and confirming every blessing that was received by the word preached, and of diffusing it to others who could not attend the public ministry. Whereas, without this religious connection and intercourse, the most ardent attempts by mere preaching have proved of no lasting use."[2]

Classes and bands became, as Wesley describes above, the "sinews" that held Methodism together. Their place in what Wesley calls "private economy," namely, that part of Methodism that occurred in smaller gatherings apart from field preaching and Methodist society meetings, is critical to understanding Wesley's evangelistic vision of offering Christ. Proclamation and maturity through discipleship are more evident in classes and so classes receive more focus in this chapter, but proclamation did occur at times in bands.

Classes and bands had some remarkable similarities and differences both in design and ends. Classes were made up of usually seven to twelve people, of mixed gender and marital status, from all "states of grace," be it awakened, convinced, justified, or sanctified. Bands usually consisted of about four people, grouped by gender, each of whom had experienced the New Birth and sought perfect love. Bands were the first small groups in the Methodist movement, and as late as 1781 he writes that "no society will continue lively without them."[3]

And yet class meetings, and not band meetings, ultimately became the defining small group experience for Methodists. Beginning in 1743 class membership was required for all Methodists, something that was not ever true of bands. Bands became less central to the movement over time, at least as determined by the number of participants, and they fell out of favor in Methodism much quicker than did classes, which continued in England and Britain for most of the nineteenth century.

This chapter marks a shift in the book to these two more "private" aspects of the Methodist structure. Field preaching was a public gathering where anyone who could get to the gathering was invited. Society meetings were still large group gatherings, though only open to people who sought to grow in their faith following the Methodist principles and patterns. Class meetings and private visitation were much more intimate, allowing the opportunity for in-depth conversation about the joys and travails of life and faith. Proclamation was integral to these two forums, and therefore both necessitate thorough analysis in this discussion of Wesley's evangelistic vision.

---

[2]*Treatises II*, Farther Thoughts upon Christian Perfection, §I.37, 13:120.

[3]*Letters* (Telford), Letter to Edward Jackson, 16 January 1781, 7:47.

HERITAGE OF SMALL GROUPS IN WESLEY'S LIFE

Unlike Methodist societies, for which there was precedent in the Church of England, the small groups that came to define Methodism, namely, classes and bands, had little, if any, precursor in British religious life. But a number of experiences helped form Wesley's understanding of the importance of discipleship in small, intimate gatherings of people committed to the pursuit of the Christian life.

Wesley's experience growing up with Samuel and Susanna Wesley as parents, along with his ten brothers and sisters, was itself instrumental in shaping his understanding. John's parents embraced the Puritan passion for the "care and cure of souls" quite strictly. His parents believed that they were responsible for their children's spiritual development. While Samuel took a more traditional role, especially as a cleric, Susanna exerted a strong influence over her children's spiritual lives. She learned from her father, who viewed the family as itself a Christian community, "where prayer, Bible-reading, catechizing, and detailed private instruction in the Christian faith" were integral to family life.[4] She spent at least one hour a week with each of her children, guiding their spiritual development. John's hour was typically on Thursday evenings, and he seems to have appreciated these times of direction and conversation.[5] Her oversight tended toward warmth and intimacy instead of formality, but it was still quite intentional.[6]

Wesley's later incorporation of classes and bands was also influenced by his time in a small community of Christians in Oxford. In 1729 he returned to Oxford to begin his appointment as a Fellow at Lincoln College. Charles was still a student at Oxford, and he, along with two other young men, gathered regularly, typically four nights a week, to read together from the classics and the Greek New Testament. Charles invited John to join the group soon after John returned, and it was not long until John assumed leadership of the group.

Within a short time John quickly changed the focus of the group. Under his leadership the group added more personal aspects of devotion, including prayer, fasting, confession, and communion, to their reading regimen. The group also initiated more public types of ministry, such as providing clothes and money for the poor. On William Morgan's initiative, the group also began visiting the sick, the elderly, and those in prison. Each of these elements became such a regular part of the group's corporate life that other students began deriding the group, calling them "The

[4]John A. Newton, *Susanna Wesley and the Puritan Tradition in Methodism* (London: Epworth, 1968), 53.

[5]Ibid., 77.

[6]Henderson, 38.

Bible Moths," "The Holy Club," and even "Methodists." While intended in a derogatory way, the final term so appropriately portrayed the group that Wesley embraced it, and his heirs claim the name to this day.

The Holy Club began as a small group of only three or four. Within a few years, though, there was a fluctuating group of ten or so who gathered regularly. In 1735 John, along with the other members of the Holy Club, was invited to go to Georgia to serve with General Oglethorpe as religious leaders in the region. Charles actually accepted the assignment first, agreeing to go to Georgia as General Oglethorpe's secretary. Charles convinced John to come along as the colonialist's chaplain. Benjamin Ingham accepted an invitation as well, joining John, Charles, and the new recruit, Charles Delamotte, all of whom departed England on October 21, 1735.

The remaining members of the Holy Club kept meeting in England for a few years, with George Whitefield taking leadership of the group. When Wesley returned from Georgia, he met with some of the members, recording in his journal:

> Soon after I returned to England I had a meeting with Messrs. Ingham, Stonehouse, Hall, Hutchins, Kinchin, and a few other clergymen, who all appeared to be of one heart, as well as of one judgment, resolved to be Bible-Christians at all events, and, wherever they were, to preach, with all their might, plain old Bible-Christianity.[7]

That original "Holy Club," which began with a cognitive emphasis on academic books but evolved to include various aspects of devotion associated with Christian discipleship, shaped Wesley's understanding of small discipleship groups.

While the Holy Club was a formative experience for Wesley, it was not the only spiritual group of this time that helped develop his understanding of the critical importance of smaller communities of committed people for ongoing discipleship. On board the *Simmonds* was a group of Moravians who came to help shape his ministry.

The Moravians, known more accurately as the Church of the Brethren, were a German Pietist movement that traced their origins to Philipp Jakob Spener. Spener made small, intense Christian study groups, which he called *collegia pietatis*, an important part of the Moravian movement. Later leaders added tangible acts of charity to the home study groups. General Oglethorpe came to know of the Moravians through the German Count Ludwig von Zinzendorf. At Oglethorpe's invitation, some twenty-six Moravians ventured to Georgia, on board the *Simmonds*, sailing on the same trip as John and Charles.

On the small ship John got to know many of the other travelers,

[7]*Societies*, "Short History of the People Called Methodists," §9, 9:369.

especially the Moravians. He grew to appreciate their hymn singing, simplicity, and devotion. Just a week out from Savannah, the ship encountered a terrible storm that solidified Wesley's admiration. As John and others became scared, the Moravians seemed calm, passing the time with singing. John records in his journal entry of January 25, 1736,

> The sea broke over, split the mainsail in pieces, covered the ship, and poured in between decks, as if the great deep had already swallowed us up. A terrible screaming began among the English. The Germans calmly sung on. I asked one of them afterwards, "Was you not afraid?" He answered, "I thank God, no." I asked, "But were not your women and children afraid?" He replied, mildly, "No; our women and children are not afraid to die."[8]

For the next few years John looked to the Moravians as a unique specimen of Christian discipleship that he sought to emulate personally, and he incorporated their practices into Methodism at some key points.

Wesley continued to meet with Moravians in Georgia, and they were to play another critical role upon his return to England. But his ministry in Georgia also helped form his understanding of classes and bands. As he established societies in Savannah and Fredericka for "the more serious" of the congregation, as noted in the previous chapter, he saw the need for even smaller groups in order to encourage discipleship. Therefore he also selected from the society "a smaller number for a more intimate union with each other, which might be forwarded, partly by our conversing singly with each, and partly by inviting them all together to our house; and this, accordingly, we determined to do every Sunday in the afternoon."[9] Once again, the importance of smaller gatherings within a larger, committed group of people seeking Christ was made evident to Wesley.

Soon after John's return to England in the spring of 1738, he became involved with the new Fetter Lane Society, which Böhler called together on May 1 of that year. A few weeks later, on May 24, Wesley had his experience at Aldersgate Street following a Bible study. The experience was so significant that, after about three weeks, he set off for Germany in order to learn more from the Moravians. He met Count Zinzendorf and observed Moravian practices in Herrnhut. He noted their division into small groups—"bands" and "classes," as they were termed—for spiritual oversight.[10] Wesley records in his journal a number of elements he found important:

[8] *Journal and Diaries I,* 25 January 1736, 18:143.

[9] Ibid., 17 April 1736, 18:157.

[10] Clifford W. Towlson, *Moravian and Methodist: Relationships and Influences in the Eighteenth Century* (London: Epworth, 1957), 185.

II. The people of Herrnhut are divided; (1) Into five male classes, viz., the little children, the middle children, the big children, the young men, and the married. The females are divided in the same manner. (2) Into eleven classes, according to the houses where they live; and in each class is an Helper, an Overseer, a Monitor, an Almoner, and a Servant. (3) Into about ninety Bands, each of which meets twice at least, but most of them three times a week, to "confess their faults one to another, and pray for one another, that they may be healed."

III. The rulers of the church, i.e., the Elders, Teachers, and Helpers (all chosen by the congregation), have a conference every week, purely concerning the state of souls, and another concerning the institution of youth.[11]

First, classes were organized by geographic location, gender, and age, meaning members often knew one another and shared personal aspects of discipleship with that smaller community. Second, confession and prayer were part of the gatherings. Third, Wesley saw how the larger society needed to be divided into classes for more personal direction, and an even more intimate gathering of bands for further oversight: "These larger are also (now) divided into near ninety smaller classes or bands, over each of which one presides who is of the greatest experience. All these Leaders meet the Senior every week, and lay open to him and to the Lord whatsoever hinders or furthers the work of God in the souls committed to their charge."[12] The result is that by the time Wesley returned to England in September of that year, he had seen the importance of small groups for more than a decade.

Upon his return to England in September 1738, he again connected with a number of societies, including the "new" Fetter Lane Society. The immediate precursors to the Methodist small groups that formed the next year in the Foundery Society were the bands that formed in the Fetter Lane Society in 1738. While the society originally seemed to have been made up of only men, by mid-October the society had both women and men on the rolls. The society as a whole met weekly for large gatherings that focused on teaching and included little or no actual discussion. But twice a week the society members gathered into gender-specific "bands" of four to eight persons. The purpose of these initial bands was more conversational and interactive than was the case in the larger meetings of the society. Bands were a place to gather to pursue both justification and sanctification. Lay leaders were guided by the specific set of questions in the *Rules* that encouraged people to share their feelings about the joys and struggles of their life of faith. All members shared their responses, and in turn other members would comment as appropriate with words

[11]*Journal and Diaries I*, 11–14 August 1738, 18:292.

[12]Ibid., 11–14 August 1738, 18:295.

of encouragement, support, and suggestions.[13] While teaching was more central to the larger society meetings, the bands included exhortation, just in a more personal and intimate way.

Wesley wrote down his "Rules of the Band Societies" in December 1738.[14] Again, the title of the document is a bit confusing because the rules are quite different from the *General Rules of the United Societies*, which Wesley recorded in 1743 and that are more closely related to the practices of Methodist bands as the movement matured. These *Rules* show the maturation of the Rules for the Fetter Lane Society, which had been adjusted at least twice since their inception.[15] The *Rules* are as follows:[16]

> The design of our meeting is, to obey that command of God, "Confess your faults one to another, and pray one for another, that ye may be healed" [James 5:16].
>
> To this end, we intend:
>
> 1. To meet once a week, at the least.
>
> 2. To come punctually at the hour appointed, without some extraordinary reason.
>
> 3. To begin (those of us who are present) exactly at the hour, with singing or prayer.
>
> 4. To speak each of us in order, freely and plainly, the true state of our souls, with the faults we have committed in thought, word, or deed, and the temptations we have felt, since our last meeting.
>
> 5. To end every meeting with prayer, suited to the state of each person present.
>
> 6. To desire some person among us to speak *his*[17] own state first, and then to ask the rest in order as many and as searching questions as may be, concerning their state, sins, and temptations.
>
> Some of the questions proposed to every one before *he* is admitted among us may be to this effect:
>
> 1. Have you the forgiveness of your sins?
>
> 2. Have you peace with God, through our Lord Jesus Christ?
>
> 3. Have you the witness of God's Spirit with your spirit, that you are a child of God?

[13] Henderson, 66.

[14] Heitzenrater, *Wesley and the People Called Methodists*, 90. Heitzenrater speculates the correct date for these may actually be 25 December 1739.

[15] *Societies*, "Rules of the Band Societies," 9:79.

[16] Ibid., 9:77–78.

[17] Ibid., 9:77. In note 2 the editors write, "The italics are used here . . . to indicate that the alternative 'her' may be substituted as necessary."

4. Is the love of God shed abroad in your heart?

5. Has no sin, inward or outward, dominion over you?

6. Do you desire to be told of your faults?

7. Do you desire to be told of all your faults, and that plain and home?

8. Do you desire that every one of us should tell you, from time to time, whatsoever is in his heart concerning you?

9. Consider! Do you desire we should tell you whatsoever we think, whatsoever we fear, whatsoever we hear, concerning you?

10. Do you desire that, in doing this, we should come as close as possible, that we should cut to the quick, and search your heart to the bottom?

11. Is it your desire and design to be on this, and all other occasions, entirely open, so as to speak everything that is in your heart without exception, without disguise, and without reserve?

Any of the preceding questions may be asked as often as occasion offers; but Wesley directed Methodists to ask the five following questions at every meeting:

1. What known sins have you committed since our last meeting?

2. What temptations have you met with?

3. How were you delivered?

4. What have you thought, said, or done, of which you doubt whether it be sin or not?

5. Have you nothing you desire to keep secret?[18]

Using the questions as a guide at each meeting, each member shared the state of his or her spiritual life, with the others in the group responding with encouragement and suggestions. While membership was open to all, any person who wanted to join had to listen to and then affirm the thirty-three articles, and then agree to a two-month trial membership. A few other highlights are worth pointing out. First, the group met regularly, at least once a week. Second, the focus is confession. Furthermore, the book of James became a consistent reference point to justify these smaller types of gatherings for the rest of Wesley's ministry.[19] Finally, the interaction in the group was quite pointed and personal. Each member was expected not only to receive challenging questions and advice but also to give it.

[18]Ibid., 9:77–78. The last five questions are not in all editions.

[19]Ibid., 9:77. See the preamble that states that the society was formed "In Obedience to the Command of God by St. James [James 5:16, 'Confess your faults to one another, and pray for one another that ye may be healed.']"

The formalizing of these rules in late 1738 helped establish the critical role of smaller communities of four to twelve persons, made up of members of the larger societies, in the Methodist framework of discipleship.

Wesley's experience with the Moravians, as well as his previous experience growing up in his family and as a member of the Holy Club at Oxford, helped him recognize that large groups such as society meetings did not themselves provide a suitable framework for ongoing discipleship. Rather, smaller, more personal communities, with specific practices and particular ends, were necessary. As Methodism developed, the two groups that came to function as a framework for such discipleship were bands and classes.

BAND MEETINGS

Development and Purpose

The first small group to develop that became part of Methodism's "private economy" were the band meetings. Wesley had observed the Moravian incorporation of small "bands" of four to eight persons as the primary small gatherings that encouraged discipleship and fellowship. In 1738 and 1739 he sought a way for those involved in the societies to "watch over" one another. One type of band, the Trial Band, provided a place for people to become acquainted with the Methodist movement before joining and officially joining a society and class. Membership in these trial bands was open to all people, whether awakened, converted, or sanctified. The bulk of the bands, however, were not trial bands, and were only for people who had experienced a certain depth of faith.

Wesley describes the development of bands in "A Plain Account of the People Called Methodists."[20] Many Methodists, having "found the pearl of great price" and being "justified by faith…felt a more tender affection than before to those who were partakers of like precious faith; and hence arose such a confidence in each other that they poured out their souls into each other's bosom." He observed many who experienced the New Birth desiring to gather together to encourage one another in seeking "closer union" with God and one another. Recognizing that "the war [with sin] was not over, as they had supposed," they gathered for confession, or as Wesley calls it here the pouring of "their souls into each other's bosoms." Thus an important purpose of these bands, at least in the beginning, was confession.

In order to provide an environment conducive to confession, Wesley divided the bands according to gender, marital status, and spiritual experience. The goal was to help one another live a holy life—to deal with one's sin so that one could live a life of perfect love for God and neighbor.

[20]Ibid., "A Plain Account of the People called Methodists," §VI–VII, 9:266–69.

Wesley describes the "chief" rules for the bands in "A Plain Account of the People Called Methodists" where he lists five of the six Rules for the Band Societies, omitting only the fifth which encouraged leaders to end meetings in prayer.[21] The goal of the bands was to provide a forum for confession and prayer, which, Wesley believed, would lead to the healing God desires.

The opening of the members' hearts and souls, part of which involved confession, was essential to the band. Margaret Austin describes the phenomenon in a letter to Charles Wesley: "The first night we met [in the band], hearing the others tell the state of their souls, it was of much strength to me to speak the state of mine."[22] Along with confession, speaking into one another's lives (what Wesley often called "searching conversations") was another significant aspect of band meetings. Band meetings were a place where band members could search one another's hearts "to the bottom." Elizabeth Sais describes Charles Wesley's personal questions during a band meeting:

> You ask'd me if I was not troubled with Self and Pride, which Struck me as Dead, for I knew not what Answer. And when I came under the word, I found it to be Quick and Powerful and Sharper than any Two Edg'd Sword…I was So Sensibly cut by it as my Body might be by a Sword, and would often wish to withdraw my Self from Such Searching.[23]

Bands were a place for people to speak to one another, sharing their challenges, failures, and successes, and receiving direction on how to improve.

A number of other gatherings took place periodically and were comprised primarily of people in various bands. Love feasts, for instance, were initially gatherings of band members in a society to partake of bread and water. Once a quarter the men would gather together, on another day women from the various bands in a society, and on a third day all the men and women from the society who were in bands would gather together.

Another group related to bands are the "select society" or "select bands." Around May 21, 1741, Wesley began grouping together people who had experienced forgiveness of sin through repentance and who were thus on the path toward Christian perfection. They, therefore, did not need rules or even much direction. In the select societies, even more

[21]Ibid., §VI.3, 9:267.

[22]"Early Methodist Volume, British Methodist Archives, John Rylands Library, Special Collections, University of Manchester," Letter from Margaret Austin to Charles Wesley, 19 May 1740, 1.

[23]Jonathan Barry and Kenneth Morgan, *Reformation and Revival in Eighteenth-Century Bristol* (Stroud, U.K.: Bristol Record Society, 1994), 97.

than in the regular bands, everyone had "equal liberty" both to speak and to "watch over [each other] in love." Wesley looked to some select band members as his confidants, and in many ways these select bands or societies became the engines of holiness in the Methodist machine.

Methodists did not universally embrace bands or classes in the beginning. Some objected that confession was "popery." Wesley responded by arguing that Methodist confession is not one person to another, but one before a group. Others objected that both groups were new additions to Methodism that had not been required in the beginning. Still others argued that both were human inventions not found in scripture. Wesley's response was that both are "prudential" helps "grounded on reason and experience, in order to apply the general rules given in Scripture, according to particular circumstances."[24] In other words, bands and classes are not themselves mandated by scripture, and are not therefore required in every age, of every Christian. Since Wesley found them helpful for discipleship in his own age, though, he thought it appropriate to build them into Methodism, including making classes mandatory throughout his life. Bands remained important to Wesley, but they were not mandatory for Methodists after the incorporation of class meetings in 1743.

Proclamation in Bands

In Wesley's vision of communal formation, band meetings were primarily a place of mutual encouragement in the pursuit of a holy life. They were not, primarily, a place of proclamation and thus are only touched upon briefly in this book. In fact, in "The Principles of a Methodist Farther Explained," Wesley states that neither band leaders nor members are "set upon expounding Scripture."[25] Nevertheless, proclamation did sometimes occur in band meetings. Wesley explicitly records, for instance, in "A Plain Account of the People called Methodists" that bands were designed so that women and men "might receive such particular instructions and exhortations as, from time to time, might appear to be most needful for them."[26] Numerous times in Wesley's journals he describes visiting bands and "exhorting" the members. He writes to one band member, "You must *search*, and find out why they are slack; exhort them to repent, be zealous, do the first works. The former you may only have to encourage, to exhort, to push forward to the mark, to bid them grasp the prize so nigh!"[27]

[24]*Societies*, "A Plain Account of the People Called Methodists," §VI.7, 9:268.

[25]Ibid., "The Principles of a Methodist Farther Explained," §III.6, 9:192.

[26]Ibid., "A Plain Account of the People called Methodists," §VI.4, 9:267.

[27]*Letters* (Telford), Letter to Jane Catherine March, 13 May 1762, 4:181.

Doughty compared Wesley's journals and diary and reports "that Wesley preached on every possible occasion and always expounded a text when meeting the Society and the Bands."[28] This type of proclamation is especially evident in some penitent band meetings. Penitent bands were for people who had strayed from Methodist teachings, and sometimes had even fallen out of justifying or sanctifying grace. When people reverted in their spiritual lives and sought sanctification once again, band members would exhort and instruct them personally or "closely," based on their spiritual need.

This is an appropriate place to discuss testimony, for testimony was an important aspect of a number of Methodist gatherings, perhaps none more so than the band meeting. Methodist testimonies were short descriptions, either verbal or written, of a person's recent spiritual experience. Many are recorded in journals of Methodist members or letters to the Wesleys, but many were also delivered in bands and other gatherings. Watson writes, "Testimonies were often contagious in early Methodism. When one person spoke of their experience of God, other people who heard the testimony often had a similar experience."[29] Testimonies are not discussed at length in this book because they emphasized a person's spiritual experience more than specific teaching or exhortation. The emphasis was more on sharing their own joys, struggles, and sin, as opposed to specifically telling the story of God as found in the Bible. But testimonies are worth touching upon at this point, because even just sharing their own experience encouraged others in a band to mature in their faith.

Most of the time the maturity is demonstrated through deeper experiences of sanctification. John Oliver recounts the nature of one band conversation:

> Some of them [society members] had just began [*sic*] to meet in band, and invited me to meet with them. Here, one of them speaking of the wickedness of his heart, I was greatly surprised; telling them, I felt no such things, my heart being kept in peace and love all the day long. But it was not a week before I felt the swelling of pride, and the storms of anger and self-will: so when I met again, I could speak the same language with them. We sympathized with each other, prayed for each other, and believed, God was both able and willing to purify our hearts from all sin.[30]

[28]Doughty, *John Wesley, Preacher*, 185.

[29]Watson, *Pursuing Social Holiness: The Band Meeting in Wesley's Thought and Popular Methodist Practice*, 133.

[30]John Oliver, "An Account of Mr. John Oliver, Written by Himself," *Arminian Magazine* 2 (1779): 419–20.

Sometimes, however, testimonies in band meetings facilitated experiences bordering on conversion for those who had not come to a point of faith and repentance. An interesting example of the role of testimony, and people's response to it, is demonstrated in a letter from Lawrence Coughlan to John Wesley. In the letter Coughlan tells of a "meeting of the Bands," perhaps a love feast, where a band member, "Old Mr. Pritchard," told of his experience at one of Wesley's sermons. Coughlan narrates Pritchard's testimony:

> For some time I [Pritchard] have been longing for a clean heart; yet I thought God would not give it to so vile a sinner. And the first night Mr. W. preached, I felt something across my heart, like an iron bar, cold and hard. But hearing Mr. W. insist on the word *now*, I said, Lord, here I am a poor sinner. I believe thou canst save me *now*, and give me a clean heart. In that moment Jesus said to my soul, *I will: be thou clean*. Immediately that bar was broken, and all my soul was filled with love: nor could I doubt but Jesus had made me clean, through the word which he had spoken to my soul.[31]

What is truly interesting for this discussion is the words that then follow. Coughlan goes on to write that immediately after Pritchard gave his testimony, "three more were enabled, before we parted, to declare the same." People responded to Pritchard's testimony with their own experience of sanctification or justification.

Examples of justification at band meetings is interesting considering that band meetings, especially after the introduction of class meetings in the early 1740s, were open only to people who experienced initial repentance and faith. Wesley initially designed regular bands (as opposed to penitent or trial bands) as a place for people who had received the gift of justification. And yet, at least before 1743, sometimes people were admitted, even if there was an acknowledgment that they shouldn't be. Watson documents two cases, those of Sarah Barber and Margaret Austin, who were admitted before they came to faith and assurance.[32] Austin writes of her justification after joining a band, "As I was arising the voice of the Lord Said to me thy Sins are forgiven twice—over I heard it a third time—Daughter be of good cheer—thy Sins are forgiven thee: then I felt old things passing away and all things becoming new."[33] As Watson demonstrates, even though bands were designed before 1743 as a place of sanctification, the reality is that there was not a proper forum for the many who

[31]Lawrence Coughlan, Letter to John Wesley, 12 April 1762, *Arminian Magazine* 4:337–38 (emphasis original).

[32]Watson, *Pursuing Social Holiness: The Band Meeting in Wesley's Thought and Popular Methodist Practice*, 108–09.

[33]Ibid., 108.

had yet to experience justification after awakening during field preaching. Therefore, at least in some cases, bands became a place for people who were "earnestly seeking forgiveness," as well as for those seeking justification.[34] But the typical person experienced awakening and conversion as a precursor to joining a band.

Sometimes even a person who joined a band needed to reexperience justification, or even awakening. Wesley was convinced that many in bands actually regressed in their faith:

> While most of these who were thus intimately joined together went on daily from faith to faith, some fell from the faith, either all at once, by falling into known, wilful sin, or gradually and almost insensibly, by giving way in what they called little things—by sins of omission, by yielding to heart sins, or by not watching unto prayer.[35]

Wesley therefore began "penitent" bands for people who had relapsed in their faith. These people needed and wanted different "hymns, exhortations, and prayers . . . adapted to their circumstances; being wholly suited to those who *did* see God, but have now lost the light of his countenance; and who mourn after him, and refuse to be comforted till they know he has healed all their backsliding."[36]

Those in penitent bands once again needed to be confronted with both the law and the gospel: "By applying both the threats and promises of God to these real (not nominal) *penitents*, and by crying to God in their behalf, we endeavoured to bring them back to the great 'Shepherd and Bishop of their souls.'"[37] The result of the penitent bands was that many reclaimed their faith:

> Many of these soon recovered the ground they had lost. Yea, they rose higher than before; being more watchful than ever, and more meek and lowly, as well as stronger in the faith worketh by love. They now outran the greater part of brethren, continually walking in the light of God, and having fellowship with the Father, and with his Son, Jesus Christ.[38]

From 1738 to 1743, bands were the only forum in which Methodists gathered regularly in small groups to mature as disciples. While bands continued for the rest of Wesley's life, and while he continued to encourage

[34]Ibid., 110. Watson cites William Seward's ms. diary, 17 September 1740. The diary is yet to be published and is held at Chetham's Library in Manchester, England, Ref: A.2.116.

[35]*Societies*, "A Plain Account of the People Called Methodists," §VII.1, 9:268–69.

[36]Ibid., §VII.2, 9:269 (emphasis original).

[37]Ibid.

[38]Ibid.

Methodists to participate in them, in 1743 another type of small group began that brought significant changes to the Methodist pattern of disciple-making: the class meeting.

CLASS MEETINGS

My brother Wesley acted wisely. The souls that were awakened under his ministry he joined in class, and thus preserved the fruit of his labour. This I neglected, and my people are a rope of sand.[39]

—George Whitefield

The single most important entrepreneurial act of Methodism was the creation of Methodist class meetings. They were the required element of Methodism's "private economy." The class meetings, which began as a building project fund-raising effort and had little or no precedent in British religious life, changed the course of the Methodist movement and shaped Methodism for generations to come. Wesley recognized the importance of classes soon after he incorporated them into Methodism. "I can never sufficiently praise God; the unspeakable usefulness of the institution [the class meeting] having ever since been more and more manifest."[40] Asbury and Coke would later refer to classes as "the pillars of our work [and] our universities for the ministry."[41] In 1948 the Methodist historian Leslie Church referred to classes as the "crowning glory" of Methodism, having "done more than any other Methodist organization to influence the world."[42] D. Michael Henderson refers to class meetings as the backbone of the Methodist reformation.[43] Kevin Watson, in his recent book that reconsiders the importance of Methodist bands, argues that a "strong case can be made that the class meeting was the single most important factor to the growth of early Methodism and to the retention of converts within Methodism."[44]

While the importance of classes is well known, the role of proclamation in them, their role in nurturing discipleship and their relationship to visitation are less established. In this section we will explore the

[39]Doughty, *John Wesley, Preacher,* 57.

[40]*Journal and Diaries II,* 25 March 1742, 19:258.

[41]Francis Asbury and Thomas Coke, *The Doctrines and Discipline of the Methodist Episcopal Church in America: With Explanatory Notes by Thomas Coke and Francis Asbury,* 10th ed. (Philadelphia: Henry Tuckniss, 1798), 140.

[42]Leslie F. Church, *The Early Methodist People,* Fernley-Hartley Lecture (London: Epworth, 1948), 153.

[43]Henderson, 28.

[44]Watson, *The Class Meeting: Reclaiming a Forgotten (and Essential) Small Group Experience* (Wilmore: Seedbed, 2014), Kindle location 372.

development of classes, their structure and purpose, and especially the role of proclamation and the nature of maturity as a disciple of Christ in classes.

Development

By late 1741 and early 1742, the Methodists in Bristol needed money. The United Society there had accumulated debt in their acquisition of a meeting place. Up to this point Methodism consisted primarily of the two United Societies in Bristol and London, as well as a number of bands scattered in those two cities and a few other places. Field preaching was commonplace in many parts of the country, but other than the few bands, and these two societies, there existed no other structural framework in which Methodists gathered. With the debt in Bristol a new plan was necessary.

Someone, perhaps Wesley himself, but more likely a Captain Foy (whom Wesley later gave the credit to), came up with an idea to pay off the debt in February 1742. His plan was to divide the society into smaller groups of about twelve people regardless of gender or marital status, all of whom lived in geographic proximity to one another. Of the twelve, one leader in whom Wesley "could most confide" would be chosen. That leader would then be responsible for visiting each class member every week in order to collect a penny from each person. Furthermore, the leader was charged, as Wesley describes in "A Plain Account of the People Called Methodists,"

> (1.) To see each person in his class, once a week at the least, in order to inquire how their souls prosper; to advise, reprove, comfort, or exhort, as occasion may require; to receive what they are willing to give, toward the relief of the poor.
>
> (2.) To meet the Minister and the Stewards of the society, in order to inform the Minister of any that are sick, or of any that are disorderly and will not be reproved; to pay to the Stewards what they have received of their several classes in the week preceding.[45]

In "Thoughts Upon Methodism" Wesley credits Foy as the person who suggested that the poorest could not give. Foy offered to take the eleven poorest in his group and to pay their penny for them, thereby encouraging other leaders to make up the difference in their classes as well.[46]

Wesley quickly embraced the practice, making it normative first

[45]*Societies*, "A Plain Account of the People Called Methodists," §I.5, 9:261. Wesley summarizes the development of the class meetings in ibid., "Thoughts Upon Methodism," 9:527–30, and ibid., *General Rules*, 9:69–71.

[46]Ibid., "Thoughts Upon Methodism," 9:528.

in Bristol and then in London. But after a few months four problems became evident. First, visiting people in their homes each week, even though they lived close to one another, was simply too time consuming, and many of the leaders struggled to visit on a weekly basis. Second, many Methodists worked as servants in homes that were not their own, and thus they had to seek permission to meet with the leaders, a request that many masters were evidently reluctant to grant. Third, those who did receive permission were often not given privacy, and therefore the leaders were not able to exhort, comfort, and reprove the members. We will come back to this topic later in the chapter because it is a significant one. After all, Wesley writes that the inability to have more private conversations "did not at all answer the end proposed, of exhorting, comforting, or reproving."

Fourth, as the leaders reported back to Wesley when they delivered the offering, Wesley became aware of quarrels between Methodists and heard stories of some Methodists lapsing in their ethical commitments. Domestic disputes and drunkenness were but two of the issues Wesley heard about that made it clear that some were not pursing holiness adequately. The system Wesley designed of field preaching, societies, bands, and these meetings of leaders with individual class members was not adequately ensuring people would continue to mature through faith and repentance and the ongoing pursuit of holiness.

Therefore Wesley made two fundamental changes to the system of Methodist classes:

> Upon all these considerations it was agreed, that those of each class should meet altogether. And by this means, a more full inquiry was made into the behaviour of every person. Those who could not be visited at home, or no otherwise than in company, had the same advantage with others. Advice or reproof was given as need required, quarrels made up, misunderstandings removed: And after an hour or two spent in this labour of love, they concluded with prayer and thanksgiving.[47]

Building on the idea of dividing the entire membership of societies into groups of about twelve, Wesley first decided to gather the group together once a week, instead of having the leaders visit each person individually. Second, Wesley expanded the spiritual activity of the group beyond the single emphasis on collecting an offering to include a few other practices that are discussed in more depth below, all of which were designed to "see how their souls prosper." After this substantive change, Wesley made class meetings the normative small group for society members.

[47]Ibid., "A Plain Account of the People Called Methodists," §I.6, 9:262.

"Thus began that excellent institution," Wesley writes, "from which we reaped so many spiritual blessings that we soon fixed the same rule in all our societies."[48] He is even clearer in affirming the value of classes in "A Plain Account of the People called Methodists":

> It can scarce be conceived what advantages have been reaped from this little prudential regulation. Many now happily experienced that Christian fellowship of which they had not so much as an idea before. They began to "bear one another's burdens" and "naturally" to "care for each other." As they had daily a more intimate acquaintance with, so they had a more endeared affection for each other. And "speaking the truth in love, they grew up into him in all things who is the head, even Christ; from whom the whole body, fitly joined together, and compacted by that which every joint supplied, according to the effectual working in the measure of every part, increased unto the edifying of itself into love."[49]

As Richard Watson writes, Wesley "turned [the original design of the class from an offering] to a higher purpose."[50] What began in the society in Bristol spread to the one in London, and despite some initial complaints in both places that Wesley was changing what it meant to be a Methodist, by the writing of the *General Rules* in 1743 the classes had become normative in Methodism. The same basic structure of the class meeting was to stay in place for the rest of Wesley's life, and the Methodist movement would never be the same. Joining a Methodist society meant joining a Methodist class. As Wesley rather tersely puts it, "Those who will not meet in class cannot stay with us."[51] As long as Wesley lived, being a Methodist meant being part of a small group of about twelve people who met weekly to "bear one another's burdens."

Structure

The structure of a class meeting was quite standardized, even if not always put into practice. Classes were designed to have around twelve members, though groups as large as twenty were not uncommon. The makeup of the classes depended on the Methodists in a particular area. Unlike bands, classes were not divided by gender or marital status; proximity to one another seems to have been the primary criterion for how a society's membership was divided into classes. The result of the emphasis on geographic divisions is that it made it easier to meet, and members had

[48]Ibid., "A Short History of the People Called Methodists," §19, 9:434.

[49]Ibid., "A Plain Account of the People Called Methodists," §II.7, 9:262.

[50]Watson, 101.

[51]*Letters* (Telford), Letter to Zechariah Yewdall, 7 December 1782, 7:154.

a better opportunity of knowing how everyone acted outside of society and class meetings.

The structure of each meeting was quite simple. Typical class meetings lasted about an hour. They began with prayer and a hymn or two. Then the leader would ask all the members to share, beginning with the leader, how they had kept the *General Rules* the previous week. Furthermore they were asked to describe the state of their souls, responding to the question, "How does your soul prosper?" or "How is it with your soul?"[52] Every person was asked to share, but those who had experienced faith and repentance and were maturing in sanctification were expected to share. Those who had not matured beyond awakening did not have to share, but they were expected to attend and listen as others shared about their experience of faith and the joys and challenges of the journey of sanctification. Based on members' responses, the leader would then "advise, reprove, comfort, or exhort, as occasion may require." Often the meeting closed with times of prayer and perhaps another hymn.

Class meetings were much more conversational and personal than society meetings or field preaching could ever be. In classes there was real conversation about the state of people's souls and about how they were maturing as disciples, be it to justification or sanctification. People in every stage—be it awakening, convinced, justified, or on the journey to sanctification—shared their success and failures in their discipleship. As Wesley describes, the classes were for "beginners and veterans" in faith. They each received personal rejoicing in their successes and direction, encouragement, and critique regarding how to mature further as a disciple. Because they were in a group of people who observed them the rest of the week, the others in the group were able to comment upon each person's outward behavior and their use of some of the means of grace. The simple format proved reproducible across Methodism and provided a small group structure for all members of Methodist societies that continued in the United States until the mid-1860s.[53]

Purpose

Wesley quickly realized classes could play an important role in discipleship beyond facilitating the taking of offerings. Classes provided a deeper level of community beyond what was offered by societies. Classes,

[52]Scott Kisker uses the question "How is your life with God?" as a contemporary substitute for Wesley's "How is it with your soul?" Elaine A. Heath and Scott Thomas Kisker, *Longing for Spring: A New Vision for Wesleyan Community* (Eugene: Cascade Books, 2010), 34.

[53]Membership in a class was required for membership in the Methodist Episcopal Church until 1864 and the Methodist Episcopal Church, South until 1866 although in each case the influence of classes had been on the wane for many decades before their formal removal as a requirement of membership.

along with societies as a whole, bands, love feasts, and other gatherings, served to help Methodists "increase our union with God and each other."[54] Thomas Walsh called the class "a little company of Christian friends, mutually agreed to meet together weekly in order to their furtherance in the way of godliness."[55]

Classes thereby facilitated further watching over one another spiritually, in small groups that Methodists thought replicated the early church practices.[56] David Lowes Watson argues that a mutual and accountable discipleship was the central purpose of the class meeting. Class members held one another accountable in the journey of discipleship. The class meeting, Watson writes, "was a prudential means of grace whereby Christians in witness to the world could sustain one another in their distinctive tasks assigned by God at a particular time and place in human history."[57] Furthermore classes were "designed to foster" an "accountability for the basics of Christian discipleship—the means of grace and the works of obedience—without which no genuine progress could be made in the Christian life."[58] Mutual accountability, Watson proposes, within the framework of Christian fellowship, was the purpose of class meetings. He grants that evangelism, fellowship, and spiritual experience were important, but experience itself became important decades after class meetings started and was not the initial point.

Accountability included oversight of a Methodist's ethical behavior. Wesley describes in the *General Rules* a more pointed purpose of the class as seen in the role of the class leader: "Let each leader carefully inquire how every soul in his class prospers. Not only how each person observes the outward rules, but how he grows in the knowledge and love of God."[59] Wesley expected Methodists to pursue an ethical life, as made plain in the *General Rules*, by doing good, not doing harm, and practicing the means of grace. Wesley outlined quite specifically the behavior he expected:

> By doing no harm, by avoiding evil in every kind—especially that which is most generally practiced. Such is:
>
> The taking the name God in vain.
>
> The profaning the day of the Lord, either by doing ordinary work thereon, or by buying or selling.

[54]Letter "From Miss A. B. to the Rev. J. Wesley," 16 April 1773, in *Arminian Magazine* 9 (1786): 284.

[55]Jackson, *The Life of Mr. Thomas Walsh*, 3:70.

[56]*Societies*, "A Plain Account of the People Called Methodists," §I.10, 9:258.

[57]Watson, 145.

[58]Ibid., 122–23.

[59]*Minutes of Conference*, §14.1, 10:847.

> Drunkenness, *buying or selling spirituous liquors*; or *drinking them* (unless in cases of extreme necessity).
>
> *Fighting*, quarrelling, or brawling; brother "going to law" with brother; returning evil for evil, or railing for railing; the "using many words" in buying or selling.
>
> The buying or selling uncustomed goods.
>
> The giving or taking things on usury.
>
> Uncharitable or unprofitable conversation, particularly speaking evil of magistrates or ministers or those in authority.
>
> Doing to others as we would not they should do unto us.
>
> Doing what we know is not for the glory of God, as,
>
> The "putting on gold or costly apparel," particularly the wearing of calashes, high-heads, or enormous bonnets;
>
> The *taking such diversions* as cannot be used in the name of the Lord Jesus,
>
> The *singing* those *songs, or reading* those *books*, which do not tend to the knowledge or love of God;
>
> Softness; and needless self indulgence;
>
> Laying up treasures upon earth;
>
> Borrowing without a probability of paying: or taking up goods without a probability of paying for them.[60]

Wesley gave directions to class leaders in the *General Rules* to discern how a person was maturing by inquiring into "how their souls prosper."[61] But observing people's behavior outside society meetings was difficult as Methodism grew, and Wesley soon recognized that such supervision would require more than just he and a few other people. As Wesley writes, "The people were scattered so wide in all parts of the town, . . . that I could not easily see what the behaviour of each person in his own neighborhood was."[62]

Unfortunately, sometimes the behavior was obviously incompatible with Christian discipleship and the directions Wesley had given. Wesley realized there was a problem in societies—not everyone who joined a society pursued holiness:

> But as much as we endeavoured to watch over each other, we soon found some who did not "live the gospel." I do not know that any hypocrites were crept in, for indeed there was no temptation. But several grew cold, and gave way to the sins which had long easily beset them. We quickly perceived, there were many ill consequences of suffering these to remain among us. It was dangerous to others, inasmuch as all sin is of an infectious nature.[63]

---

[60] *Societies, General Rules*, §4, 9:70–72.

[61] Ibid., §3, 9:70.

[62] Ibid., "A Plain Account of the People Called Methodists," §II.2, 9:260.

[63] Ibid., §II.1, 9:260.

Wesley knew that most people, even those with the best intentions, when left on their own to pursue Christian discipleship would eventually stumble, if not fail outright. Most needed a community to support them, as well as a leader who would specifically ask the difficult questions.

The question was how to provide that support and oversight. For Wesley, the answer became clear. "There could be no better way," he writes, "to come to a sure, thorough knowledge of each person, than to divide them into classes."[64] Wesley describes the period right after the formation of class meetings when he became aware that class leaders, as they began conversing with Methodists regularly and collecting the offering, observed that people's actual lives did not match the discipleship Wesley desired:

> In a while, some of these [class leaders] informed me, they found such and such an one did not live as he ought. It struck me immediately, "This is the thing; the very thing we have wanted so long." I called together all the Leaders of the classes, (so we used to term them and their companies,) and desired, that each would make a particular inquiry into the behaviour of those whom he saw weekly. They did so. Many disorderly walkers were detected. Some turned from the evil of their ways. Some were put away from us. Many saw it with fear, and rejoiced unto God with reverence.
>
> As soon as possible, the same method was used in London and all other places. Evil men were detected, and reproved. They were borne with for a season. If they forsook their sins, we received them gladly; if they obstinately persisted therein, it was openly declared that they were not of us. The rest mourned and prayed for them, and yet rejoiced, that, as far as in us lay, the scandal was rolled away from the society.[65]

Wesley almost immediately recognized that class meetings provided the forum for the spiritual oversight of maturity that he sought. Classes were a way for Wesley to overcome "the great difficulty I had long found of knowing the people who desired to be under my care."[66] He wanted to know the "behaviour of each person in his own neighbourhood," and thereby discern "where they [society members] are indeed working out their own salvation."[67] Francis Asbury and Thomas Coke, two of the early Methodist leaders in North America, understood the class meeting as a way to gain a "free inquiry into the state of the heart."[68] Classes offered a way to truly see if Methodists lived as they professed. Those who obeyed the rules were praised, and anyone no longer living up to

[64]*Journal and Diaries II*, 25 March 1742, 19:258.

[65]*Societies*, "A Plain Account of the People Called Methodists," §II.3–4, 9:260–61.

[66]*Journal and Diaries II*, 25 March 1742, 19:258.

[67]*Societies, General Rules*, §3, 9:69.

[68]Asbury and Coke, 140.

Methodist ethical standars either began doing so once again or was removed from membership.

This emphasis on community and accountability worked hand in hand with the disciplinary function of classes. Dean argues:

> Continued membership depended on personal conduct rather than on one's state of grace or even one's progress toward a conversion experience... The class meeting must be evaluated as a disciplinary mechanism rather than as an opportunity for fellowship. Fellowship could and did occur in a vibrant class meeting, but the purpose of the meeting was not fellowship as such.[69]

In Watson's interpretation this disciplinary function was just as important as the mutual accountability members provided one another. The class leader was to inform the minister "of any that are sick, or of any that walk disorderly, and will not be reproved."[70]

Wesley affirms the disciplinary nature of the class structure when he quotes in the *Arminian Magazine* a portion of Charles Perronet's description of the purpose of the class meeting as:

> To know who continue Members of the Society;
>
> To inspect their Outward Walking
>
> To enquire into their inward State
>
> To learn, what are their Trials? And how they fall by, or conquer them?
>
> To Instruct the ignorant in the first Principles of Religion: if need be, to repeat, explain, or enforce, what has been said in public Preaching.
>
> To stir them up to believe, love, obey; and to check the first spark of Offence or Discord.[71]

In a postscript to the essay, Wesley supports Perronet's affirmation: "I earnestly exhort all Leaders of Classes and Bands, seriously to consider the preceding Observations, and to put them in execution with all the Understanding and Courage that God has given them."[72] The point was not just to point out inappropriate behavior, but rather to motivate people in their discipleship. As Wesley wrote, "I am under a necessity of uniting them together, and of dividing them into little companies, that they

---

[69]Dean, 178.

[70]*Societies, General Rules*, §3, 9:70.

[71]Charles Perronet, "Of the Right Method of Meeting Classes and Bands, in the Methodist-Societies," *Arminian Magazine* 4 (1781): 604.

[72]Ibid., 605–06.

may provoke one another to love and good works."[73] Only through the disciplined oversight of the leaders was pursuit of the spiritual life made possible.

Proclamation in Class Meetings

Proclamation was also an important aspect of Methodist classes. A number of types of proclamation are evident in class meetings, including advice or counsel, exhortation, and instruction. Wesley lists these in the *General Rules*, writing that it is the class leaders' business "to advise, reprove, comfort, or exhort as occasion may require."[74] These words come immediately after Wesley directs leaders to inquire into the members' souls. Perronet, as noted earlier, echoes this charge: "To Instruct the ignorant in the first Principles of Religion: if need be, to repeat, explain, or enforce, what has been said in public Preaching." Inquiry, therefore, has a purpose: one is to inquire so that one can then give advice, direction, and instruction. In the first place, to give advice and counsel was a critical responsibility of each leader. After enquiring into the state of a class member's soul, the leader was to share "friendly and pious counsel."[75] And Wesley was not alone in thinking that the members would profit from receiving such counsel; the members themselves thought so. In a journal entry dated February 2, 1747, Wesley includes the text of a note received from John Hague, a class leader, who writes, "It seems to me, we all want advice that is plain and cutting, awakening, and shaking."[76]

The purpose of offering advice in the class was in part instructive. Leslie Church cites a 1784 Methodist class leader from Ditcheat, in Somerset, who describes the instructive element of a class meeting: "I think this to be the most useful means (except preaching) that we (Methodists) enjoy; it is instructive, it unites us together, it stirs us up to press forward."[77] Wesley identifies the teaching element of the class leader quite specifically. He writes of the need to "instruct... according to their several necessities."[78] He also notes that the instruction or teaching is specifically focused on Christian doctrine. He writes in a letter to John King, "If any of the Class-Leaders teaches strange doctrine, he can have no more place among us.

[73] *Sermons IV*, Sermon 121, "Prophets and Priests," §15, 4:81.

[74] *Societies, General Rules*, §3, 9:70.

[75] Richard Watson, *The Life of the Rev. John Wesley*, 14th ed. (London: Wesleyan Conference Office, 1831), 14.

[76] *Journal and Diaries III*, 2 February 1747, 20:154.

[77] Leslie F. Church, *The Early Methodist People*, Fernley-Hartley Lecture (London: Epworth, 1948), 164.

[78] Watson, *The Life of the Rev. John Wesley*, 15.

Only lovingly admonish him first."[79] Again, Perronet sees teaching as central to the classes, writing that class leaders are "to instruct the ignorant in the first Principles of religion."[80] Albin argues that the class meetings offered early Methodists "clear instruction in the central truths of the Christian faith. But this doctrinal instruction was supplemented by practical guidance in Christian living, that is, by the enforcement of the General Rules and by the leader's deliverance of earnest exhortations and reproofs to the members."[81] While formal lecturing was not part of the class, instruction certainly was.[82]

David Lowes Watson quotes at length a description of a class meeting from Thomas Martin's *Thoughts*, which appeared in the *Independent Methodist Magazine* in 1826.[83] The citation demonstrates the interchange between the leader and each member, with each member sharing their experience, followed by specific instruction from the leader. In each case the leader followed a member's sharing with direction from a specific Bible verse as a source of encouragement or reproof, but the point is education. As Watson writes, "exchanges in the class meeting were essentially catechetical between the leader and each member of the group. The process was one of question and answer, with the leader articulating what was felt to be the point which would most profitably be shared by the other members."[84] Methodist classes were not designed to convey large amounts of information, as might happen in a sermon or educational classroom. Rather, the point was to give pointed instruction, depending on what class members shared regarding their discipleship during a previous week.

The type of proclamation that Wesley describes most frequently in classes is exhortation. In the *Rules* Wesley writes that the business of a class leader is in part "To advise, reprove, comfort, or exhort, as occasion may require."[85] One unique example of exhortation was given by Lydia Vandome as she neared her death:

> On Tuesday evening last, she desired us to set her up in bed, to meet her class. Her voice faltered much. She earnestly exhorted them all to live near

[79]*Letters* (Telford), Letter to John King, 31 October 1787, 8:20.

[80]Charles Perronet, "The Right Method of Meeting Classes and Bands, in the Methodist-Societies," *Arminian Magazine* 20 (1797): 131.

[81]Albin, "'Inwardly Persuaded': Religion of the Heart in Early British Methodism," 45.

[82]Henderson, 96. Henderson also argues that preaching was not part of class meetings. While preaching was unusual, proclamation was common.

[83]Watson, 111–15.

[84]Ibid., 115.

[85]*Societies, General Rules*, §3, 9:70.

> to God, and to keep close together; adding, "I shall soon join the church above." She spoke no more; all was silent rapture, till, on Friday morning, without sigh or groan, she resigned her spirit to God.[86]

During his time in Germany with the Moravians, Wesley observed the weight they gave to exhortation in class, and he seems to have made it a priority for Methodists as well. In his journal of August 1738, Wesley gives an overview of the structure and discipline of the Church of Herrnhut. He describes the Sunday morning gatherings:

> On Sunday morning the Service begins at six; at nine, the Public Service at Bertholdsdorf; at one, the Eldest gives separate exhortations to all the members of the Church, divided into fourteen little classes *for that purpose*, spending about a quarter of an hour with each class; at four, begins the Evening Service at Bertholdsdorf, closed by a conference in the church; at eight, is the usual Service; after which the young men, singing praises round the town, conclude the day.[87]

Other Methodists noted the importance of exhortation in class meetings as well. "In the discipline of Methodism," Richard Watson writes, "the division of the society into classes is an important branch. Each class is placed under a person of experience and piety, who meets the others once a week, for prayer, and inquiry into the religious state of each, in order to administer exhortation and counsel."[88]

Exhortation in classes was more focused and personal than the preaching and exhortation that took place in the fields. Classes, along with bands, offered the opportunity for "particular exhortation."[89] The particularity of the exhortation came in its response to a person's testimony. At class meetings, as well as band meetings, people would "testify" to their experience of God. In turn, leaders would give brief feedback on how to progress in their spiritual life based on what the leader heard in the testimony. Appropriate shorter commentary that included advice, reproof, comfort, and exhortation was part of the class leader's responsibility.[90] The point was to provide personal and direct feedback on a class member's spiritual experience, feedback that was difficult if not impossible in the larger society meetings or gatherings at field preaching.

[86]Wesley, *Works* (Jackson), 3:352.

[87]Ibid., August 1738, 1:142 (emphasis mine).

[88]Watson, *The Life of the Rev. John Wesley*, 114.

[89]*Treatises II*, "Farther Thoughts upon Christian Perfection," §I.37, 13:120.

[90]*Societies*, "A Plain Account of the People Called Methodists," §II.6, 9:262. Wesley writes here that class meetings were sometimes a "labour of love" where "Advice or reproof was given as need required, quarrels made up, misunderstandings removed."

This catechetical nature of the class continued into the nineteenth century both in the United States and England.[91] In England the Methodist preacher John Atkinson, just over one hundred years after Wesley's death, still encourages leaders to "make a few terse and suggestive remarks illustrating and enforcing the words (of scripture) read, and opening the way for the speaking of the members. He (the leader) should relate modestly and in few words his own experience and not discuss matters that are not relevant to the meeting."[92] Brevity is important, since one way to ruin a class is for the leader to take up to "ten to fifteen minutes in an exhortation."[93] In the United States Father Reeves fretted over the loss of his ability to "enlarge" upon the biblical narrative when classes became too large.[94]

Proclamation in classes built on proclamation that took place in the fields as well as the society meetings. Perronet points this out in his directions to class leaders to instruct class members"in the first Principles of Religion . . . what has been said in public Preaching."[95] The class leader is called to exhort in "particular" ways so that the preaching that has occurred in society meetings and field preaching can be confirmed, especially for those who attended regular preaching. But even for those who did not attend the formal preaching, class meetings were a place where the message could be repeated so that those who didn't hear the preaching could still engage the content. Proclamation, when it takes place in a class, allowed members to reengage what was preached in the fields and societies, having it explained and enforced, but at a more intimate level than societies and field preaching allowed for.[96] The point of proclamation in classes was to "reinforce" what had been preached in the field and society, so that people could make a more informed decision about Christ and mature in discipleship.

The Bible was proclaimed in such a way that people could be challenged in specific ways according to their circumstances. Thomas Walsh writes, "If any had fallen into sin, they were reproved; if tempted, they were comforted and encouraged; and those who ran well, adorning their profession in all things, were exhorted still to press forward, and give

[91]Philip F. Hardt, "The Evangelistic and Catechetical Role of the Class Meeting in Early New York City Methodism," *Methodist History* 38, no. 1 (1999): 23–26.

[92]John Atkinson, *The Class Leader: His Work and How to Do It* (New York: Nelson & Phillips, 1874), 197.

[93]Ibid.

[94]Edward Corderoy, *Father Reeves, the Methodist Class Leader: A Brief Account of William Reeves* (London: A. Heylin, 1854), 81.

[95]Perronet, "Of the Right Method of Meeting Classes and Bands, in the Methodist-Societies," 604.

[96]Dean, 157.

glory to God."[97] Class members heard not only the proclamation directed at them but also that which was directed at others. The result was that classes provided a forum in which proclamation took place in a variety of ways. In Wesley's mind, however, proclamation itself was not the goal. It was simply a primary means to the end, which was for Methodists to respond with the next stage of discipleship, namely faith and repentance leading to justification or to further sanctification.

Responses to Proclamation

Many Methodists attested to importance of response in class meetings. John Mason wrote a letter to Wesley that was published in the *Arminian Magazine* in 1780. In it he describes the joys and challenges of being a class leader. A central labor of the class leader, he writes, is "to help them [class members] forward in the ways of the kingdom."[98] Perronet, as quoted earlier, describes the leader's task in similar fashion. For him the task of the leader was "to stir them [class members] up to believe, love, obey."[99] Another writes that "every sentence he [the class leader] utters, either in prayer of counsel, Reproof, or Exhortation, should have a tendency to draw his people to a present Sense of the divine presence—and immediate Application of Soul to the Father thro' the Son—& an entire dedication of their all to Him."[100]

Members of classes were just like members of societies in that the only spiritual requirement was awakening, not faith and repentance leading toward conversion and sanctification. Some members of classes did not exhibit "awakened" lives. For instance, Wesley comments after visiting one class, "I met the classes, and found many therein who were much alive to God. But many others were utterly dead."[101] Therefore, maturing "forward" or being "stirred up" to believe typically meant maturing beyond awakening into either of these latter two responses, but sometimes people needed to be reawakened.

That the first response, namely, faith and repentance leading to justification, was desired is evident in not only Wesley's writing but also that of numerous other early Methodists. On numerous occasions, Wesley describes conversions in or as a result of classes. A typical example is found

97Jackson, *The Life of Mr. Thomas Walsh,* 3:70.

98John Mason, "Some Account of the Life of Mr. John Mason: In a Letter to the Rev. Mr. John Wesley," *Arminian Magazine* 3 (1780): 653.

99Perronet, "Of the Right Method of Meeting Classes and Bands, in the Methodist-Societies," 604.

100David Lowes Watson, "The Origins and Significance of the Early Methodist Class Meetings" (PhD diss, Duke University, 1978), 407.

101*Journal and Diaries IV,* 29 June 1761, 21:332.

in his journal entry from July 26, 1761: "About one I preached to the usual congregation at Birstall. What a work is God working here also! Six in one class have, within this week, found peace with God; two this morning in meeting the class."[102] The early Methodist Benjamin Rhodes reports that people often "found a sense of forgiveness" in Rhodes's class meetings.[103] Sarah Ryan relates her own conversion story:

> For three weeks I had expected it in every means of grace, when being one night at my class, with my sister, who was in great distress, I felt the burden of her soul laid upon mine in an inexpressible manner: and while I was exhorting her to believe, the power of God overwhelmed my soul, so that I fell back in my chair, and my eye-sight was taken from me: but in the same moment the Lord Jesus appeared to my inward sight, and I cried out three times, "O the beauty of the lovely Jesus, Behold him in his vesture dipt in blood!" A little after, my leader asked me, "Do you now believe?" I faintly answered, "Yes."[104]

Ryan continues that she still wavered in her faith, but that the next morning the words "Thy sins are cast as a stone into the deep waters" were "applied with power," and then she could write, "Now I do believe. Now I know my sins are forgiven me."[105] Another example is found in a letter Isaac Duckworth wrote to Sarah Ryan, in which he describes the number of conversions in his class alone in the previous weeks:

> I bless God he is more greatly reviving his work among us. I believe in less than 2 weeks I have heard of 6 people that has found Christ [unreadable word] in my own class and many more that... are longing greatly for full Redemption. 4 young men I have that meets [sic] with me that has [sic] a clean sense that God has saved them from sin.[106]

Tom Albin's research on early Methodism informs contemporary conceptions of evangelism in important ways. Albin demonstrates that, at least in those he studied, almost half of the early British Methodists experienced the New Birth after they had completed their time on trial and entered full membership in the class meeting.[107] Furthermore,

[102]Ibid., 21:338.

[103]Benjamin Rhodes, "An Acount of Mr. Benjamin Rhodes, Written by Himeslf," *Arminian Magazine* 2 (1779): 364.

[104]Sarah Ryan, "Account of Mrs. Sarah Ryan," *Arminian Magazine* 2 (1779): 302.

[105]Ibid.

[106]Undated ms. letter from Isaac Duckworth to Sarah Ryan, *MARC*, Fletcher-Tooth Collection, Box MAM Fl 2.7/9.

[107]Albin, "'Inwardly Persuaded': Religion of the Heart in Early British Methodism," 45.

the majority of conversions took place either alone or in societies, and a significant number took place in class meetings or following a class meeting.[108] In addition, the length of time it took for most people to repent and believe after joining a class is significant. Instead of the instantaneous response that many contemporary evangelists advocate, early Methodists took on average two and half years to ponder and struggle with their faith before responding to the story of God in Christ with repentance and faith.[109]

The preponderance of examples of conversion in classes leads many contemporary scholars to emphasize the role of conversion in class meetings. Knight argues that the experience of the New Birth was also important in class meetings and signified that spiritual progress was central to the class.[110] The role of conversion was so significant that some scholars, such as Philip Hardt, argue that the class meetings really were designed more for nonbelievers than for believers.[111] In Hardt's mind the conversion came "as a result of the class leader's weekly instruction and the veteran class members' personal testimonies."[112]

In *A History of the Methodist Church in Great Britain*, Davies, Rupp, and George point out the evangelistic purpose of the class meeting as noted at the 1820 Liverpool conference, which urged the societies to reclaim the evangelistic component of classes: "Let us... attempt the formation of new classes in suitable neighbourhoods, where we may hope by that method to gather some people who are 'not far from the kingdom of God' but who need special invitation, and are not to give themselves fully to the Lord."[113]

Others demonstrate the central place of conversion in classes as well. William Carvosso, a mid-nineteenth-century American class leader, noted the same situation. He emphasized the evangelistic role of the class meeting as he encouraged people at preaching service to attend class meetings, not necessarily to convert on the spot at the preaching service.[114] Dean, having read many biographies of early Methodists class leaders, notes that "the frequency with which references, allusions, and hints appeared

[108]"An Empirical Study of Early Methodist Spirituality," 278–79.

[109]Hardt, 19.

[110]Knight III, *The Presence of God in the Christian Life: John Wesley and the Means of Grace*, 98–100.

[111]Hardt, 15.

[112]Philip F. Hardt, *The Soul of Methodism: The Class Meeting in Early New York City Methodism* (Lanham, MD: University Press of America, 2000), 16.

[113]Rupert Eric Davies, E. Gordon Rupp, and A. Raymond George, *A History of the Methodist Church in Great Britain*, 4 vols. (London: Epworth, 1965), 4:368. See also Hardt, 16. Hardt notes the evangelistic emphasis on classes through the 1820 Liverpool Conference.

[114]William Carvosso, *A Memoir of Mr. William Carvosso, Sixty Years a Class Leader* (New York: Lane and Tippett, 1846), 65.

in these sources to an evangelistic role is striking."[115] The class leaders knew that they would engage people in each stage of discipleship. Therefore some leaders kept notes on how many of their people were convinced of sin or awakened, how many had been converted, how many were on the path to holiness, and how many were backsliders. One example, from 1832, is Father Reeves, a noted class leader, who records one day that in his class, sixty were convinced of sin, forty had found peace, six backsliders had recovered, and two found happy deaths.[116] Needless to say his class had more members than the usual twelve.

The most convincing evidence of conversion as central to the life of the class meeting comes from the work of William Dean. In the biographies he studied, he discovered that before 1820, no conversions took place in a preaching service or prayer meeting. He discovered that many who wrote that field preaching, prayer meetings, or preaching services were important to their conversion, actually meant that they continued thinking and praying about what they heard in those gatherings, but the conversions themselves typically took place in solitude. Of all the conversions he studied, "more than half happened either in a class meeting, or following a class meeting, or under the influence of a class leader."[117] In other words many if not most of the conversions that took place occurred not in field preaching or in societies, but in classes, a phenomena again that Wesley himself was cognizant of.[118]

But conversion was not the only response to proclamation. Many people responded with the deeper repentance and faith leading to sanctification. The story of Mrs. Ann Gilbert is one example. "She experienced," one account records, "the perfect love of God, and she seems to have lived in the enjoyment of this liberty, for some time before she heard a single sermon on the subject of Christian perfection."[119]

Andrew Thompson's recent work documents quite clearly that "the class became a preparatory forum for justification and a facilitative vehicle for sanctification."[120] He argues that David Watson's assertion that mutual accountability was the primary goal of class meetings is incomplete. While accountability is certainly an aspect of the class meeting, it is neither the goal nor the end.[121] "The class meeting," he writes, "was not

[115]Dean, 307.

[116]Corderoy, 52.

[117]Dean, 303.

[118]*Letters III*, Letter to Sarah Crosby, 14 June 1757, 27:86.

[119]George Coles, *Heroines of Methodism; or, Pen and Ink Sketches of the Mothers and Daughters of the Church* (New York: Carlton & Porter, 1857), 303.

[120]Thompson, 177.

[121]Ibid., 167.

just a means for facilitating mutual accountability; it was also a communal means of grace whereby men and women came to experience the reality of sanctification and the myriad levels of transformation that it entailed."[122] Thompson continues:

> The testimonies of both Wesley and early class members about class meetings indicate that experiences of new birth and progressive sanctification were demonstrably occurring…class meetings were…the forum in which lives were inwardly and outwardly transformed—where holiness of heart and life was inculcated—by the Holy Spirit over time.[123]

In sum, sanctification and conversion were important responses in the classes.

The Relationship between Proclamation and Response in Classes

Proclamation played a critical role in helping people respond to Christ, leading to justification and sanctification in class meetings. Proclamation through teaching, exhortation, and testimony helped "press" people forward in their faith. Encouraging people forward was a specific function of the class leader.[124] As people heard biblical themes, they were called to take the next step of faith. Simply hearing others verbalize their stories of repentance and faith helped those who had yet to have such experiences seek and find that response. As Joseph Sutcliffe points out, an advantage of class meetings is "the holy emulation and courage with which it tends to inspire the penitent upon hearing of the grace and comfort that others have received of the Lord."[125] Margaret Austin expresses a similar sentiment in a 1740 letter to Charles Wesley: "The first night we met [in class], hearing the others tell the state of their souls, it was of much strength to me to speak the state of mine." Later she received spiritual counsel from Charles Wesley and others, which gave her the courage to pray "to the Lord to show me my heart."[126] People heard the gospel proclaimed, as well as people's narration of how they experienced the gospel, and they frequently responded with faith and repentance as well as awakening.

---

[122]Ibid., 168.

[123]Ibid., 169.

[124]Hardt, "The Evangelistic and Catechetical Role," 14. See also Dean, 307.

[125]Joseph Sutcliffe, *The Mutual Communion of Saints: Shewing the Necessity and Advantages of the Weekly Meetings for a Communication of Experience* (Trowbridge: Abraham Small, 1794), 45.

[126]Ms. letter from Mrs. Margaret Austin to Charles Wesley, 19 May 1740, *MARC*, Early Methodist Volume.

The relationship between proclamation and these two responses leads many to argue that classes were remarkably evangelistic in nature. Dean, for instance, argues that evangelism was one of the primary functions of the class meeting and it encouraged people to continue to mature in their faith.[127] Boraine argues that classes were "agencies" or "instruments" of evangelism.[128] Evangelism, rather than a one-time act that occurred in the fields, was an ongoing activity that started in the fields, was nurtured in societies, and was fostered still further in class meetings. Class meetings complemented society meetings and field preaching in their evangelistic task. They were another context of ministry in which people experienced multiple stages of discipleship because multiple modes of evangelism were incorporated into the ministry's structure. Classes were not only designed to sustain the responses that occurred in fields and societies, they were also evangelistic mechanisms that encouraged and facilitated conversion and sanctification.

CONCLUSION

Field preaching and society meetings themselves were inadequate to ensure the pursuit of holiness of heart and life. The message preached had to be further explicated in the more personal forums of the classes. The small size of the class meeting encouraged deep fellowship with other class members and especially deep conversation with the class leader. Class meetings provided an opportunity for greater reflection and personal dialogue than did either field preaching or society meetings. The classes to a greater degree, along with bands to some degree, provided the means to confirm the word preached first in the fields and then in the societies.

And yet Wesley became convinced that an even more personal forum was needed for proclamation so that people could respond to the gospel. This final forum worked in conjunction with field preaching, societies, and classes to close the loop on proclamation and the call to holiness that defined the Methodist movement. It is to this final forum that our conversation now turns.

[127]Dean, 298, 300.

[128]Boraine, 247. Boraine correctly argues that classes and societies were "agencies" or "instruments" of evangelism that "promoted holiness."

CHAPTER 7

VISITATION

> *In many places the work of God seems to stand still. What can be done to revive and enlarge it?...Do we visit from house to house, according to the plan laid down in the Minutes? Have you done this?...What hinders? Want of time?...Spend half the time in this visiting which you spend in talking uselessly, and you will have time enough. Do this, particularly in confirming and building up believers. Then, and not till then, the work of the Lord will prosper in your hands.*[1]

The late 1760s was an important time for Methodism. The small group of students who started meeting in the 1720s at Oxford had grown into a community of thousands in England and was starting to reach into the colonies across the Atlantic. And yet there were signs that the movement was waning in parts of Britain. Membership in Methodist societies, classes, and bands, while thriving in some places, was uneven across the country. On August 16, 1768, Methodist leaders and preachers gathered in Bristol for Conference as they did every summer to hear from their leader, John Wesley, to converse, and to worship together. As at previous conferences, Wesley led the Methodists through a series of questions as a way to provide his response to the opportunities and challenges of the day. Many questions were essentially repeated from year to year, but in 1768 question 23, the question above, was new. The Methodist movement was not growing as it had, and Wesley thought there were many reasons why it had stalled. He proceeded to make a number of unsurprising recommendations, such as getting Methodists to read more Methodist books, encouraging preachers to preach more often in the fields, insisting that Methodists meet more faithfully in their bands, and instructing all to fast more consistently. At the end, however, Wesley offered a prescription for reviving the work of God that typically surprises contemporary laity and clergy alike in most Methodist traditions, if only because the practice is rarely mentioned in the literature on Methodism over the past two hundred years. His prescription: Methodists must visit people in their homes if the ministry is to thrive.

[1]*Minutes of Conference*, 1768, 10:364.

Wesley repeated the same basic injunction in subsequent *Large Minutes*.[2] In fact, throughout his writings, Wesley emphasizes the importance of visiting from house to house. Almost a decade before the 1768 Conference, on January 29, 1759, Wesley reflected on the Methodist society in Colchester: "I found the society had decreased...; and yet they had had full as good Preachers. But that is not sufficient: By repeated experiments we learn, that though a man preach like an angel, he will neither collect, nor preserve a society which is collected, without visiting them from house to house."[3]

About six weeks later, Wesley, again in Colchester, describes how visitation helps to keep Methodists connected to the ministry: "I rode to Colchester, and found that out of the hundred and twenty-six I had left here last year, we had lost only twelve; in the place of whom we had gained forty. Such is the fruit of visiting from house to house!"[4] When Wesley lists questions to new helpers he asks: "Will you preach every morning and evening; endeavouring not to speak too long, or too loud? Will you diligently instruct the children in every place? Will you visit from house to house?"[5] Late in his life he identifies three requirements for increasing the work of God in Scotland. Wesley: "(1.) Preach abroad as much as possible. (2.) Try every town and village! (3.) Visit every member of the society at home."[6] On hundreds of occasions, Wesley highlights the importance of visitation, private instruction, or some other type of individual conversation between a leader and a member of a Methodist society for the purpose of encouraging greater discipleship. In Wesley's mind, visitation is the most "important branch of the pastoral office."[7]

These statements by Wesley often astound Methodists today. Early Methodism's vitality is often seen as flowing from the field preaching, societies, classes, or even bands. That Wesley understood visitation as the ministry's bedrock is simply shocking to many contemporary Methodists. For many Western Methodists visitation, rather than being a time of spiritual encouragement, is primarily either a social occasion at a person's home or a pastoral visit in response to illness or death. Visitation is most often seen as a time-consuming relic of a previous age with no relevance to contemporary Christian communities. Therefore, not surprisingly, when United Methodist candidates for ordination are asked as a group by their bishop the historic Wesleyan question, "Will you visit from house to house?" the response is

[2]Wesley repeats the same basic injunction in *Minutes of Conference, Large Minutes*, 1770–72, §79, 10:907, and *Large Minutes* 1780–89, §13, 10:912.

[3]*Journal and Diaries IV*, 29 January 1759, 21:175.

[4]*Societies*, "Short History of the People Called Methodists," §73, 9:469.

[5]*Minutes of Conference, Large Minutes*, 1770–72, §60.1, 10:893.

[6]Ibid., *Large Minutes*, 1780–89, §58, 10:928–29.

[7]*Journal and Diaries V*, 11 January 1774, 22:396.

often a communal sheepish "Yes," accompanied by smiles and chuckles. Wesley was different. He believed visitation is the climactic forum in which evangelistic proclamation occurs. This chapter explores why.

The chapter begins with an overview of the heritage of pastoral visitation in England that influenced Wesley. Then follows an analysis of visitation in early Methodism and an overview of Wesley's emphasis on the practice. The remainder of the chapter investigates the role of proclamation in visitation and the responses such proclamation elicited. Wesley's evangelistic vision, and to a certain degree Methodism as a whole, cannot be adequately understood apart from the role of visitation and proclamation in it.

HERITAGE OF VISITATION

Wesley learned the practice of having spiritual conversations in people's homes that encourage maturity in discipleship from a number of people, perhaps most importantly his father. Wesley records his father's practice:

> My Father's method was to visit all his parishioners, sick or well, from house to house, to talk with each of them on the things of God and observe severally the state of their souls. What he then observed he minuted down in a book kept for that purpose. In this manner he went through his parish (which was near three miles long) three times.[8]

Wesley's father in turn learned the practice from others as visitation was a common, if underutilized, clerical practice in seventeenth- and early eighteenth-century England. For example Wesley notes Joseph Allein's practices, and in turn encourages Methodist's to practice them, when he includes some of Allein's writings in *A Christian Library* that he provided to his preachers and encouraged them to read. Wesley specifically highlights Allein's emphasis on visitation, pointing out that Allein

> used to spend five afternoons every week in these exercises, from one or two o'clock till seven: in which space he used to visit three or four families, sometimes more, as they were greater or less. Thus he went through the whole town, and then presently began again: and he did often bless God for the great success he found in those exercises, saying, that God made him hereby an instrument to the good of souls as by his public ministry.[9]

Perhaps the most important influence on Wesley's understanding is the seventeenth-century Puritan Richard Baxter. In his influential book

---

[8] *Letters II*, Letter to a Gentleman, 16 November 1742, 26:90.

[9] "A Christian Library: Consisting of Extracts from and Abridgments of the Choicest Pieces of Practical Divinity Which Have Been Published in the English Tongue," v. 14, *Extracts From The Works Of Mr. Jospeh Allein*, http://wesley.nnu.edu/john_wesley/christian_library/vol14/CL14Part1.htm.

The Reformed Pastor, Baxter argues that visitation is crucial to the pastoral task. It allows for private and personal instruction that gives Christian leaders direct insight into congregants' lives so that leaders can "see how you live, and examine how you profit, and direct you in the Duties of your Families."[10] Visiting allows preachers to systematically "watch for souls" of a parish through personal and pointed spiritual care for people.[11]

Wesley's heritage demonstrated to him not only that visitation was important but also that proclamation itself is a vital aspect of visitation. For example, late in his life James Hervey expressed his regret for not visiting more frequently: "O! . . . how much has Christ done for me; and how little have I done for so loving a Saviour! If I preached once a week it was at last a burden to me. I have not visited the people of my parish as I ought to have done; and thus have preached as it were from house to house. I have not taken every opportunity of speaking for Christ."[12]

The prominent Church of England cleric Bishop Ken (1637–1711), in a pastoral letter to his clergy, encourages them to carry out a number of pastoral tasks during Lent in order to prepare themselves and their parishioners for Easter. One practice Ken encourages is to daily reread their own ordination vows, the same vows Charles and John made, to "teach publickly, and from House to House."[13]

Wesley observes this essential aspect of visitation in those who inform his practice of ministry—namely proclamation. Allein, Baxter, and others mention its importance. Allein, for instance, is described by Gillies as not being satisfied with pulpit preaching so he, "constantly went from house to house, and there dealt both with governors, children, and servants, instructing them . . . [and] exhorting them to diligence, both in their general and particular callings."[14]

Wesley notes the importance Allein places on visitation in great detail,

> He inspected, as far as he could, the state of every particular person, and reproved, comforted, and encouraged, as he found occasion; . . . he instructed the younger sort in the principles of religion, by asking questions out of the

[10]Richard Baxter and William Orme, *The Practical Works of the Late Reverend and Pious Mr. Richard Baxter*, 4 vols. (London: Thomas Parkhurst, 1707), 3:ii.

[11]Richard Baxter and Samuel Palmer, *The Reformed Pastor; a Discourse on the Pastoral Office... Abridged and Reduced to a New Method* (London: J. Buckland, 1766), 41. Visiting on a regular basis allows for oversight of many in the parish: "We spend Monday and Tuesday (from the morning almost to night) in the work; taking about fifteen or sixteen families in a week, that we may go through the parish (in which there are above eight hundred) in a year," 164.

[12]James Hervey, *A Collection of the Letters of the Late Reverend Mr. James Hervey... To Which Is Prefixed, an Account of His Life and Death* (Edinburgh, 1763), 9–10.

[13]William Wogan, *The Right Use of Lent: Or, a Help to Penitents... To Which Is Added, Bishop Kenn's Pastoral Letter* (London: C. Rivington, 1732), 208 (emphasis original).

[14]John Gillies, *Historical Collections Relating to Remarkable Periods of the Success of the Gospel*, 2 vols. (Glasgow: Robert and Andrew Foulis, 1754),1:233.

Catechism, and explaining the answers. He was accustomed also to inquire of them about their spiritual state, laboring to make them sensible of the evil and danger of sin, the corruption of our natures, and the misery of an unconverted state; provoking them to look after the true remedy, to turn from all their sins to GOD, to close with CHRIST upon his own terms, to follow after holiness, to watch over their hearts and lives, to mortify their lusts, to redeem their time, and to prepare for eternity. These things he explained to their understandings, and pressed upon their consciences with the most forcible arguments and considerations; showing what great privileges they enjoyed, the many gospel-sermons they did or might hear, the many talents they were entrusted with, and the great account they were to give to GOD of the same. Besides, he left with them several counsels and directions, to be care-fully remembered and practiced for the good of their souls.[15]

Baxter especially emphasized the role of instruction and exhortation in house-to-house visitation:

It is the duty of the Minister not only to teach the people committed to his charge in publick [*sic*], but Privately and Particularly to admonish, exhort, reprove and comfort them upon all reasonable occasions, so far as his time, strength, and personal safety will permit. He is to admonish them in time of health to prepare for death: And for that purpose, they are often to confess with their Minister about the estate of their souls, etc.[16]

The justification for including proclamation during a visit was found in New Testament practices. William Allen, for instance, emphasizes that Paul is the model, and specifically the apostle's example of preaching house to house: "St. Paul gave this account to the Elders of the Church of Ephesus, both of method and substance of his Preaching publickly, and from house to house when he told them, that he had testified both to the Jews and also the Greeks."[17]

Hervey reminds his readers that Paul "taught the people publickly, and from house to house."[18] Baxter writes, "Paul taught them also from house to house, Day and Night with Tears [Acts 20:20–21]."[19] In the *Minutes*, Wesley included Baxter's assertion that, "Undoubtedly this private

[15]Wesley, "A Christian Library: Consisting of Extracts from and Abridgments of the Choicest Pieces of Practical Divinity Which Have Been Published in the English Tongue," v. 14, *Extracts From The Works Of Mr. Jospeh Allein*, http://wesley.nnu.edu/john_wesley/christian_library/vol14/CL14Part1.htm.

[16]Richard Baxter, et al., *Gildas Salvianus: The Reformed Pastor Shewing the Nature of the Pastoral Work* (London: Robert White, 1656), 2.

[17]William Allen, Richard Kidder, and John Williams, *The Works of Mr. William Allen, Consisting of Thirteen Distinct Tracts on Several Subjects* (London: Walter Kettilby etc., 1707), 293.

[18]Baxter and Palmer, 41.

[19]Baxter and Orme, 3:ii.

application is implied in those solemn words of the Apostle: 'I charge thee before God and the Lord Jesus Christ, who shall judge the quick and the dead at his appearing, preach the Word, be instant in season, out of season; reprove, rebuke, exhort, with all long-suffering and doctrine.'"[20]

Even Whitefield, whose emphasis was clearly on field preaching, saw the value of visitation in general and the role of proclamation during visitation in particular. In Tucker's book on George Whitefield, he quotes Whitefield writing to a fellow preacher, "catechise and visit from House to House, live as *Christ lived*, teach as he taught."[21] Whitefield himself writes that he taught from "house to house" as part of his ministry.[22] Wesley even acknowledged Whitefield's stress on visitation when Wesley preached his funeral sermon.[23]

Considering the legacy of visitation it is unsurprising that Wesley quickly recognized the Moravian emphasis on visitation during his trip to Hernhuth in 1738:

> On the first Saturday in the month the Lord's Supper is administered. From ten in the morning till two, the Eldest speaks with each communicant in private, concerning the state of his soul; at two, they dine, then wash one another's feet; after which they sing and pray; about ten, they receive in silence without any ceremony, and continue in silence till they part at twelve.[24]

Some of the reason many in the traditions that Wesley drew from seem to emphasize the role of proclamation in visitation as a deep-rooted uncertainty in the ability of public preaching alone to facilitate adequate discipleship. Baxter asserts, for instance, that "private oversight" is a minister's most important task and that public preaching is the "least part of a minister's work."[25] Bishop Wilson echoes Baxter's sentiment when he writes that visiting parishioners, especially those who do not regularly attend worship, is important in order to "take an account of the state and condition of your particular Flocks... visit[ing] and deal[ing] in private with those upon whom your Sermons have probably had no influence."[26] William Al-

[20]*Minutes of Conference, Large Minutes*, 1770–72, §17.4, 10:879. Here Baxter refers to the Apostle Paul's command to Timothy in 2 Timothy 4:1-2.

[21]Josiah Tucker, *The Life and Particular Proceedings of the Rev. Mr. George Whitefield* (London, 1739), 71.

[22]George Whitefield, *Fifteen Sermons Preached on Various Important Subjects* (Paisley: J. Neilson, 1794), 120.

[23]*Sermons II*, Sermon 53, "On the Death of George Whitefield," §1.7, 2:332.

[24]*Journal and Diaries I*, 11–14 August 1738, 18:293.

[25]Baxter and Orme, 3:ii.

[26]Thomas Wilson, *Parochialia; or, Instructions to the Clergy, in the Discharge of Their Parochial Duty* (Bath: R. Cruttwell, 1788), 20.

len claimed that visiting "from house to house was of very great use for their [church parishioners'] profiting in Religion, yea so great, that some of you have thought you did more good that way, than by your publick Ministration."[27] Bishop Burnet wrote in the late seventeenth century that doctrine was confirmed best through personal conversations in people's homes: "He [the parish priest] ought to admonish, to reprove, and to comfort them [parishioners], not only by his general Doctrine in his Sermons, but from House to House; that so he may do these Things more home and effectually, than can be done from the Pulpit."[28] Wesley discovered in his heritage the conviction that pulpit preaching is a vital tool for encouraging discipleship but that in isolation it fails to guide all people into the holy life the Spirit desires. Therefore visitation that included examination and proclamation became an essential part of the religious milieu from which Wesley drew.

FAMILY RELIGION

Visitation and family religion (sometimes called family worship) are closely related concepts in Wesley's mind. Wesley encouraged parents to closely oversee their children's spiritual development. Family religion in Wesley's day was the practice of families gathering for corporate worship, prayer, Bible study, and even proclamation. The task of leading the time was typically given to the father or governor, but sometimes women led family worship as well. Family religion was not unique to Methodists. Whitefield encouraged it. In his sermon "The Great Duty of Family Religion," Whitefield writes, "it is the duty of every governor of a family to take care, that not only he himself, but also that those committed to his charge, should serve the Lord."[29] For as Whitefield continues, "Every house is as it were a little parish, every governor . . . a priest, every family a flock: And if any of them perish through the governor's neglect, their blood will God require at his hands."[30]

Wesley shared the same basic sentiment. He echoes Baxter's view that part of the preacher's task is to ensure that family worship plays a regular

[27]Allen, Kidder, and Williams, 483.

[28]Gilbert Burnet, "A Discourse of the Pastoral Care" (1692), http://anglicanhistory.org/england/burnet/care/01.html.1.

[29]George Whitefield, *Sermons of George Whitefield*, ed. Evelyn Bence (Peabody: Hendrickson, 2009), 27.

[30]Ibid., 28. Whitefield continues that ignoring this responsibility is as "odious" as a minister disregarding "teaching his people publicly, and from house to house." To do so, he continues, "Is no worse than (a governor) who thinks himself obliged only to save his own soul, without paying any regard to take souls of his household. For... every house is as it were a parish, and every master is concerned to secure, as much as in him lies, the spiritual prosperity of every one under his roof, as any minister whatever is obliged to look to the spiritual welfare of every individual person under his charge."

part in family life. The preacher should check up on the governor to make sure family worship is adequate:

> Get certain information how each family is ordered, and how God is worshipped in them: that you may know how to proceed in your carefulness for their future good . . . Go now and then among them, when they are like to be most at leisure, and ask the master of the family whether he pray with them, or read the Scriptures, or what he doth? And labour to convince the neglecters of their sin.[31]

Wesley writes in his journal, "I strongly inculcated family religion, the *grand desideratum* among the Methodist."[32] In the "Directions Given to the Band-Societies" for society members, Wesley writes, "To use private prayer every day; and family prayer, if you are at the head of a family."[33] Furthermore, Methodists should let no "day pass without family prayer, seriously and solemnly performed."[34]

Methodists continued to follow this advice for years. They adopted Wesley's belief that children could have significant spiritual experiences, that all of a household could grow spiritually, and that children especially should be nurtured spiritually. Yet sometimes Methodists did not take family religion seriously enough in Wesley's eyes. In the 1766 *Minutes* Wesley warns that "family religion is shamefully wanting" in Methodism. In the 1765 *Minutes* Wesley asks, "Is not family worship partly neglected, partly performed in a dull, formal manner? A. It is. Therefore strongly recommend both in public and private the having [of] family prayer morning and evening, after reading a chapter [of scripture], and that in the most lively manner."[35]

Years later some Methodists wondered why parents still took this task so lightly. Jacob Moore writes in 1826,

> It is a matter of regret that there should be any need to adduce arguments to show the obligation of family worship. But many private persons, who make pretensions to Christianity, deny its obligation, and neglect it altogether. . . . All heads of families are bound, by natural and moral obligation, to worship God in and with their families.[36]

[31]Baxter, et al, 84.

[32]*Journal and Diaries V,* 16 November 1766, 22:68, (emphasis mine).

[33]*Societies*, "Directions Given to the Band-Societies," §III.3, 9:79.

[34]*Sermons III,* Sermon 94, "On Family Religion," §3.5, 3:340.

[35]*Minutes of Conference*, 1765, 313.

[36]Jacob Moore, "An Essay on the Obligation of Family Worship," *Methodist Magazine* 9 (July 1826): 255.

Stephen Olin writes in the late 1840s that religious training is "one of the plainest and least controverted of duties" and that "the highest of the parent's obligations finds its sphere in the moral and religious training of his offspring."[37] And yet, he continues:

> Many parents, whose ordinary administration of family government is judicious and firm, often act upon a vague theory, that in all matters related to Christian faith and practice, their children should be left free from control. They will advise, but nothing further. Hence the children are allowed to grow up in irreligious habits, much as they know and hear of religious principles and duty.[38]

Parents, Olin argued, were giving their children direction in everything but the spiritual life. A writer in the *Methodist Magazine* made a similar point in 1821:

> How strange is the conduct of parents who bestow less labour on the intellects of their offspring, than they would acknowledge sufficient to bring forward a good production among their vegetables! They attentively watch the growth of the plant, and carefully pluck the obtruding weed that it may not undermine its roots, or cast an unseemly shade over its fair blossoms; but leave the growing mind to its own bent, or to take the course which chance may give it![39]

Characteristics of Methodist Visitation

By the late 1760s Wesley recognized the Methodist movement had a problem. Some outside the movement critiqued Methodists for being "no better than other people."[40] Wesley disputes this in part, but writes the assertion "is nearer the truth than we are willing to imagine."[41] Wesley's evidence that many Methodists fail to live demonstrably holy lives is twofold. First:

> Personal religion, either toward God or man, is amazingly superficial among us…
>
> How little faith is there among us! How little communion with God! How little living in heaven, walking in eternity, deadness to every creature!

[37]Stephen Olin, "Religious Training," *Methodist Quarterly Review* 31 (April 1849): 304.

[38]Ibid., 314.

[39]"On Family Religion," *Methodist Magazine* 4 (December 1821): 472.

[40]*Minutes of Conference, Large Minutes*, 1770–72, §17.1, 10:876.

[41]Ibid.

> How much love of the world; desire of pleasure, of ease, of getting money! How little brotherly love! What continual judging one another! What gossiping, evil-speaking, tale-bearing! What want of moral honesty![42]

Furthermore:

> Family religion is shamefully wanting…The Methodists in general will be little better till we take quite another course…For what avails public preaching alone, though we could preach like angels? We must instruct them "from house to house." Till this is done, and that in good earnest, the Methodists will be little better than other people.[43]

Beginning with these words in the *Minutes* from the late 1760s and early 1770s, as well as his 1786 sermon "On Visiting the Sick," Wesley began to formalize for Methodists expectations that had to that point been forthright, but not fully clarified. Wesley, building on his heritage, especially Richard Baxter's influential *Gildas Salvianus,* formalized the practice of visitation and the characteristics that helped define it.[44]

The Time and Place of Visitation

A number of characteristics helped define Methodist visitation. Typically, visitation took place best either after a Methodist society or class meeting or during a visit to a Methodist home. In this first case, a leader or preacher would speak in "close" (personal, direct, or searching conversation), with some or all Methodists in small groups or in private after a communal gathering, be it a society, band, or class meeting.[45] On occasion leaders would alternate weeks meeting with married persons and then single people.[46] In the second case, preachers, class leaders, or Wesley himself would visit a person at their home. Visits could occur at any time of the day. Sometimes they followed an evening meal in which the family could be present. Other times preachers and leaders would set up regular times that were convenient to all. For instance Wesley writes: "I

[42]Ibid.

[43]Ibid., *Large Minutes,* 1770–72, §17.1, 10:877.

[44]Ibid., 1766, 10:332. Beginning in the 1766 edition of the *Minutes,* Wesley asks, "Can we find a better method of doing this [instructing from house to house] than Mr. Baxter's? If not, let us adopt it without delay. [It] is well worth a careful perusal." In the 1770–72 *Minutes* (10:876), Wesley cites the "unspeakable need" (876) for visiting people in their home and abridges Baxter's process for how to do so adequately on pages 877–83.

[45]Ibid., *Large Minutes,* 1753–63, §16.1, 10:848. See also *Large Minutes,* 1770–72, §17, 10:876. Wesley's first answer in the *Minutes* to the question, "How can we farther assist those under our care?" is to examine them more closely at the "meetings of the classes" (1753–63), or at each "Visitation" (1770–72).

[46]Ibid., *Large Minutes,* 1770–72, §17, 10:876.

began visiting my parishioners in order from house-to-house, for which I set apart the time when they could not work, because of the heat, namely from twelve to three in the afternoon."[47] Visits in homes began with a corporate time of "words spoken to all in the house," followed frequently with private meetings in another room.[48]

Visiting the Physically and Spiritually Sick

Wesley urges Methodist leaders, preachers, and members to visit Methodists who are physically or spiritually sick. Unlike in many churches today, where visitation is seen primarily, if not solely as a clerical service for those who are physically ill, Wesley viewed it as a pastoral practice of all Methodists towards those sick in body and spirit. This is perhaps most evident in Wesley's sermon "On Visitation": "By the sick, I do not mean only those that keep their bed, or that are sick in the strictest sense. Rather I would include all such as are in a state of affliction, whether of mind or body; and that whether they are good or bad, whether they fear God or not."[49] Wesley's focus in this sermon is not one's physical ailments but rather in assisting with a person's "spiritual wants."[50] When visiting he suggests beginning a conversation by addressing a person's "outward condition," asking if they "have the necessaries of life," whether food, clothing, fuel, and are receiving medical advice.[51] But after inquiring into their physical health, Wesley says, the visitor may move on "to the things of greater importance," namely an examination of a person's spiritual health.[52]

Spiritual Examination

From its earliest days as a formal movement, Wesley integrated spiritual examination into Methodist practice. As early as 1744 Wesley writes that part of a leader's task is "to inquire into the state of their [Methodists'] souls, and advise 'em as occasion may require... to inquire into the their disorder, and procure advice for 'em."[53] Wesley's sermon "On Visiting the Sick" is instructive. Examples of questions are "Have you ever

[47]*Societies*, "Short History of the People Called Methodists," §6, 9:429.

[48]*Minutes of Conference, Large Minutes*, 1770–72, §17.7, 10:881.

[49]*Sermons III*, Sermon 98, "On Visiting the Sick," §1.1, 3:387. Wesley does not denigrate physical illness, but his emphasis is clearly on spiritual sickness. His priority is evident in this sermon where he writes that spiritual visitation offers a "more excellent kind" of help than just physical comfort (Ibid., 387–89).

[50]Ibid., §1.5, 3:389.

[51]Ibid., §2.2, 3:390.

[52]Ibid., §2.4, 3:391.

[53]*Minutes of Conference*, 1744, §79, 10:143.

considered that God governs the world? That his providence is over all? And over *you* in particular? Does anything then befall you without his knowledge? Or without his designing it for your good?"[54] This questioning is then followed by an examination of the person's outward and inward life, followed by an explanation of justification and holiness. Once the person "begins to understand the nature of holiness, and the necessity of the New Birth, then you may press upon him 'repentance toward God, and faith in our Lord Jesus Christ.'"[55] Then Wesley recommends the visitor offer various writings, depending on a person's spiritual state. For instance, he suggests "some plain tracts," such as "Instructions for Christians," "Awake, thou that Sleepest," and the "Nature and Design of Christianity."

Subsequent visits should pick up where the visitor left off, questioning whether the person remembered and understood the previous conversation. The visitor can then in these later meetings continue to "enforce" what had been taught and "impress it on their hearts."[56] All visits should conclude with prayer, preferably a personal one "without a form" but for those who have not broken "through this backwardness" of not knowing how to pray extemporaneously.[57]

The questions noted above are not ones typically associated with an inquiry into a person's physical health. The questions are, rather, profoundly spiritual in nature. Through examination leaders and preachers grew to know Methodists under their care in body and soul and then provided a setting by which Methodists could encourage one another toward their pursuit of holiness. Wesley sometimes refers to this spiritual care as "looking upon" people in love or "watching over" one another. In his sermon "On Visiting the Sick," Wesley writes, "The word which we render 'visit' in its literal acceptation means to *look upon*."[58] Baxter set the tone that Wesley emphasizes later when he writes, "We should know every person that belongeth to our charge. For how can we take heed to them, if we do not know them?"[59] Atkinson demonstrates that at least some kept up this pattern long after Wesley's death:

> He (the class leader) must watch his flock like a shepherd. If he simply hold class-meeting once a week, and look no further after his members,

[54]*Sermons III*, Sermon 98, "On Visiting the Sick," §2.4, 3:391.

[55]Ibid.

[56]Ibid., §2.5, 3:392.

[57]Ibid., §2.4, 3:391.

[58]Ibid., §I.2, 3:387.

[59]Baxter, et al, 60.

> his knowledge of them will be very imperfect. He should know them, not simply in the class room, but in their daily life, their company, diversions, business; in their besetments, perplexities, discouragements; their temptations, falls, and uprisings. He should know their peculiarities of character, temperament, and condition, and so be able to rightly admonish, advise, and encourage them.[60]

The point of visitation was for the visitor to converse about a Methodist's deep joys, doubts, and struggles, namely, to have a spiritual conversation that would be difficult, if not impossible, in the larger gatherings during field preaching, society, and class meetings. Wesley wanted access to the deeper recesses of a person's soul, not the trivialities that so often mark superficial conversations. Wesley makes this point in a letter to Mrs. Elizabeth Bennis on September 10, 1773: "I hope you will encourage every Preacher to visit the whole society in order, from house to house: Dinner, or drinking tea, does not answer the same intention. This may and ought to be done over and above."[61] Meeting for tea and generic conversation is not the point. Deep spiritual conversation about a person's core beliefs and life is the point.

Sometimes what was discovered was shocking. Wesley describes in the *Minutes* an example from an earlier Church of England cleric, Rev. Thomas Lupton. Wesley once heard his son relate a story Wesley found all too familiar:

> My father, visiting one of his parishioners, who had never missed going to church for forty years, then lying on his death-bed, asked him, "Thomas, where do you think your soul will go?" "Soul? Soul?" said Thomas. "Yes. Do not you know what your soul is?" "Ay, surely," said he: "Why, it is a little bone in the back that lives longer than the rest of the body." So much Thomas had learned by often hearing sermons, yea, and exceeding good sermons, for forty years![62]

Even after years of listening to public preaching, some people still did not know the basics of the Christian faith and life. Only through examination could a leader help determine a person's spiritual maturity, a determination of which was necessary in order to help people mature in discipleship by proclaiming to them the next appropriate step as a disciple.

---

[60]Atkinson, 16–17.

[61]*Letters* (Telford), Letter to Mrs. Elizabeth Bennis, 10 September 1773, 6:40.

[62]*Minutes of Conference*, 1766, 10:332.

All Methodists Are to Visit and Receive Visits

Wesley hoped all Methodists would themselves visit other Methodists. In his sermon "On Visiting the Sick," Wesley emphasizes that visiting is "a plain duty, which all that are in health may practice."[63] Whether young or old, rich or poor, male or female, all who visit are "blessed" and shall "inherit the kingdom," while those who don't visit are "cursed" and will "depart into everlasting fire."[64] Visiting is not left to clergy or preachers or leaders alone, but is part of every Christian's ministry.

Not only are all Methodists to visit, all Methodists should be visited. Some did not want to be visited so Wesley makes sure to include Baxter's observation that, "Too many of them [those visited] will be unwilling to be taught till we conquer their perverseness by the force of reason and the power of love. [Furthermore] many are so dull that they will shun being taught, for fear of showing their dullness."[65] Neither of these are excuses according to Baxter:

> Their willfulness will not excuse us from our duty: If we offer them not our help, how know we who will refuse it? Offering it is our part, and accepting is theirs.... If some refuse our help, others will accept it, and the success with them may be so much, as may answer all our labour were it more. It is not all that are wrought on by our public preaching, and yet we must not therefore give it over as unprofitable.[66]

The same is true for children. Indeed Wesley believed that the continuation of the Methodist movement would be in part determined by how well the children were "watched over" and nurtured in their own spiritual journey. Wesley asks in the 1768 *Minutes*, "What can we do for the *rising generation*? Unless we can take care of these the present revival of religion will be *res unius aetatis*. It will last only the age of a man."[67] Wesley's response, echoing Baxter, is to focus particularly on children:

> (i) Spend an hour a week with the children in every large town, whether you like it or no.

[63]*Sermons III*, Sermon 98, "On Visiting the Sick," §1.4, 3:386.

[64]Ibid., §III.1, 3:392. Wesley concludes the sermon writing to those who do not begin visiting immediately, "Begin, my dear brethren, begin now; else the impression which you now feel will wear off; and, possibly, it may never return! What then will be the consequence? Instead of hearing that word, 'Come, ye blessed!—For I was sick, and ye visited me;' you must hear that awful sentence, 'Depart, ye cursed!—For I was sick, and ye visited me not!'" (§III.9, 3:397).

[65]*Minutes of Conference, Large Minutes*, 1770–72, §17.3, 10:878.

[66]Baxter, et al, 406.

[67]*Minutes of Conference*, 1768, 10:364.

(ii) Talk with them every time you see any at home.

(iii) Pray in earnest for them.

(iv) Diligently instruct and vehemently exhort all parents at their own houses.[68]

Methodists had a responsibility to care for the spiritual development of all their members, even their youngest participants. For Wesley, visitation is a responsibility of all Christians—not only the elite, or the leaders, or the preachers. Wesley expected leaders and preachers to visit, but not only them. While Wesley emphasizes the role of preachers and class leaders in visitation, all Methodists should see visiting as part of their ministerial task.

Personal and Private

A visit is preferably as personal and as private as possible. Sometimes if a Methodist is "disabled by pain or weakness," and the need is only physical, then bodily comfort, such as food or clothing, can be sent.[69] But if the need is a spiritual one then the visit must be personal. "Looking upon" people's spiritual needs, Wesley writes, "cannot be done unless you are present with them," and it cannot be "left undone."[70] It must be done in person and "cannot be done by proxy."[71]

Privacy also encourages sharing about one's spiritual journey. Visitation is preferably done one on one, though if necessary others could be in the same room, but certainly none should "be present but those who are familiar with each other."[72] Visitation is the most intimate of the four forums for proclamation discussed in this book. Whereas the other three forums are always group-oriented—from potentially many thousands in the case of field preaching, to many hundreds in society meetings, to usually less than twelve in class meetings—visitation, at its core, is designed to facilitate a personal conversation. Even on occasions when a visit starts with a familial gathering, as discussed below, Wesley encourages preachers and leaders to include time for one-on-one conversations with each member of a household, typically in a private room. Wesley uses the term "close" to describe personal and pointed conversations where people can share their souls and where the preacher or leader can give specific direction on how to mature spiritually. These close conversations are much more likely in visitation than in the other three forums.

[68]Ibid., *Large Minutes*, 1770–72, 10:365.

[69]*Sermons III*, Sermon 98, "On Visiting the Sick," §III.9, 3:397.

[70]Ibid., §I.2, 3:387.

[71]Ibid., §I.5, 3:389.

[72]*Minutes of Conference*, *Large Minutes*, 1770–72, §17.7, 10:881.

Repetitive Practice

A principle of Wesley's visitation is that it is a repetitive practice. Reflecting on the importance of multiple conversations over a period of time, Wesley writes:

> Make every particular plain to their understanding. Fix it in their memory. Write it in their heart. In order to [do] this, there must be "line upon line, precept upon precept." I remember to have heard my father asking my mother, "How could you have the patience to tell that blockhead the same thing twenty times over?" She answered, "Why, if I had told him but nineteen times, I should have lost all my labour." What patience, what love, what knowledge is requisite for this![73]

Spiritual maturity comes through ongoing engagement with other disciples. Wesley encourages visitation annually at the minimum, and preferably at least quarterly. These repetitive visits allow visitors to continually follow up with a Methodist's questions, concerns, or issues they were struggling to either retain or believe.

Gentle and Graceful Spiritual Direction

Through its personal and conversational nature, visitation allowed the preacher or leader to provide a direct feedback that was impossible in larger group settings. Sometimes this meant redirecting those who erred to the right path, encouraging a change in behavior.[74] Other times it meant encouragement. But each time, the leader was to give directions in love. Wesley writes, "Be sure to deal gently with them, and take off all discouragements as effectually as you can... Let your dealing with those you begin with be so gentle, winning, and convincing, that the report of it may move others to desire your coming."[75] Wesley writes in another place, "Be plain and open in dealing with souls. Be mild, tender, patient."[76]

[73]Ibid., §34.2, 10:888.

[74]Isaac Lim, "Wesleyan Preaching and Small Group Ministry: Principles and Practice," *Asia Journal of Theology* 3, no. October (1989): 519. Correcting behavior was still understood as part of visitation late into the nineteenth century. Atkinson writes, "How many are lost... because their Class Leaders do not visit them!" He continues, "Fidelity in visiting and restoring the erring members of his flock is one of the highest excellences of a Class Leader." Atkinson, 97, 100.

[75]*Minutes of Conference, Large Minutes*, 1770–72, §17.6, 10:881.

[76]Ibid., 1744, §80, 10:144. Baxter writes of a number of critiques of private instruction through visitation, though they do not sway his commitment to it. One is that visiting people in their homes, "Will take up so much time that a man shall have no time to follow his studies." Another is that it, "Will destroy the health of our bodies, by continual spending the spirits and allowing us no time for necessary recreations; and it will wholly lock us up from any civil friendly visitations, so that we must never stir from home nor take our delight at home one day with our friends, for the relaxation of our minds; but as we shall seem discourteous and more so to others, so we shall tire our selves, and the bow that is still bent will be in danger of breaking at last." Baxter, et al, 388, 391.

The point was to provide gentle yet pointed direction based on the examination, so that Methodists were encouraged to continue maturing in the life of discipleship. Wesley believed it is easy to regress in discipleship. Christian maturation, he held, is not guaranteed, and many Methodists are quite tentative in their discipleship. In the *Minutes* Wesley quotes Baxter's warning that if preachers do not visit from house to house, the gospel will not be fixed "on their [convert's] heart, without which all our labour is lost...And when we have made some impressions on their hearts, if we look not after them, they will soon die away."[77]

The Challenge of Visitation

One consistent characteristic of visitation is its difficulty, a fact both Wesley and his preachers freely acknowledged. In one place, Wesley calls it so "grievous to flesh and blood" that he can only "prevail on a few, even of our Preachers, to undertake it."[78]

Despite this difficulty, Wesley's stance in favor of visitation remained firm through his life. He agrees with Baxter that some preachers are unfaithful in their ministries, being dull and lazy, and too focused on "man-pleasing... [willing] to let men perish rather than lose their love. We let them go quietly to hell lest we should anger them."[79] Some preachers argued that the time required by visitation inhibited adequate study. Wesley's solution was for preachers to sleep less, study in the morning, and visit in the afternoons, for "Gaining knowledge is a good thing; but saving souls is better."[80]

Unfortunately, Wesley seemed to struggle to get preachers to visit with the consistency he desired. Dean writes, "Wesley's preachers never placed the same emphasis on house-to-house visitation that he did, and often must not have taken as much care in the quarterly visitations, either. He increasingly urged the preachers to visit."[81] Nineteenth-century Methodist leaders continued the call for preachers to visit, but again, to little avail.[82]

---

[77]*Minutes of Conference, Large Minutes,* 1770–72, §17.3, 10:878.

[78]*Journal and Diaries V,* 12 January 1774, 22:396. Two years earlier Wesley wrote that visiting is a "heavy cross, no way pleasing to the flesh and blood. But I already saw how unspeakable useful it will be to many souls" (ibid., 30 September 1772 22:394).

[79]*Minutes of Conference, Large Minutes,* 1770–72, §17.2, 10:877.

[80]Ibid., §17.5, 10:880.

[81]Dean, 293.

[82]Ibid., 231. Dean examines a number of pamphlets that describe the "almost universal complaint" of Methodist members regarding the lack of visitation by preachers: "Exhortations to the preachers to visit and frequent complaints that they did not do so are plentiful in Conference records and other literature in the nineteenth century." One preacher's response in a pamphlet that Dean cites on page 293 is telling, "But we fear too much is expected. The strictly secular duties, which have gradually surrounded the ministerial office, often compel a neglect of pastoral claims that would gladly be satisfied, if it were possible."

PROCLAMATION

Each of the characteristics of visitation mentioned above are important, but the most significant one for the purpose of this discussion is the integral relationship between visitation and proclamation. We have seen the importance of the role of proclamation through exhortation, instruction, teaching, and even preaching in visitation throughout this chapter. But the priority of proclaiming the law and the gospel in visitation cannot be overemphasized and is worth exploring to a greater degree.[83]

As noted earlier, Wesley cites Baxter at length in the *Minutes*, directing preachers to "go to each house" and give "with suitable exhortation and direction" the *Instructions for Children*.[84] Baxter continues that the preacher is to "advise the grown persons to see that they understand them. And enlarge upon and apply every sentence as closely as you can."[85] After a thorough conversation regarding each person's spiritual state, Baxter says to:

> Instruct them yourself...If a man understand the fundamentals fall on what you perceive he most needs, either explaining further some doctrine of the gospel, or some duty, or showing the necessity of something he neglects, as may be most edifying to him. If it be one that is grossly ignorant, give him a short recital of the Christian religion in the plainest words. And if you perceive he understands not, go over it again till he does, and if possible, fix it in his memory.[86]

Finally, Baxter writes to conclude "with a strong exhortation on 1. The duty of the heathen to receive Christ and, 2. The avoiding of former sins."[87] Baxter's, and thus Wesley's, point is clear. Teach the people under your care the basics of the Christian faith. He wants to make sure the people under his care know the story of God in Christ and its implications for their lives, and this requires a verbal announcement, or proclamation, through instruction and teaching.

Wesley incorporates Baxter's linclusion of proclamation in visitation throughout his ministry. For Wesley, proclamation in visitation includes exhortation, teaching, instruction, reproof, and even preaching. A variety

[83]*Letters II*, Letter to an Evangelical Layman, 20 December 1751, 26:486. Both law and gospel can be the content of proclamation in a one-on-one setting. This final forum is the only one in which Wesley believed the gospel apart from the law is appropriately proclaimed: Wesley writes that the only time that the gospel alone should be preached, without any connection to the law, is, "In private converse with a thoroughly convinced sinner."

[84]*Minutes of Conference, Large Minutes*, 1770–72, §17.6, 10:881.

[85]Ibid., §17.6, 10:881.

[86]Ibid., §17.7, 10:882.

[87]Ibid., §17.7, 10:883.

of examples will suffice. A typical example of Wesley's encouragement of people to proclaim in multiple ways is found in a letter from Wesley to Richard Steel where Wesley tells him to "examine, instruct, reprove, exhort" when going house to house.[88] Another example is Wesley's letter to Miss Stokes on February 11, 1772:

> You are not sent thither for nothing, but in order to do, as well as to receive, good; and that not to one family only, or to those four of your acquaintance; nay, but you have a message from God, (you and—Eden too,) to all the women in the society. Set aside all evil shame; all modesty, falsely so called. Go from house to house; deal faithfully with them all; warn every one; exhort every one. God will everywhere give you a word to speak; and his blessing therewith.[89]

Still another example of exhortation in visitation is found in one author's commentary on Methodist preachers: "He [the minister] prays, reproves, and exhorts from house to house."[90]

Wesley also mentions teaching and instruction as part of visitation. In his sermon "On Visiting the Sick" Wesley encourages Methodists to instruct those they visit: "In the first principles of religion; endeavouring to show them the dangerous state they are in, under the wrath and curse of God through sin, and point them to the Lamb of God."[91] In the *Large Minutes* Wesley writes, "This [instruction in homes] has never been effectually done yet," and that where it has, the blessings are great both to those who hear and those who speak.[92] He continues, "Do all you can herein, if not all you would. Inquire in each house, 'Have you family prayer? Do you read the Scripture in your family? Have you a fixed time for private prayers?' Examine each as to his growth in grace, and discharge of relative duties."[93]

Perhaps the best example is Wesley's command in the *Large Minutes* that precedes his abridgement of Baxter's *Gildas Salvianus*. Wesley writes that "We must instruct them 'from house to house.' Till this is done, and that in good earnest, the Methodists will be little better than other people."[94] Therefore offer "suitable exhortation and direction" for both

[88] *Letters* (Telford), Letter to Richard Steel, 24 April 1769, 5:132.

[89] Ibid., Letter to Mary Stokes, 11 February 1772, 5:305.

[90] *The Detector Detected, or the Plowman's Defense of Methodism* (London, 1796), 32.

[91] *Sermons III*, Sermon 98, "On Visiting the Sick," §I.5, 3:389.

[92] *Minutes of Conference, Large Minutes*, 1753–63, §16.5, 10:848. See also ibid., *Large Minutes*, 1770–72, §17, 10:876.

[93] Ibid., *Large Minutes*, 1753–63, §16.5, 10:848.

[94] Ibid., *Large Minutes*, 1770–72, §17.1, 10:877. In earlier versions of the minutes Wesley substitutes the phrase "every travelling Preacher" for "We."

children and adults.[95] Wesley continues: "It may be well, after a few loving words spoken to all in the house, to take each person singly into another room, where you may deal closely with him, about his sin, and misery, and duty." Wesley then moves to a series of theological questions, asking, for example, "Do you believe you have sin in you? What does sin deserve? What remedy has God provided for guilty, helpless sinners?"; or "What is repentance?...What is faith?"; or "How do you think your many and great sins will be pardoned?"; or "Can you be saved without the death of Christ?"[96] If someone did not know an answer, instead of being condemning, Baxter, and thus Wesley, suggests offering the answer.[97] The point is not to burden the person but to discern where his or her knowledge and practice were inadequate and then to share the correct answer. Wesley writes, "If you perceive them troubled that they cannot answer, step in yourself, and take the burden off them, answering that question yourself; and then do it thoroughly and plainly, and make a full explication of the whole business to them."[98]

Even more enlightening is Wesley's clear inclusion of preaching in visitation. As in other areas, some of the religious milieu of the time helped lead Wesley to embrace preaching in visitation. Wesley was certainly aware of Baxter's entreaty that "a master of a family may preach to his own family."[99] Furthermore before Wesley left for Georgia, Dr. Burton advised him that preaching is part of visitation: "The apostolic manner of preaching from house to house will, through God's grace, be effectual to turn many to righteousness."[100] Wesley also believed that the practice is rooted in the New Testament. The NIV translation of Acts 20:20 is, "You know that I have not hesitated to preach anything that would be helpful to you but have taught you publicly and from house to house." Reflecting on this verse in his *Explanatory Notes Upon the New Testament*, Wesley comments, "For even an apostle could not discharge his duty by public preaching only. How much less can an ordinary pastor!"[101] According to Wesley, the task of preaching house to house is a part of every pastor's duty.

Other people, both Methodist and otherwise, discuss the Methodist

[95]Ibid., §17.6, 10:881.

[96]Ibid., §17.7, 10:881–82.

[97]Ibid., §17.7, 10:882. For example, if someone could not adequately answer the question, "What is repentance?" Wesley suggests providing the answer, "Sorrow for sin, or a conviction that we are guilty helpless sinners?"

[98]Ibid.

[99]Baxter, et al, 79.

[100]Doughty, *John Wesley, Preacher*, 15.

[101]Wesley, *Explanatory Notes Upon the New Testament*, 243.

emphasis on preaching in visitation. The Methodist preacher John Pawson, for instance, uses the word *preach* when he asks the question in his address to young preachers, "In our conversation with them (those we visit), are we not sometimes too light and trifling? Should we not endeavour to preach out of the pulpit, as well as in it?"[102] Christopher Hopper, another Methodist preacher during Wesley's lifetime, was said to go "from town to town, and from house to house, singing, praying, and preaching the word."[103] The Anglican priest Samuel Clapham notes that Methodists recognize the important ways visitation can serve to reinforce the message preached, and laments his own tradition's failure to do so:

> One cause, which exceedingly promotes [Methodism's] success, is the very little religious intercourse which is too often found to subsist between the pastor and his flock, in our own Church. The preachers among the Methodists maintain a regular communication with their people; they enquire how far their sermons are understood from the pulpit, and what improvement they produce on the minds of their hearers. Unless we in some degree renew the pastoral intercourse with our parishioners which our forefathers maintained, our ministerial labors will not, I fear, be very forceful, and Methodism will assuredly continue to increase.[104]

The fact that even preaching is part of early Methodist visitation illuminates the role of proclamation in visitation.

Wesley's letter to Richard Steel is again instructive as it further illustrates the role of proclamation in visitation:

> In every town, visit all you can from house to house. I say "all you can," for there will be some whom you cannot visit; and if you examine, instruct, reprove, exhort as need requires, you will have no time hanging on your hands. It is *by this means* that the Societies are increased wherever Thomas Ryan goes: he is preaching morning to night; warning every one, that he may present every one perfect in Christ Jesus.[105]

In just this one letter instruction, exhortation, and even preaching are clearly documented as part of visitation. The point is clear—the proclamation that begins in the relative anonymity of the fields becomes progressively more personal through Methodist society meetings, the class meetings, and finally in visitation.

[102]John Pawson, *A Serious and Affectionate Address to the Junior Preachers in the Methodist Connection* (London, 1798), 7.

[103]Jackson, *The Life of Mr. Christopher Hopper*, 1:198.

[104]Samuel Clapham, *How Far Methodism Conduces to the Interests of Christianity, and the Welfare of Society; Impartially Considered* (Leeds: J. Binns, 1794), 29.

[105]*Letters* (Telford), Letter to Richard Steel, 24 April 1769, 5:132 (emphasis mine).

RESPONSES TO PROCLAMATION IN VISITATION

For Wesley, the point of visitation was not simply inquiry into and determination of a person's spiritual state, followed by proclamation on themes in which people had insufficient knowledge. The point of visitation is to encourage maturity in discipleship, and ultimately holiness of heart and life. Wesley identifies the role of response in Allein's ministry:

> He used also to enquire of them about the spiritual estate, labouring to make them sensible of the evil and danger of sin, of the corruption of our natures, the misery of an unconverted state; provoking them to look after the true Remedy, to turn from all their sins to God, to close with Christ upon his own terms, to follow after holiness, to watch over their hearts and lives, to mortify their lusts, to redeem their time, and to prepare for eternity... he left with them several counsels and directions to be carefully remembered and practiced for the good of their souls.[106]

Once again, Wesley's inclusion of portions of Baxter's *Gildas Salvianus* offers significant insight into Wesley's understanding of how Methodists respond to the gospel in visitation:

> Private instruction... is absolutely necessary. For, after all our preaching, many of our people are almost as ignorant as if they had never heard the gospel. I speak as plain as I can, yet I frequently meet with those who have been my hearers many years, who know not whether Christ be God or man. And how few are there that know the nature of repentance, faith, and holiness! Most of them have a sort of confidence that God will justify and save them, while the world has their hearts and they live to themselves. And I have found by experience, that one of these has learned more from one hour's close discourse than from ten years' public preaching.[107]

In this one citation Wesley describes awakening, repentance and faith, and holiness in the private instruction that can occur during visitation.

Those who know "not whether Christ be God or man" had not yet made the first step of maturity. This is a bit surprising since awakening was a requirement of being a Methodist in the first place. But the reality is that some people had not actually awakened or had reverted from being "awakened" back into the State of Nature. As noted earlier, Wesley believed that it is not only easy to regress in discipleship, but also never to make much progress in discipleship. In his view, Christian maturation is not guaranteed, and many Methodists are quite tentative in their discipleship. After all, it is hard "to fix [spiritual] things on their heart, without

[106]Gillies, 233.

[107]*Minutes of Conference, Large Minutes*, 1770–72, §17.4, 10:878–79.

which all our labour is lost...And when we have made some impressions upon their hearts, if we look not after them, they will soon die away."[108] Setting those first impressions of awakening is an integral aspect of visitation.

Responding with repentance and faith that leads first to justification and then to sanctification is also a critical aspect of visitation in early Methodism. Wesley's quotation of Baxter regarding how few know the nature of repentance and faith demonstrates that Wesley knew that people respond with faith and repentance during visitation. This was especially true of children, as John W. Prince demonstrates when he argues that Wesley's "chief work was to cultivate in them a sense of their sinful nature and a desire for a cure...namely, repentance and faith" and thereby knowing if people are converted or not.[109] Wesley articulates the process of encouraging faith and repentance in visitation later in the quotation from Baxter:

> Next, inquire into his state, whether convinced, or unconvinced, converted or unconverted. Tell him, if need be, what conversion is. And then renew and enforce the inquiry. If you perceive he is unconverted, your next business is to labour with all your skill and power to bring his heart to a sense of his condition. Set this home with a more earnest voice than you spoke before—for if you get it not to the heart, you do nothing. Conclude all with a strong exhortation, which should contain two parts: 1. The duty of the heart, in order to receive Christ. 2. The avoiding former sins, and constantly using the outward means [of grace]. And here be sure, if you can, to get their promise to forsake sin, change their company, and use the means. And do this solemnly; reminding them of the presence of God, that hears their promises and will expect the performance.[110]

The importance of both awakening and conversion through visitation is evident in nineteenth-century Methodism. Carvosso, for instance, notes the importance of visitation in ensuring both awakening and salvation: "I remained here [Saltash] three weeks, meeting the classes and visiting the people from house to house; and some souls were awakened and saved."[111]

Perhaps Wesley's instruction in his sermon "On Visiting the Sick" offers the best example of how Wesley understood proclamation in visitation to lead to justification and sanctification. After caring for a person in body, Wesley says the next step is to care for one's soul:

[108]Ibid., §17.3, 10:878.

[109]John W. Prince, "Wesley on Religious Education: A Study of John Wesley's Theories and Methods of the Education of Children in Religion" (PhD diss., Yale University, 1926), 97, and 134–35.

[110]*Minutes of Conference, Large Minutes*, 1770–72, §17.7, 10:882–83.

[111]Carvosso, 106.

> May you not begin with asking, Have you ever considered, that God governs the world? That his providence is over all? And over you in particular? Does any thing then befall you without his knowledge? Or without his designing it for your good? He knows all you suffer; he knows all your pains; he sees all your wants. He sees not only your affliction in general, but every particular circumstance of it. Is he not looking down from heaven, and disposing all these things for your profit? You may then inquire, whether he is acquainted with the general principles of religion. And afterwards, lovingly and gently examine, whether his life has been agreeable thereto. Whether he has been an outward, barefaced sinner, or has had a form of religion. See next whether he knows anything of the power [of godliness]; of worshipping God "in spirit and in truth." If he does not, endeavour to explain to him, "Without holiness no man shall see the Lord;" and "Except a man be born again, he cannot see the kingdom of God." When he begins to understand the nature of holiness, and the necessity of the new birth, then you may press upon him "repentance toward God, and faith in our Lord Jesus Christ."[112]

Wesley knew that some Methodists had yet to repent and believe in Christ long after they joined a society and class. Therefore visits that included private instruction provided a most intimate setting in which Methodists were encouraged to mature as disciples.

Finally, visitation offers a forum in which people can grow in holiness. Many Methodists never matured to holiness, the apex of the Christian life in Wesley's mind. Visitation completed the cycle that started in field preaching, of encouraging maturity as a disciple, but was all too often still incomplete after some Methodists had long participated in society and class meetings. This very "work of the Lord" is best, and perhaps only, possible when visitation is a vibrant part of Methodist communities.

CONCLUSION

Visitation, this most "unspeakably useful" practice as Wesley describes it, offers the most private space between two people in which in which the Spirit works to nurture holiness.[113] Wesley knew that many Methodists never matured to holiness, the apex of the Christian life, despite years of participating in classes and societies. Public reaching alone, Wesley was convinced, does not ensure that every Methodist grows in holiness. To think otherwise, Wesley concludes, ignores the true difficulty of Christian discipleship.

Wesley makes his conviction known in the 1768 *Minutes* he grieves: "How far from entire sanctification are we still?"[114] The next phrase is a

[112] *Sermons III*, Sermon 98, "On Visiting the Sick," §2.4, 3:391.

[113] *Journal and Diaries V*, 30 September 1772, 22:349.

[114] *Minutes of Conference*, 1768, 10:364.

poignant one: "The religion of the Methodists in general is not internal; at least not deep, universal, uniform, but superficial, partial, uneven." He then offers only one solution—"visit from house to house." Not in useless talking but "particularly in confirming and building up believers," toward sanctification. "Then, and not till then," Wesley insists, "the work of the Lord will prosper in your hands."[115] Wesley expresses the same sentiment at the conclusion of a letter to John Mason: "Labour on, especially by visiting from house to house, and you will see the fruit of your labour."[116] The fruit of Methodist ministry is a people maturing from the natural state into the holy image of God marked by holiness of heart and life. Encouraging Methodists to mature beyond awakening, toward an ongoing posture of faith and repentance that results first to justification and then sanctification, is the point of Methodism and the reason for visitation.

Those seeking Christ need a person who will come alongside them to help direct them to maturity as followers of Christ.[117] In personal conversations a visitor can ask the challenging questions that discourage complacency in the Christian life. In return, the person being visited can share deep-seated concerns and challenges that are often hard to express in public settings. Wesley believed the personal interaction that visitation encourages allows Methodists to discover a person's spiritual state and then caringly encourage them in the next stage of discipleship, even if that meant teaching, exhortation, or even preaching the story of God to a person one-on-one.

For Wesley, visitation was not simply a chance to take care of someone's physical ailments. Rather it was the culmination of the Methodist practice of announcing the good news of God in Christ. The proclamation that began in the fields continued in societies, became more pointed in classes, and was most personal in visitation. Proclaiming the story of God in Christ during a personal and private visit made it possible to confirm all the work that took place in the previous three forums. In this way proclamation in visitation serves as the heart of Wesley's evangelistic vision.

[115]Ibid.

[116]*Letters* (Telford), Letter to John Mason, 21 November 1776, 6:240. See also Wesley's 6 August 1768 letter to Mason, "Take pains, likewise, with the children, and in visiting from house to house; else you will see little fruit of your labour." Ibid., 5:100; Wesley's 3 December 1771 letter to Mrs. Bennis of Limerick where describes the necessity of preachers going house to house, telling her to, "Thrust him [brother C.] out to visit the whole society, (not only those that can give him meat and drink,) from house to house, according to the plan laid down in the Minutes of Conference: Then he will soon see the fruit of his labour." Ibid., 5:291.

[117]*Appeals, Further Appeal to Men of Reason and Religion,* Part II, §34, 11:246.

Conclusion

In 1764 Wesley corresponded with a man who liked the idea of being a Methodist but did not want to follow the method of discipleship Wesley prescribed. The man appreciated attending field preaching and wanted to be a Methodist, but did not want to go further and join a society or a class. It is hard to imagine that he would have entertained the even more intimate conversation that came with personal instruction in his house. In essence, he wanted to be Methodist in spirit but not in practice. Wesley writes to the gentleman, stating that, "This *joining half-way*, this being a friend to, but not a member of, the society [is an] imperfect union."[1] Only when one embraces the essential practices of Methodism, of becoming a member of a society and attending society meetings, classes, and receiving visits, can one get the "benefit of the advices and exhortations at the meeting of the society; and also of provoking one another, at the private meetings, to love and to good works."[2]

There is no doubt that the early Methodist movement was evangelistic in nature. Nineteenth-century evangelists, who still shape concepts of evangelism today, would unfortunately have us believe that Wesley's evangelism consisted only of preaching for an immediate conversion. More recent scholarly inquiry is right to challenge this assertion. But many today go wrong with the diagnosis they provide—that proclamation by itself cannot constitute the whole of evangelism—and in the remedy they suggest—expanding the concept of evangelism to include many other aspects of the church's mission (such as social justice). The problem with evangelism today is not when a person or community limits the essential act evangelism to a specific announcement of the story of God in Christ. Rather it is when they see conversion as the only legitimate response to the gospel story and thereby ignore awakening and sanctification.

Wesley understood this well. If Wesley were here today he would, I believe, argue that the essential act of evangelism is best understood as the proclamation of the story of God in Christ as found in the Bible, and that proclamation occurs in a variety of ways, including preaching, teaching, and exhortation. The story of God in Christ is one that Wesley believed

[1]*Letters III*, Letter to an Unidentified Man, 13 July 1764, 27:377–78 (emphasis original).

[2]Ibid., 27:377.

had to be specifically articulated. The Spirit is free to move miraculously in the lives of those who have never heard the story of Jesus, but that is not the normal pattern. The normal pattern is for Christians to tell the story in a variety of ways that engages people's hearts and minds, thus facilitating the work of the Spirit. For Wesley, proclamation is no superficial or optional activity; it is the glue that binds together field preaching, society meetings, class meetings, and visitation—and as such it is integral to any accurate understanding of John Wesley's evangelistic vision.

But Wesley would also say, I believe, that evangelism is best conceived not only as the act of proclaiming but also the response it seeks. Repentance and faith that results in a conversion to Christ is never the apex of Christian discipleship in Wesley's mind. It is a critical moment, but it is neither the first nor last response to an encounter with God in Christ. The Spirit typically works in partnership with proclamation of the story of God, to encourage first an awakening to the presence of God. Then the Spirit continues that same work, through ongoing encounters with that same word, to encourage both initial and subsequent experiences of faith and repentance that results first in justification, and then deeper and deeper experiences of sanctification. Wesley's evangelistic vision is thus a dynamic partnership between proclaimer, the word, and the Spirit that is operative throughout every human life whether a person is a Christian or not and whether a person has encountered that grace for the first time or for the thousandth time.

Thus this book challenges contemporary assertions that evangelism can ever be reduced to one's own ethical behavior or acts of charity. A commitment to "doing good" is certainly a "necessary branch of true Christianity," as Wesley calls it, which is critical to the faith.[3] Furthermore, part of Christian perfection, which in Wesley's understanding is perfect love, includes actively demonstrating love for God and neighbor through social ministry. Such demonstrations are signs of love for God and for one's neighbor. As Barclay writes, "It is abundantly clear that to [Wesley] love was not merely passive sentiment... but positive volition—active and outgoing, finding expression in service."[4]

But these demonstrations are not acts of evangelism in and of themselves; rather; they are a Christian's response to the gospel becoming real in his or her life. People who demonstrate charitable acts—what Wesley often called works of mercy—"testified" to the truth of Jesus "by their lives as well as their words" only when the "sound of the gospel" had already gone forth.[5] In this way proclamation served as a critical component

[3]*Sermons I,* Sermon 24, "Sermon on the Mount: Discourse IV," §I.4, 1:534.

[4]Barclay, 1.xxviii.

[5]*Sermons I,* Sermon 24, "Sermon on the Mount: Discourse IV," §II.6, 1:541.

of the works of mercy in early Methodism, for to be Methodist was to love people in body and soul.[6] Thus charitable work or high personal ethics only become evangelistic in nature when specifically linked to the gospel.

The story of God in Christ is truly *the* story of history in Wesley's mind. When people hear the gospel, engage it, and then let it form them completely, their lives are never the same. His brother Charles agreed: "My late discourses had worked different effects. Some were wounded, some hardened and scandalized above measure. I hear of no neuters. The Word has turned them upside down...I found as did others that He owned me."[7] At the heart of John Wesley's evangelistic vision is the conviction that when the word of God is proclaimed no one can remain neutral. The word turns us all upside down and inside out, for God owns us and calls for a response.

[6]*Sermons III*, Sermon 92, "On Zeal," 3:314.

[7]Baker, *Charles Wesley as Revealed by His Letters*, Letter to John Wesley, March 1740, 38.

BIBLIOGRAPHY

Abraham, William J. *The Logic of Evangelism*. Grand Rapids: Eerdmans, 1989.

Albin, Thomas R. "An Empirical Study of Early Methodist Spirituality." In *Wesleyan Theology Today: A Bicentennial Theological Consultation*, edited by Theodore Runyon, 275–90. Nashville: Kingswood, 1985.

———. "'Inwardly Persuaded': Religion of the Heart in Early British Methodism." In *"Heart Religion" in the Methodist Tradition and Related Movements*, edited by Richard B. Steele, xlv, 317. Lanham, MD: Scarecrow, 2001.

Allen, William, Richard Kidder, and John Williams. *The Works of Mr. William Allen, Consisting of Thirteen Distinct Tracts on Several Subjects*. London: Walter Kettilby etc., 1707.

Arias, Mortimer. *Announcing the Reign of God: Evangelization and the Subversive Memory of Jesus*. Philadelphia: Fortress, 1984.

Asbury, Francis. *The Journal of the Rev. Francis Asbury, Bishop of the Methodist Episcopal Church, from August 7, 1771, to December 7, 1815*, vol. 2. New York: N. Bangs and T. Mason, 1821.

Asbury, Francis, and Thomas Coke. *The Doctrines and Discipline of the Methodist Episcopal Church in America: With explanatory Notes by Thomas Coke and Francis Asbury*. 10th ed. Philadelphia: Henry Tuckniss, 1798.

Atkinson, John. *The Class Leader: His Work and How to Do It*. New York: Nelson & Phillips, 1874.

Baker, Frank. *Charles Wesley as Revealed by His Letters*. London: Epworth, 1948.

———. *John Wesley and the Church of England*. London: Epworth, 1970.

———. "The People Called Methodists: 3. Polity." In *A History of the Methodist Church in Great Britain*, edited by Gordon Rupp Rupert Davies, 213–55. London: Epworth, 1965.

Barclay, Wade Crawford. *History of Methodist Missions, Part 1: Early American Methodism: 1769–1844*, vol. 1. New York: The Board of Missions and Church Extension of the Methodist Church, 1949.

Barry, Jonathan, and Kenneth Morgan. *Reformation and Revival in Eighteenth-Century Bristol*. Stroud, U.K.: Bristol Record Society, 1994.

Baxter, Richard, and William Orme. *The Practical Works of the Late Reverend and Pious Mr. Richard Baxter*, 3 vols. London: Thomas Parkhurst, 1707.

Baxter, Richard, and Samuel Palmer. *The Reformed Pastor; a discourse on the pastoral office...Abridged and Reduced to a New Method*. London: J. Buckland, 1766.

Baxter, Richard, Robert White, Nevill Simmons, and William Roybould. *Gildas Salvianus: The Reformed Pastor Shewing the Nature of the Pastoral Work*. London: Robert White, 1656.

Bede. *The Ecclesiastical History of the English Nation. Everyman's Library*, edited by Vida Dutton Scudder. London: J. M. Dent & Sons, 1910.

Benefiel, Ron. "John Wesley's Mission of Evangelism." Paper presented at the Missio Ecclesia, Missio De: A Wesleyan Perspective on the Church in Mission, Point Loma Nazarene University, 12 March 2012.

Bentham, Daniel. *Memoirs of James Hutton: Compromising the Annals of His Life, and Connection with the United Brethren*. London: Hamilton, Adams, and Company, 1856.

Boraine, Alexander L. "The Nature of Evangelism in the Theology and Practice of John Wesley." PhD diss., Drew University, 1969.

Boswell, James. *The Life of Samuel Johnson, LL.D.*, 2 vols. Oxford: Talboys and Wheeler; William Pickering, 1826.

Burnet, Gilbert. "A Discourse of the Pastoral Care." 1692. http://anglicanhistory.org/england/burnet/care/01.html.

Campbell, Ted. *John Wesley and Christian Antiquity: Religious Vision and Cultural Change*. Nashville: Kingswood, 1991.

Carvosso, William. *A Memoir of Mr. William Carvosso, Sixty Years a Class Leader*. New York: Lane and Tippett, 1846.

Catalogue of the Early Preachers Collection, Methodist Archives and Research Centre (MARC), John Rylands University Library of Manchester. Manchester, England.

Catalogue of the Wesley Family Letters, Methodist Archives and Research Centre (MARC), John Rylands University Library of Manchester. Manchester, England.

Chapman, Stephen B., and Laceye C. Warner. "Jonah and the Imitation of God: Rethinking Evangelism and the Old Testament," *Journal of Theological Interpretation* 2, no. 1 (2008): 43–69.

Chilcote, Paul W. "Evangelism in the Methodist Tradition." In *T & T Clark Companion to Methodism*, edited by Charles Yrigoyen. London: T & T Clark, 2010.

Chilcote, Paul Wesley. *Early Methodist Spirituality: Selected Women's Writings*. Nashville: Kingswood, 2007.

———. *She Offered Them Christ: The Legacy of Women Preachers in Early Methodism*. Eugene, OR: Wipf and Stock, 2001.

Church, Leslie F. *The Early Methodist People*, Fernley-Hartley Lecture. London: Epworth, 1948.

———. *More About Early Methodist People*. London: Epworth, 1949.

Clapham, Samuel. *How Far Methodism Conduces to the Interests of Christianity, and the Welfare of Society; Impartially Considered*. Leeds: J. Binns, 1794.

Coles, George. *Heroines of Methodism; or, Pen and Ink Sketches of the Mothers and Daughters of the Church*. New York: Carlton & Porter, 1857.

Corderoy, Edward. *Father Reeves, the Methodist Class Leader: A Brief Account of William Reeves*. London: A. Heylin, 1854.

Crosby, Bernard. "Methodist Evangelism, 1800–1820," *The London Quarterly and Holborn Review* 6, no. 13 (Jan/Oct 1944): 289–305.

Crosby, Sarah. "The Grace of God Manifested in an Account of Mrs. Crosby," *Methodist Magazine* 29 (1806).

Davies, Rupert Eric, E. Gordon Rupp, and A. Raymond George. *A History of the Methodist Church in Great Britain*, 4 vols. London: Epworth, 1965.

Dean, William W. "Disciplined Fellowship: The Rise and Decline of Cell Groups in British Methodism." PhD diss., University of Iowa, 1985.

Deist in London. *The True Character of the Rev. Mr. Whitefield*. London: Mrs. Dodd, Nutt, Cook, Bartlett, 1739.

The Detector Detected, or The Plowman's Defense of Methodism. London, 1796.

Doughty, William L. "Charles Wesley, Preacher," *The London Quarterly and Holborn Review* 182 (October 1957): 263–67.

———. *John Wesley, Preacher*. London: Epworth, 1955.

Downey, James. *The Eighteenth Century Pulpit: A Study of the Sermons of Butler, Berkeley, Secker, Sterne, Whitefield and Wesley*. Oxford: Clarendon Press, 1969.

Dygoski, Louise Annie. "The Journals and Letters of John Wesley on Preaching." PhD diss., University of Wisconsin, 1961.

Early Methodist Volume, British Methodist Archives, John Rylands Library, Special Collections, University of Manchester. Manchester, England.

Ensley, Francis Gerald. *John Wesley, Evangelist*. Nashville: Methodist Evangelistic Materials, 1958.

Etheridge, John Wesley. *The Life of the Rev. Adam Clarke*. London: John Mason, 1858.

———. *The Life of the Rev. Adam Clarke*. Nashville: Southern Methodist Publishing House, 1859.

Felleman, Laura Bartels. *The Form and Power of Religion: John Wesley on Methodist Vitality*. Eugene, OR: Cascade Books, 2012.

Gibson, William. *The Church of England, 1688–1832: Unity and Accord*. London: Routledge, 2001.

Gillies, John. *Historical Collections Relating to Remarkable Periods of the Success of the Gospel*, 2 vols. Glasgow: Robert and Andrew Foulis, 1754.

Green, Joel B., and William H. Willimon. *The Wesley Study Bible*. Nashville: Abingdon, 2009.

Green, Richard. *John Wesley: Evangelist*. London: Religious Tract Society, 1905.

Hardt, Philip F. "The Evangelistic and Catechetical Role of the Class Meeting in Early New York City Methodism," *Methodist History* 38, no. 1 (1999): 4–26.

———. *The Soul of Methodism: The Class Meeting in Early New York City Methodism*. Lanham, MD: University Press of America, 2000.

Hatch, Nathan O., and John H. Wigger, eds. *Methodism and the Shaping of American Culture*. Nashville: Kingswood, 2001.

Heath, Elaine A., and Scott Thomas Kisker. *Longing for Spring: A New Vision for Wesleyan Community*. Eugene, OR: Cascade Books, 2010.

Heitzenrater, Richard P. "John Wesley's Principles and Practice of Preaching." Paper presented at the Center for Methodist Studies at Bridwell Library: Lectures on Several Occasions, Dallas, 1997–1999.

———. *Wesley and the People Called Methodists*. Nashville: Abingdon, 1995.

Hempton, David. *Methodism: Empire of the Spirit*. New Haven: Yale University Press, 2005.

Henderson, David Michael. *John Wesley's Class Meeting: A Model for Making Disciples*. Nappanee, IN: Evangel, 1997.

Hervey, James. *A Collection of the Letters of the late Reverend Mr. James Hervey … To which is prefixed, an account of his Life and Death*. Edinburgh, 1763.

Hone, Richard Brindley. *Lives of Eminent Christians [in English]*. London: John W. Parker, 1843.

Hong, John Sungschul. *John Wesley the Evangelist*. Lexington: Emeth, 2006.

Hunter, George. "John Wesley as Church Growth Strategist," *Wesleyan Theological Journal* 21, no. 1–2 (1986): 25–33. http://wesley.nnu.edu/fileadmin/imported_site/wesleyjournal/1986-wtj-21.pdf.

Jackson, Jack (Thomas Glenn III). "St. Francis: Patron Saint of Evangelism through Social Ministry?" *Witness* 23 (2007–2009): 22–33.

Jackson, Thomas. *The Lives of Early Methodist Preachers*, 3rd ed., 6 vols. London: Wesleyan Methodist Book Room, 1865.

Jones, Scott J. *The Evangelistic Love of God and Neighbor: A Theology of Witness and Discipleship*. Nashville: Abingdon, 2003.

Kidder, Richard. *The Life of the Reverend Anthony Horneck, D.D., Late Preacher at the Savoy*. London: J. H. for B. Aylmer, 1698.

Kisker, Scott Thomas. *Foundation for Revival: Anthony Horneck, the Religious Societies, and the Construction of Anglican Pietism*. Lanham, MD: Scarecrow, 2008.

Kissack, Reginald. "Two Hundred Years of Methodist Field Preaching," *The London Quarterly and Holborn Review* (April 1939).

Klaiber, Walter. *Call and Response: Biblical Foundations of a Theology of Evangelism*. Nashville: Abingdon, 1997.

Knight III, Henry H. "The Means of Grace and the Promise of New Life in the Evangelism of John Wesley." In *Considering the Great Commission: Evangelism and Mission in the Wesleyan Spirit*, edited by Stephen W. Gunter and Elaine A. Robinson, 135–46. Nashville: Abingdon, 2005.

———. *The Presence of God in the Christian Life: John Wesley and the Means of Grace*, Pietist and Wesleyan Studies. Metuchen: Scarecrow, 1992.

Kurewa, John Wesley Zwomunondiita. *Drumbeats of Salvation in Africa: A Study of Biblical, Historical and Theological Foundations for the Ministry of Evangelism in Africa*. Mutare, Zimbabwe: Africa University Press, 2007.

Lemay, J. A. Leo. *The Life of Benjamin Franklin*, 3 vols. Philadelphia: University of Pennsylvania Press, 2013.

Liden, Johan H. "Extract from the Journal of Professor John Henrick Liden," *Proceedings of the Wesleyan Historical Society* 17, no. 1 (1929–30): 1–4.

Lim, Isaac. "Wesleyan Preaching and Small Group Ministry: Principles and Practice," *Asia Journal of Theology* 3 (October 1989): 509–23.

Lloyd, Gareth. "Scipio Africanus: The First Black Methodist," *Wesley and Methodist Studies* 3 (2011): 87–95.

Maddox, Randy L. *Responsible Grace: John Wesley's Practical Theology*. Nashville: Kingswood, 1994.

———. "The Rule of Christian Faith, Practice, and Hope: John Wesley on the Bible," *Methodist Review* 3 (2011): 1–35.

Mason, John. "Some Account of the Life of Mr. John Mason: In a Letter to the Rev. Mr. John Wesley," *Arminian Magazine* 3 (1780): 650–55.

Matthews, Rex. "'With the Eyes of Faith': Spiritual Experience and the Knowledge of God in the Theology of John Wesley." In *Wesleyan Theology Today*, edited by Theodore Runyon, 406–15. Nashville: Kingswood, 1985.

McCarthy, Daryl. "Early Wesleyan Views of Scripture," *Wesleyan Theological Journal* 16, no. 2 (1981): 95–105.

Meadows, Philip R. "Embodying Conversion." In *Conversion in the Wesleyan Tradition*, edited by Kenneth J. Collins and John H. Tyson, 223–39. Nashville: Abingdon, 2001.

Meadows, Phillip. "The Journey of Evangelism." In *Oxford Handbook of Methodist Studies*, edited by William J. Abraham and James E. Kirby. Oxford: Oxford University Press, 2009.

Moore, Jacob. "An Essay on the Obligation of Family Worship," *Methodist Magazine* 9 (July 1826): 254–57.

Newport, Kenneth G. C., ed. *The Sermons of Charles Wesley: A Critical Edition, with Introduction and Notes*. Oxford: Oxford University Press, 2001.

Newton, John A. *Susanna Wesley and the Puritan Tradition in Methodism*. London: Epworth, 1968.

Olin, Stephen. "Religious Training," *Methodist Quarterly Review* 31 (April 1849): 303–21.

Oliver, John. "An Account of Mr. John Oliver, Written by Himself," *Arminian Magazine* 2 (1779): 419–20.

"On Family Religion," *Methodist Magazine* 4 (December 1821): 468–75.

Outler, Albert C. *Evangelism and Theology in the Wesleyan Spirit*. Nashville: Discipleship Resources, 1996.

———. *John Wesley's Sermons: An Introduction*. Nashville: Abingdon, 1991.

Outler, Albert Cook, ed. *John Wesley*. New York: Oxford University Press, 1964.

Overton, John Henry. *Life in the English Church, 1660–1714*. London: Longmans, 1885.

Parkes, William. "John Wesley: Field Preacher," *Methodist History* 30 (July 1992): 217–34.

Pawson, John. *A Serious and Affectionate Address to the Junior Preachers in the Methodist Connection*. London, 1798.

Perronet, Charles. "Of the Right Method of Meeting Classes and Bands, in the Methodist-Societies," *Arminian Magazine* 4 (1781).

———. "The Right Method of Meeting Classes and Bands, in the Methodist-Societies," *Arminian Magazine* 20 (1797).

Plumb, J. H. *England in the Eighteenth Century: Pelican History of England*, vol. 7. London: Penguin Books, 1963.

Priestley, Joseph. *Original Letters by the Rev. John Wesley and His Friends*. 1791.

Prince, John W. "Wesley on Religious Education: A Study of John Wesley's Theories and Methods of the Education of Children in Religion." PhD diss., Yale University, 1926.

"Proceedings." Wesley Historical Society.

Rack, Henry D. *Reasonable Enthusiast: John Wesley and the Rise of Methodism*, 3rd ed. London: Epworth Press, 2002.

Rhodes, Benjamin. "An Acount of Mr. Benjamin Rhodes, Written by Himeslf," *Arminian Magazine* 2 (1779).

Rogers, Hester A. *An Account of the Experience of Hester Ann Rogers: And Her Funeral Sermon*. New York: Carlton & Porter, 1857.

Ruth, Lester. *Early Methodist Life and Spirituality: A Reader*. Nashville: Kingswood, 2005.

Rutherford, Thomas. "An Account of Mr. Thomas Rutherford," *Methodist Magazine* 31 (1808): 433–42.

Ryan, Sarah. "Account of Mrs. Sarah Ryan," *Arminian Magazine* 2 (1779): 298–310.

Schlimm, Matthew R. "Defending the Old Testament's Worth: John Wesley's Reaction to the Rebirth of Marcionism," *Wesleyan Theological Journal* 42, no. 2 (2007): 28–51.

Seward, William. William Seward Letter Book, *Methodist Archives and Research Centre* (*MARC*), John Rylands University Library of Manchester. Manchester, England.

Simon, John S. *John Wesley and the Religious Societies*. London: Epworth, 1921.

Snyder, Howard A. *The Radical Wesley and Patterns for Church Renewal*. Pasadena: Wipf & Stock, 1996.

———. *Yes in Christ: Wesleyan Reflections on Gospel, Mission, and Culture. Tyndale Studies in Wesleyan History and Theology*. Toronto: Clements Academic, 2010.

Soper, Donald. "Wesley the Outdoor Preacher." In *John Wesley: Contemporary Perspectives*, edited by John Stacey. London: Epworth, 1988.

Souza, Luis Wesley de. "The Wisdom of God in Creation: Mission and the Wesleyan Pentalateral." In *Global Good News: Mission in a New Context*, edited by Howard A. Snyder, 138–52. Nashville: Abingdon, 2001.

Stevenson, George J. *Memorials of the Wesley Family*. London: S. W. Partridge and Co., 1876.

Stone, Bryan. *Evangelism after Christendom: The Theology and Practice of Christian Witness*. Grand Rapids: Brazos, 2007.

Sutcliffe, Joseph. *The Mutual Communion of Saints: Shewing the Necessity and Advantages of the Weekly Meetings for a Communication of Experience*. Trowbridge: Abraham Small, 1794.

Taylor, Isaac. *Wesley and Methodism*. New York: Harper and Brothers, 1852.

Telford, John. *The Life of John Wesley*. London: Epworth, 1924.

———, ed. *Wesley's Veterans: Lives of Early Methodist Preachers Told by Themselves*, 6 vols. London: Robert Culley, 1910.

Thompson, Andrew C. "'To Stir them up to Believe, Love, Obey'—Soteriological Dimensions of the Class Meeting in Early Methodism," *Methodist History* 48, no. 3 (2010): 160–78.

Towlson, Clifford W. *Moravian and Methodist: Relationships and Influences in the Eighteenth Century*. London: Epworth, 1957.

Tucker, Josiah. *The Life and Particular Proceedings of the Rev. Mr. George Whitefield*. London, 1739.

Tyerman, Luke. *The Life and Times of the Rev. John Wesley*, 2 vols. London: Hodder and Stoughton, 1870–71.

———. *The Life and Times of the Rev. John Wesley, M.A., founder of the Methodists*. New York: Harper & Brothers, 1872.

———. *The Life of the Rev. George Whitefield*, 2 vols. New York: Anson D. F. Randolph, 1877.

Tyson, John R., ed. *Charles Wesley: A Reader*. Oxford: Oxford University Press, 1989.

Warner, Laceye C. *Saving Women: Retrieving Evangelistic Theology and Practice*. Waco, TX: Baylor University Press, 2007.

———. "Spreading Scriptural Holiness: Theology and Practices of Early Methodism for the Contemporary Church," *The Asbury Journal* 63, no. 1 (2008): 115–38.

Watson, David L. *The Early Methodist Class Meeting: Its Origins and Significance*. Nashville: Discipleship Resources, 1992.

———. "The Origins and Significance of the Early Methodist Class Meetings." PhD diss, Duke University, 1978.

Watson, Kevin M. *The Class Meeting: Reclaiming a Forgotten (and Essential) Small Group Experience*. Wilmore: Seedbed, 2014.

———. *Pursuing Social Holiness: The Band Meeting in Wesley's Thought and Popular Methodist Practice*. Oxford: Oxford University Press, 2014.

Watson, Richard. *The Life of the Rev. John Wesley*, 14th ed. London: Wesleyan Conference Office, 1831.

———. *The Life of the Rev. John Wesley*, 14th ed. New York: T. Mason and G. Lane, 1840.

Watts, Isaac. *The Arminian Magazine: Consisting of Extracts and Original Treatises on Universal Redemption*, 21 vols. London: Fry, J. and Co., 1778.

Wedgwood, Julia. *John Wesley and the Evangelical Reaction of the Eighteenth Century*. London: MacMillan and Co., 1870.

Wesley, Charles. *The Journal of the Rev. Charles Wesley*. Grand Rapids: Baker, 1980.

———. *The Letters of Charles Wesley: A Critical Edition, with Introduction and Notes*, v. 1, 1728–56. Edited by Kenneth G. C. Newport and Gareth Lloyd. Oxford: Oxford University Press, 2013.

Wesley, John. *The Bicentennial Edition of the Works of John Wesley*. 35 vols. projected. Edited by Frank Baker, Richard P. Heitzenrater, and Randy L. Maddox. Nashville: Abingdon, 1984–. (Volumes 7, 11, 25, and 26 originally appeared as the *Oxford Edition of the Works of John Wesley*. Oxford, U.K.: Clarendon, 1975–83.)

———. "A Christian Library: Consisting Of Extracts From And Abridgments Of The Choicest Pieces Of Practical Divinity Which Have Been Published In The English Tongue." Northwest Nazarene University, http://wesley

.nnu.edu/john_wesley/christian_library/index.htm.

———. *A Compendium of Natural Philosophy: Being a Survey of the Wisdom of God in the Creation*. 3 vols. London: Thomas Tegg and Son, 1836.

———. *Explanatory Notes Upon the New Testament*. New York: J. Soule and T. Mason, 1818.

———. *The Letters of the Rev. John Wesley*, 8 vols. Edited by John Telford. London: Epworth, 1931.

———. *The Works of John Wesley*, 3rd ed., 14 vols. Edited by Thomas Jackson. Grand Rapids: Baker, 1872, repr. 1978.

Whitefield, George. *Fifteen Sermons Preached on Various Important Subjects*. Paisley: J. Neilson, 1794.

———. *George Whitefield's Journals*. Edinburgh: Banner of Truth, 1960.

———. *A Journal of a Voyage from London to Savannah in Georgia*, 5th ed. London: James Hutton, 1739.

———. *Letters of George Whitefield: For the Period 1734–1742*. Edinburgh: Banner of Truth Trust, 1976.

———. *Sermons of George Whitefield*, edited by Evelyn Bence. Peabody: Hendrickson, 2009.

Wigger, John H. *Taking Heaven by Storm: Methodism and the Rise of Popular Christianity in America*. Urbana: University of Illinois Press, 2001.

Wilson, Thomas. *Parochialia; or, Instructions to the Clergy, in the Discharge of their Parochial Duty*. Bath: R. Cruttwell, 1788.

Wogan, William. *The Right Use of Lent: Or, a help to Penitents... To which is added, Bishop Kenn's Pastoral letter*. London: C. Rivington, 1732.

Wood, A. Skevington. *The Burning Heart: John Wesley, Evangelist*. Minneapolis: Bethany House, 1978.

Woodward, Josiah. *An Account of the Rise and Progress of the Religious Societies in the City of London*, 4th ed. London: M. Downing, 1712.

———. *An Account of the Societies for Reformation of Manners in London and Westminster, and other parts of the Kingdom*. London: RA Simpson, 1698.

www.ingramcontent.com/pod-product-compliance
Lightning Source LLC
Chambersburg PA
CBHW011744290426
44113CB00017BA/2647
* 9 7 8 1 5 0 1 8 1 4 2 2 8 *